teach yourself... DOS 6.0

by Al Stevens

MIS: PRESS

A Subsidiary of
Henry Holt and Co., Inc.

a subsidiary of Henry Holt and Company, Inc.
115 West 18th Street
New York, New York 10011

ISBN 1-55828-253-X

Printed in the United States of America

10 9 8 7 6 5 4 3 2

MIS:Press books are available at special discounts for bulk purchases for sales, promotions, premiums, fundraising, or educational use. Special editions or book excerpts can also be created to specification.

For details contact: Special Sales Director
MIS:Press
a subsidiary of Henry Holt and Company, Inc.
115 West 18th Street
New York, New York 10011

TRADEMARKS:
Throughout this book, trademarked names are used. Rather than put a trademark symbol after every occurrence of a trademarked name, we used the names in an editorial fashion only. Where such designations appear in this book, they have been printed with initial caps.

Development Editor: Cary Weinberger
Editor: Dawn Erdos
Layout: Dawn Erdos

Dedication

To Tyler, Landon, and Kellie

Table of Contents

Preface

This book allows you as a new user to teach yourself MS-DOS 6.0, the latest version of the disk operating system that drives the IBM PC and other compatible computers. DOS 6.0 is an upgrade from earlier versions of DOS with several improvements and new features over version 5.0. Even though DOS 6.0 builds on prior versions, this book does not assume that you know anything about DOS. Teach Yourself DOS 6.0 begins at the beginning and covers everything you need so that you can learn DOS 6.0 at a graduated pace.

You will teach yourself enough the first time out to allow you to use the PC in the simplest ways. You will learn to move around through the DOS file system, and to run your programs and DOS commands. Then, as your experience with DOS 6.0 grows, you will learn more advanced DOS concepts and commands.

What This Book Teaches You

This self-help DOS 6.0 tutorial teaches you to use DOS 6.0 in your daily use of your PC. The tutorial enables you to teach yourself DOS 6.0 by explaining concepts and offering exercises that you can perform as you read. After you install DOS 6.0, you will need nothing more than your PC and a single, blank, formatted floppy diskette to run the exercises. The first part of the book teaches you the basics and the second part teaches you the things you need to know to become a power user. Appendix A provides a command summary and Appendix B is a glossary.

As PCs and DOS become more sophisticated, a greater need arises for this kind of book—one that starts with the basics and delivers the primary lessons necessary for a new user to confidently learn DOS 6.0.

This book covers the following topics:

- For New Users:
    - Introduction to DOS 6.0
    - Diskettes
    - Installing DOS 6.0
    - DOS 6.0 commands
    - DOS 6.0 path
    - Printing
    - DOSSHELL program
- For Power Users:
    - Filters, pipes, and input/output redirection
    - Advanced topics and commands
    - DOSKEY program
    - Text editing: EDLIN and EDIT
    - Batch files
    - Memory management and optimizing
    - Disk and file management.

How This Book Differs from a Reference Manual

Teach Yourself DOS 6.0 is not the same type of reference manual that you received when you purchased DOS 6.0. A reference manual assumes that you already know what a disk operating system is and what the commands are. When you want to know the details of a command, you look up the command in an alphabetic list and read about its syntax and effects. This works well for the veteran user who knows the commands. However, new users need more help than that. New users are not only unfamiliar with the commands, they might not know that a PC has commands. If you do not know what a disk directory is, how can you know that you can display one—or that you want to?

Section 1: The New DOS 6.0 User

This section helps new users who are ready to learn DOS 6.0. Soon you will be running the exercises that let you teach yourself DOS 6.0. Chapter 1 is an introduction. Chapter 2 begins the section and has no exercises, but it explains some of the basics. Chapter 3 takes a side trip to explain the differences between diskette formats. Chapter 4 teaches you how to install DOS 6.0. When you get into Chapter 5, the exercises and the fun begin.

Chapter 1

Introduction

Microcomputers come in many varieties, with many names: PC, XT, AT, 386, Laptops, and Clones. These machines have many differences, but a feature they share is that they all use the Disk Operating System called DOS (MS-DOS or PC-DOS—the names are synonymous). As a new user, you need to learn how to use DOS 6.0 to get the most out of your machine. From now on, this book refers to the computer as a *PC* and the operating system as *DOS 6.0*.

How did you come to be a new DOS 6.0 user? Perhaps you are newly retired and writing your memoirs. Maybe your boss confiscated your typewriter and replaced it with a PC. Or maybe you reported to a new job and found that your duties include using a PC. It could be that PCs have nothing to do with your work, but are a newfound hobby. Perhaps you are just trying to keep up with your kids. What do you do next? Read on.

Why This Book?

A new DOS 6.0 user will find an abundance of advanced DOS reference books. You might not want to undertake such an extensive study of the subject. You might prefer instead to simply learn enough to apply the computer to some useful task. Most DOS books contain information that is too advanced for your initial entry into its use.

This book, therefore, is about operating DOS 6.0 well enough to get some work done. You sit at a PC so you can do work, typically running programs such as word processing, spreadsheets, and databases. While the object of your efforts is the work, the path to that work is by way of DOS 6.0, something you need to understand at least well enough to do the work. There is a lot to know about DOS 6.0 if you want to become what has come to be known as a *power user.* There is a smaller body of knowledge that you need to have to get your work done.

Users

In this book, *users* refers to the person learning and using DOS 6.0. To be a user, you must run the programs. To run the programs, you must know how to start them and how to point them to their respective data files. To run programs and use data files, you must understand the mechanism inside the PC that supports those processes. That mechanism is DOS 6.0, which finds the programs and runs them. DOS 6.0 finds the data files for the programs and reads and writes them. In one way or another, you tell DOS 6.0 when and how to do these things by issuing commands.

Power Users

Most books about using DOS are aimed at the person who has come to be known as the power user. The power user extracts the maximum performance from the PC, using and understanding a complex set of mechanisms including expanded memory, memory-resident pop-up utilities, RAM disks, caches, disk compressors, and other DOS-specific things that are unrelated to but support the word processing, database, and spreadsheet applications. Power users can get caught up in the technology. They like to talk about the various technical aspects of their PCs—their memory size, disk capacity, and speed in Megahertz.

New Users

Teach Yourself DOS 6.0 is for the new user (NU). The NU is not yet a power user (PU). The NU wants to get the PC running well enough to get a job done.

Many NUs become PUs. Whether or not you want to become a PU, Teach Yourself DOS 6.0 is the first step to take in getting what you really need right now—an understanding of the elementary principles of using DOS 6.0. Section II discusses the parts of DOS 6.0 that interest the PU. These subjects are not all that difficult, but you can ignore them for now. Later, when you are a seasoned NU, on the brink of PU-hook, you will find good use for them. However, from now on, and until you get into Section II, there are no further distinctions between new and power users.

A Brief History of DOS

When IBM entered the personal computer market in 1981, they made numerous design decisions that shaped the way personal computing would look for years to follow. Among those decisions was the selection of an operating system. The first PC was introduced in 1981, and buyers were told they had a choice of three operating system environments. You could order CP/M-86, USCD Pascal, or DOS. Most potential buyers were interested in CP/M-86 because its predecessor, CP/M, was the dominant operating system for the generation of personal microcomputers that preceded the IBM PC. For one reason or another, CP/M-86 was not immediately available, and IBM displayed a commitment to DOS as its operating system of choice. DOS had a command structure similar to CP/M. Microsoft had acquired the original software package from its developers and modified it to run on the PC. It was available, looked like CP/M, and most users bought it.

DOS has progressed through several versions to become the DOS 6.0 that you are learning now. Each new version is a superset of the one that preceded it. The command structure has remained the same. The file organization has been the same since version 2.0. Each successive version added features, commands, and support for devices. DOS 5.0 culminated the evolution of DOS by using the hardware features of the more advanced PCs of today while retaining the ability to effectively operate in the smaller, slower machines of earlier times. DOS 6.0 adds to that power by including memory optimization and virus detection in the operating system package.

Some Assumptions

To teach yourself DOS 6.0, you need a PC that will run DOS. The exercises that you will use require your participation with such a PC. That PC could be configured many ways, and a book such as this one cannot cover every possible configuration. Therefore, this book makes a certain assumptions about your PC.

You Have a Hard Disk Drive Named C:

Throughout the lessons and examples in this book, you will see this format:

```
C><command>
```

The C> is the DOS prompt that DOS 6.0 displays to tell you it is waiting for a command. The *<command>* is what you type. Unless the exercise tells you otherwise, always assume that you press **Enter** at the end of each command.

This book uses the C> DOS prompt because it assumes that you have a hard disk and that the disk drive letter is C. If you do not have a hard disk, the letter would be A. In this case, substitute A> wherever you see C>. You will learn about disk drive letters and their relation to the prompt in Chapter 4.

You Have a Floppy Diskette Drive Named A:

Many of the exercises use the floppy diskette drive for you to build examples on. These exercises will frequently use this format:

```
A><command>
```

Establish an Environment

You need to understand DOS 6.0 well enough to set up a system to teach yourself DOS 6.0. But, at this point, you might not. You will have to trust the instructions given in these exercises to get that preliminary job done for you. Sometimes you will enter some commands that you have not learned yet. The purpose for that is to establish an environment that supports the current exercise. In those cases, follow the instructions. You will learn the reasons later.

The DOS 6.0 Shell

When you turn on the PC, you might see a screen that is similar to Figure 1.1. This is the DOS 6.0 Shell. If you see this screen, hold down **Alt** and press **F4** to exit the Shell and go to the DOS command line. The Shell is supposed to make things easier. It does, but you need to learn DOS 6.0 from the more primitive view of the command line first. Why? First, not all DOS 6.0 commands are available from the shell. Second, you might find yourself someday at a PC that has an earlier version of DOS and no helpful Shell. You need to understand the command line. Third, the command line syntax is the basis for all of the DOS features. The Shell came after the command line syntax.

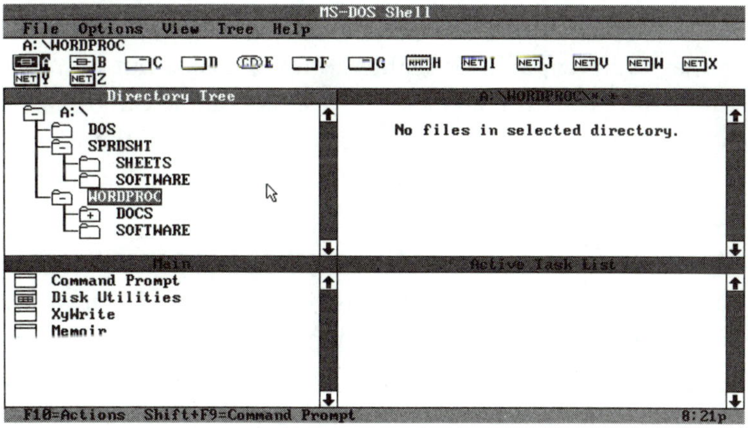

Figure 1.1 *The DOS 6.0 Shell*

Perhaps your PC was installed with a different shell or menu program. One such program is the Norton Commander. Others are available from commercial, public domain, and shareware sources. Public domain programs are free. Shareware programs are ones that you may try out before you decide to purchase them—usually at a low price. Many system installers install their own custom menu programs. If you are using such a program, find out how to get out of it and do so. If you can locate the system installers, have them disable it. You might want it later, but you do not want it getting in the way while you teach yourself DOS 6.0.

Once you know DOS 6.0 well enough, you may never again need or want such a shell. Then again, you might prefer it. The use of a shell is a personal choice, and you should not let the opinions of others dissuade you from using one if you want. For now, you need to learn the basics of DOS 6.0 and an understanding of the DOS command line.

Chapter 8 describes the use of the DOS 6.0 Shell program in detail.

Get In Command

When computer technology was young, the disciplines of computer operation were exercised exclusively by computer programmers and computer operators. The programmers designed the operator interface to be a concise and cryptic command language. The reasons for this design are found in the complex nature of older computers that were difficult to operate. They were capable of highly complex tasks, but they cost a lot of money to run. The languages were just as complex and consisted of short cryptic sequences of commands. The brevity of these operations kept operator time at a minimum and therefore reduced work force and processor costs. At least, that was the idea.

Users did not operate the computers in those days. Users provided input data (usually on paper) and received printed output reports, delivered from the computer room by hand.

As desktop computers came into use, some of this cryptic command mentality came with them. This circumstance was due to the fact that the first microcomputer programmers came from the world of the large mainframe computers and it was all they knew. This influence is seen even today in the DOS command line.

The designers of other computer operating environments have taken directions to provide more symbolic and intuitive command languages. Similarly, there are the shell programs mentioned above that attempt to make the use of DOS 6.0 easier by providing menus and pictorial representations of the file structures. While we inherited the cryptic command methods from the old computers, we also inherited their main advantage: a concise command language that, once learned, is the fastest and most efficient way to use DOS 6.0.

Some people argue that lay users should not be required to learn a cryptic command language. That argument had validity in the days when there was no standard for such a language. The PC, by virtue of its overwhelming acceptance by small computer users, has become the accepted standard desk top computer. On its coattails rides DOS 6.0, the universally acknowledged operating system. There is no good reason to avoid learning DOS 6.0 if you are going to have computers as a part of you life. To learn DOS 6.0 is to learn its command line conventions.

Once you know DOS 6.0 from the command line perspective, you are in command.

The Command Line Prompt

When you exit the Shell or menu program or start up DOS 6.0, you might see a command line prompt that looks something like this:

```
C:\>
```

or this:

```
C:\DOS>
```

DOS 6.0 installs itself to always tell you something you are not ready for. Turn off the unwanted help by typing this command immediately following whatever prompt you see:

```
prompt
```

The prompt shown just below is what you want to see each time you enter a session of Teach Yourself DOS 6.0:

```
C>
```

The reason for disabling the helpful prompt is so that your PC behaves as much like the examples in this book as possible. Later, you can decide if you want to keep that feature.

The Tutorial Objective of This Book

Teach Yourself DOS 6.0 provides you with a structured tutorial approach to the lessons. The objective is to introduce new material at the point where you are ready to learn it. For this reason, except for a brief listing in Appendix A, you will not find the DOS 6.0 commands listed in alphabetical order or arranged functionally. If you know the name of a command and want to find the exercises that explain it, look in Appendix A or the index for a reference to its exercises. The tutorial material is in the order in which you should learn it. Each lesson progresses and assumes that you have learned the lessons that precede it.

The exercises help you to build and change a diskette, which you will call the *TYD Learning Diskette*. You must follow the exercises in the order in which they are presented so that the diskette is always configured the way the next exercise expects it. You should be able to take that diskette and this book from computer to computer and continue with your lessons from the place where you interrupted them. It will not matter whether DOS 6.0 is installed at the computer where you use the diskette. The diskette will hold everything you need to run the exercises, including DOS 6.0.

Often you will learn a concept that is not complete. A power user might expect more detailed information in the lesson. However, there is a good reason for providing only the necessary information in a lesson. Many aspects of DOS 6.0 require circular understanding. You must understand subject C to understand subject B, which requires an understanding of subject A, which cannot possibly be explained until subject C is understood. Such is the nature of complex systems. For this reason, the first explanation of subject A would be incomplete because you have not learned subject C yet. Subject A is revisited when the lessons of subject C are complete. This is the structure of a good tutorial.

Call for Help

From time to time the book asks that you make sure of something that you might not be equipped to know. For example, in Chapter 3, you are advised to determine if your diskette drive is high or low density. You are told that if you do not know, you should ask someone. This is a common piece of advice, and unless you live in a remote area, you should be able to find a nearby PC expert. Some PC users like to be helpful, but be careful not to let their enthusiasm get away from you. They might start modifying your system, installing all kinds of software—such as menu shells—that will get in the way of your objective, which is to teach yourself DOS 6.0 with a minimum of fuss

Find a friendly fellow user who knows more than you and who does not mind answering a question from time to time.

About Tutorials

Tutorials have a responsibility to the student. It is not enough to teach you how something works. A good tutorial should tell you why and under what circumstances you would want to use it. For example, you might see this command:

```
C>dir t*.*
```

You might learn that the command displays a directory of all files that have a *t* as the first letter. Left with that, you might well ask, "So, what?" and never know why you would need to perform such as task. Therefore, where it is appropriate and possible, these lessons give you examples of when and why you might use the DOS 6.0 features being taught.

Tests, Midterms, and Finals

These lessons and exercises have no tests or questions for you to answer. The exercises all have their results fully displayed and explained when the exercise is presented. You should run each exercise on your PC to see that the results are correct, to get practice, and to gain experience and confidence with DOS 6.0. However, do not fear the end of the chapter, anticipating a test of your knowledge. You will not find one. If you are motivated to learn DOS 6.0, that is enough.

Examples and Experience

This tutorial approach lets you learn by example and, more important, by doing. You need a PC to learn these lessons because you are going to run the exercises, and they involve operating the PC with DOS 6.0. You do not learn to fly an airplane, deliver a baby, or cook a chicken by reading a book. You learn by doing. There are books that explain the basics, but you will never know those procedures until you use them. You are born knowing how to do some things. Running DOS 6.0 is not one of them.

Chapter 2

Introduction to DOS 6.0

If you are going to teach yourself DOS 6.0, you need to know just what DOS 6.0 is and what its component parts do for you. You will learn that DOS 6.0 is just another computer program, although an important one.

This chapter teaches you:

- The purpose of DOS 6.0
- How DOS 6.0 loads into memory
- What a file is
- How files are named
- What a program is
- What a DOS 6.0 command is

What Is DOS 6.0's Purpose?

When you use a PC or any other kind of computer, you run computer programs. *Computer programs* are sequences of instructions that tell the computer how to do something, and they are created by computer programmers. A computer program is usually stored on disk waiting for you to run it. Then the program is loaded into the computer's main memory to be executed.

DOS 6.0 is the master computer program that manages the files on the disk file system and runs programs at your request. DOS 6.0 creates, reads, changes, copies, and deletes files whenever you or one of your programs instructs it to do so.

The DOS 6.0 command line is on the screen at the place where the C> prompt and the cursor are displayed. As long as no programs are running, DOS 6.0 is waiting for a command. Eventually, you type a command into the DOS command line so that DOS 6.0 performs an action. What DOS 6.0 does could be something as simple as showing you the current time. However, it could be something as complex as running programs to post a year's worth of general ledger journal entries, printing a report of all the sales year to date, or scheduling an oil change for the company car.

DOS 6.0 provides a common interface between you and the PC for the execution of programs, and a common way for programs to get loaded into memory and executed.

DOS 6.0 provides a common interface between the programs and the data files that are stored on disk. Thanks to DOS 6.0, each application program does not have to contain the code that keeps track of where the data files get stored and how they get found, read, written, and deleted.

By working in a DOS-supported environment, users have a measure of compatibility among their PCs. Disk data files and programs that work on one PC work on another because the PCs use the same DOS 6.0, and DOS 6.0 is the proprietor of standard formats for data files and programs among PCs.

Loading DOS 6.0

When you first turn on the PC, it runs a program that is permanently stored in the PC's memory. That program is called *Basic Input/Output System* (BIOS), and it is always there, whether or not you have any diskettes loaded and even when the power is turned off. BIOS does many things to support the PC's operations, but you need to know only that, upon startup, BIOS automatically looks for the PC's Disk Operating System, or DOS 6.0.

Power-up Boot

When you power up the PC, BIOS locates DOS 6.0 on the primary disk medium, which is the hard disk if you have one. If you do not have a hard disk, or if a diskette is inserted in the A: diskette drive, BIOS looks to the A: drive for DOS 6.0. BIOS reads the first block of memory from the disk medium into the computer's memory and executes it. That block is commonly called the *boot block*, and it contains another small computer program that loads DOS 6.0 from elsewhere on the disk into the computer's memory and executes it. After that, DOS 6.0 takes care of executing all of the other programs. This process is called *bootstrapping*, or *booting* for short. The term originated long ago as a metaphor that related the computer's ability to load programs into itself to the old adage about pulling one's self up by one's own bootstraps.

Some PCs have a reset button on the front or back of the computer case. The reset button executes the equivalent of a power-on boot but without requiring you to turn the power off and then back on.

Ctrl-Alt-Del Boot

You can boot DOS 6.0 after the PC is already running by holding down **Ctrl** and **Alt** and pressing **Delete**. This procedure is sometimes called rebooting. Another more whimsical name for it is the three-fingered salute.

The DOS 6.0 Command Line Prompt

We call DOS 6.0 the master program because it is the vehicle with which we run other programs. There are utility programs that come with DOS 6.0 and applications programs that you get from other places. They all run under the DOS 6.0 umbrella.

When DOS 6.0 loads, it may display many different messages on the screen depending on how DOS 6.0 has been configured by the installer. Eventually though, when the loading is done, DOS 6.0 displays its command line prompt, which looks something like this:

```
C>
```

The cursor (a blinking underline character) will be just to the right of the greater than (>) character.

Files and Commands

In the view of the user, DOS 6.0's main purpose is to support data files and user commands. There is a common thread that runs between the two. To understand commands, you need to know how the files are organized and named. To organize and name files, you need to understand the commands that achieve those purposes. You need to understand both to understand either one. Although it may sound complicated, many commands are programs and all programs are disk files. The following sections explain this concept, one step at a time.

Files

The concept of "files" is an important one. The contents of a DOS 6.0 disk volume (the disk itself) are organized into files. Everything is in a file. Word processing documents are files. So are spreadsheets and databases. The programs that comprise the word processing, spreadsheet, and database software systems are files. DOS 6.0 itself is stored on the disk in files.

The floppy diskette that you hold in your hand and the hard disk that spins inside the cabinet of your PC both can contain many files. There are no architectural differences between the files on the two media. The floppy diskette does not have the capacity of the hard disk, but the floppy diskette is removable while the hard disk is not. Other than for those two differences, everything you will learn about disks and their files applies equally to floppy diskettes and hard disks.

Think of your PC as a file cabinet. Think of each hard disk drive or floppy diskette as a drawer in a file cabinet that is capable of holding many file folders. Each disk file is a file folder. Think of the data records in the disk files as letters, documents, and forms in the file folders. The big difference between the file cabinet and your disk filing system is this: you can go to the file cabinet, pull anything out, and look at it without help. However, you cannot see or use the files and records on the disk without the cooperation of the PC, DOS 6.0, and your applications programs.

File Names

Every file has a file name. Later, you will learn the significance of the unique properties of file names. For now, it is enough to know that a file name has this format:

```
<name>.<extension>
```

The name is from one to eight characters. The extension is optional, but if it exists it has from one to three characters. Typical file names are:

```
LETTERS.TXT
WP.EXE
AUTOEXEC.BAT
```

You name many of the files yourself. Others are named for you by the developers of the applications software you purchase. Still others are named by Microsoft and are included when you purchase DOS 6.0 itself.

File names can consist of letters, numbers, and some special characters. The letters are case-insensitive. That is, if you create a file as

LETTERS.TXT, you can refer to it later as letters.txt. You can even mix cases, as in LeTTeRs.TxT, but you probably never will.

Naming Files

Do not worry about your responsibility for naming files. There is nothing mysterious or cryptic about the process. A letter to Aunt Milly composed in your word processor might be named MILLY.LTR. You could as easily name it FERN.DOC or BLITZ.FRP. DOS 6.0 would not care. You would care later, however, when you looked at those meaningless file names and wondered what was in the files with the funny names. Try to select names that reflect the purposes of the files. Give it some thought. It's worth the time to get it right.

File Name Extension Conventions

Remember that file names consist of a name and an extension. The name can be up to eight characters long and the extension can be up to three characters long. The name and extension are separated by a period like this:

```
NAME.EXT
```

The name part usually identifies the particular file. The extension usually identifies a category of files. For example, files with the extension of .DOC might be word processing documents. This would be a convention that you would choose or that is chosen by the developer of the applications software.

There are conventions that specify certain defined extensions to some file names. DOS 6.0 has its conventions, and those who develop applications programs must comply with them. Many programs also impose file naming conventions, usually allowing you to pick a file name to be combined with a defined extension. Others leave you all the latitude you want. Look at some examples. These three-character extensions are some of those used by DOS 6.0. (You will learn about each of these and their purposes soon.) The extensions include:

- **.BAT**—a batch command file
- **.EXE**—an executable program
- **.COM**—an executable program
- **.SYS**—primarily a DOS 6.0 device driver program

You could use these extensions for your own file names. However, you should know how DOS 6.0 handles files that have these extensions in their names. You should avoid using those extensions to keep from confusing your files with files that have a defined purpose in DOS 6.0. With these conventions, you can look at a file's name and know something about the purpose for the file.

You might consider developing your own file extension conventions. If you named that letter MILLY.LTR, why not name all of your letters with the .LTR extension?

Conventions for the File Name

If you write a letter to Aunt Milly every month, you might name them MILLY01.LTR in January, MILLY02.LTR in February, and so on. When January rolls around again, you'll need to either move those files somewhere else to reuse the file name MILLY01.LTR or use a different convention.

Later, when you learn about file name wild cards, you will see how helpful such practices can be.

File Types

There are three basic kinds of disk files. They are:

- Data files
- Program files
- Subdirectory files

Data Files

These files are what you might expect. They contain records of data that are created, retrieved, and modified by applications programs. They take many forms and have many different functions.

A word processor will have a number of different data files. The ones you will be most familiar with are the letters and documents that you type. However, others are equally important. There are printer definition files that specify the characteristics of the printer you have chosen. Printers are so different that it takes a complex file of configuration statements to describe the way the printer works to the program. There are font files that let you use many different character formats in your publications. These files do not change often, and you can usually disregard them, taking their presence for granted.

Other programs will have their own data files. An accounts receivable system will have a file of vendors, a file of invoices, and a file of payments. A desktop publishing program will have files that describe page formats. A paintbrush program will have files of graphics images that represent the pictures you paint.

Most programs have configuration data files that describe the unique way you want them to run. You may be able to select screen colors, custom keystrokes, and functional options. DOS 6.0 itself has several such configuration data files.

Many applications programs use files of help text to give you helpful information while you are running the program.

These are just some of the different kinds of data files that a DOS 6.0 system manages for its applications programs. There are many more, but to DOS 6.0, they all look the same. A program can create, read, update, and delete files, and DOS 6.0 provides the means to do that. What the applications program does with them beyond that is its business and yours, and DOS 6.0 is not involved.

Program Files

There are six kinds of programs that DOS 6.0 stores in disk files. Two of them are functionally identical and others are not for you, the user, to worry about at first. However, you need to know about all of them so that you recognize them when you see them. Soon you will see how programs are executed from the command line. For now, consider how DOS 6.0 stores programs in disk files.

When you purchase a software package, it usually comes on a diskette, although many programs come on the CD-ROM medium now. The diskette or CD-ROM has files that comprise the software package. You already learned what some of the data files are. The other files are the software program. DOS 6.0 stores software programs in files with these file name extensions:

- .EXE
- .COM
- .BAT
- .SYS
- .BAS
- .OVL

These file extensions represent six different kinds of DOS 6.0 programs. This book mentioned four of them earlier. The .EXE and .COM files are the same as far as you are concerned. There are technical differences that programmers know about, but to the user, they are the same. If, for example, you see the file named WP.EXE, you may assume that the file is a program that you can run.

As with any rule, there are exceptions. Some software packages distribute executable .EXE files that will not run correctly from the command line. They expect to be run automatically from within another program. The documentation that accompanies a software package will identify which programs you may run from the command line.

The .BAT file is a text file with a batch of DOS 6.0 commands in it. Chapter 13 is about batch file processing and how you can build your own files of batched DOS 6.0 commands. For now, if you see a file with the .BAT extension, you will know that it is operationally equivalent to the .EXE and .COM files. The extension indicates a program that you can run.

The .SYS file is a DOS 6.0 device driver program. You do not run this program yourself. DOS 6.0 runs it when you turn on the PC's power. If you add an applications program or a hardware device to your system, you might need to install a .SYS file into DOS 6.0. There is a special file named CONFIG.SYS that is not itself a device driver program, but figures prominently in the installation of other .SYS files. The .SYS files are discussed later in the book.

The .BAS file is a file of QBasic program source code. The QBASIC command executes this file to run the program. Few programs are distributed in this format. Basic was a popular programming language several years ago, but its popularity has waned with the availability of better software development tools.

The .OVL file is a program file that contains program overlays. Sometimes a program is so big that it will not fit into a computer's memory. The program's developers divide it into overlays—segments of the program that overlay one another when they execute. You do not run an overlay program file. The program itself manages the execution of its own overlays.

Subdirectory Files

The third kind of disk file is the subdirectory. You will learn about subdirectories in Chapter 5.

DOS 6.0 Commands

A command is something you type when the cursor is at the screen command line. To execute the command, you type its name and perhaps some parameters. Then the command makes the computer do something.

A command can be one of three general types: internal DOS 6.0 commands, program file commands, and batch file commands. They may all look alike at first, but to DOS 6.0 they work differently. Eventually, you will need to know this difference to know how and when you can use the different kinds of commands.

Internal DOS 6.0 Commands

In Chapter 4, you will begin to execute commands in earnest. However, you can try one now. Enter this command:

```
C>time
```

DOS 6.0 displays the current time from the computer's time-of-day clock and prompts you to enter a new setting for the clock. You can press Enter if you do not want to change the time. The TIME command is an example of an internal DOS 6.0 command. The command is built into DOS 6.0 and no disk file with the .COM, .EXE, or .BAT extension exists to execute the command. Now enter this command:

```
C>dir
```

What you see depends on how your computer is set up, but whatever it is, take notice. The directory command is probably the most frequently used of the internal DOS 6.0 commands. This command displays a list of disk files. There are several variations on this command, and you will learn and use them all.

Program File Commands

You run a program by typing its name on the command line. For example, to run a program named FOO.EXE or one named FOO.COM, you type this command:

```
C>FOO
```

Program file commands are found in files with the .COM and .EXE extensions. To execute these commands, DOS 6.0 must be able to find the file. For example, you could type this command on the command line:

```
C>hello
```

If DOS 6.0 finds a file named HELLO.COM or HELLO.EXE, DOS 6.0 reads that file into memory and executes the program that is stored in the file. When the program finishes, it returns control to you at the DOS 6.0 command line.

Batch File Commands

Batch file commands are found in files with the .BAT extension. A batch file is a file of text that you can prepare with a text editor program or with some word processors. The text in the file has commands that DOS 6.0 recognizes just as if you typed them yourself on the command line.

If, in the example just given for program file commands, DOS 6.0 did not find HELLO.COM or HELLO.EXE, then DOS 6.0 would look for a file named HELLO.BAT. If DOS 6.0 finds that file, DOS 6.0 reads the file a line at a time and executes the commands in the file. The .BAT file is a batch file that contains a series of DOS 6.0 commands. You will learn about batch files in Chapter 13. For now, you need to know that if you see a file with the extension .BAT, it is like a program to you and you can execute it just as you can the .EXE and .COM files.

There is one important difference between .COM, .EXE, and .BAT files. DOS 6.0 assigns them a precedence. You can have three files with the same file name, but with these three extensions. For example, you can have FOO.COM, FOO.EXE, and FOO.BAT. If you attempt to run FOO, DOS 6.0 takes the .COM file over the .EXE and .BAT files. If there is no .COM file, the .EXE file takes precedence. This common file naming is not a good practice and is seldom intentionally used.

Batch files provide a way for you to put frequently used sequences of commands into a procedure that you execute with just one command name. You can put a complex series of commands into a named batch file and execute all of those commands by typing the batch file's name.

Chapter 13 provides details about how you build batch files.

Invalid Commands

A fourth kind of command is the invalid one. If you type a command that DOS 6.0 does not recognize, you will see this message:

```
Bad command or file name.
```

That message means that DOS 6.0 does not recognize the command as being one of its internal ones and cannot find a matching .COM, .EXE, or .BAT file to load and execute. Try it now. Type any string of nonsense and press **Enter**.

The DOS 6.0 Directory Structure

By now, you know that DOS 6.0 keeps files on disks. You learned the different kinds of files along with the suggestion that DOS 6.0 manages those files by allowing you and your programs to create, retrieve, change, and delete them. Remember the analogy of the file cabinet where the PC was the cabinet and the disk was the drawer full of files. The analogy goes further, however. With the high capacity of the hard disk, it is possible to have so many files that you cannot keep track of them. You need a filing system that lets you organize your files into functional separators.

The PC can handle many different applications, but only one at a time. You can have many different kinds of files on your disk. It would be to your advantage to segment the file folders into functional groups to make things easier to find.

DOS 6.0 provides a hierarchical structure of directories and subdirectories into which you can store files. You design the hierarchy, and DOS 6.0 manages it under your direction. Every disk starts out with nothing on it. Someone must prepare it for use by DOS 6.0. Later, you will learn how to prepare it with the FORMAT command, but for now assume that it has been done. A formatted disk has the beginnings of a hierarchical directory structure with the top of the hierarchy, which is called the *root directory*. What goes below that is up to you, and Figure 2.1 shows a typical DOS 6.0 hierarchical disk directory structure.

```
\ ................................... (Root Directory)
│
├── command.com
├── autoexec.bat
├── WORDPROC ........................ (Word Processing)
│     ├─ SOFTWARE ................... (Word Processing Software)
│     │     └── wp.bat
│     └─ DOCS ....................... (Word Processing Documents)
│          ├── LETTERS .............. (Letters)
│          │     ├── milly01.ltr
│          │     └── milly02.ltr
│          └── MANUSCRP ............. (Manuscripts)
│                └── novel.doc
├── SPRDSHT ......................... (Spreadsheets)
│     ├── SOFTWARE .................. (Spreadsheet Software)
│     │     ├── ss.bat
│     └── SHEETS .................... (Spreadsheet data files)
│           └── taxes92.sps
└── DOS ............................. (DOS Utility Programs)
      ├── chkdsk.exe
      ├── diskcopy.com
      └── etc.
```

Figure 2.1 *DOS 6.0 Directory Structure*

This figure represents a directory structure. Such a structure will figure significantly in the lessons that follow in the chapters to come.

Summary

This chapter explained the basic ideas behind these subjects:

- What DOS 6.0 is and how it is loaded
- How DOS 6.0 manages files, runs programs, and provides the command line user interface
- What a DOS 6.0 file is
- File names and file naming conventions
- The file types: data, program, and subdirectory
- DOS 6.0 internal commands
- Command files

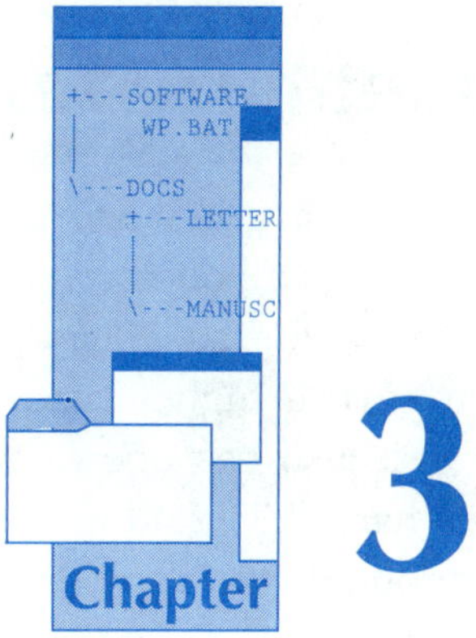

Diskettes

There are many different kinds of diskettes, and you need to know what kind you have so you can get on with the lessons. This chapter teaches you about:

- Diskette drives
- Sizes of diskettes
- Compatibility issues

Diskette Drives

Some PCs have diskette drives only. A *diskette drive* accepts a floppy diskette, which you can remove and replace with another diskette at any time. Most PCs have hard disk drives, which cannot be removed and which have a higher capacity than the diskettes. Usually, a PC with a hard disk also has one or two diskette drives as well. Rarely does a PC have a hard drive and no diskette drives at all. Most commercial software is distributed on floppy diskettes, and you need a diskette drive to install such software.

There is a category of PC called the *diskless workstation*, which has no disk drives at all, but which is connected to a local area network where some other PC, called a file server, has all of the disk power for everyone on the network.

This book assumes that you have at least one floppy diskette drive in your PC.

The History of the Diskette

In the early seventies, IBM invented the diskette as a portable medium for small-scale data storage. The first diskette was 8 inches wide, about the size of a 45 RPM record. The diskette was a paper disk coated with a magnetic emulsion. The disk was sealed inside a square paper envelope with openings to expose the recording surface. Early personal computers used this 8-inch diskette as their primary mass storage device.

In the late seventies, well before the introduction of the IBM PC, diskette manufacturers designed a smaller diskette, one that was 5.25 inches wide. This diskette became the standard for the IBM PC in 1981, and, as a result, a standard for practically everyone else.

A third physical diskette format was introduced about the same time the IBM AT came out. This diskette is 3.5 inches wide, and its protecting envelope is made of rigid plastic with a sliding metal shield that protects the recording surface when the diskette is out of the drive. This diskette is the handiest of the three types because it is more durable and fits neatly into your shirt pocket, its most endearing attribute.

Some PCs support 5.25-inch diskettes, others support the 3.5-inch diskettes, and others still include one drive of each format. Most laptop computers support the 3.5-inch diskette size. The 8-inch diskette is all but extinct.

Diskette Capacities

The two diskette sizes come in five different capacities. A diskette's capacity is expressed in characters, also called *bytes*. The standard units of measure are *K bytes* (kilobytes) where K is equal to 1024 and *M bytes* (megabytes) where M is equal to 1024K. The notations for these measures are K and MB. This is a shorthand that is used for convenience.

It would be better if users could be spared such technical jargon, but these expressions are common and necessary when you converse with other users. Besides, you will need to know these terms to talk to the sales person where you will buy your diskettes.

The 5.25-Inch Diskettes

The 5.25-inch diskettes are found in two common sizes, 360K, and 1.2MB, and an obsolete size, 160K. All three formats have a small square notch on the upper right edge of the diskette envelope. This notch, when covered with an adhesive tab, *write-protects* the diskette so that the computer cannot write to it.

160K: Single-Sided

The first PC came with a diskette drive that recorded on one side of the 5.25-inch diskette. These diskettes had a capacity for 160K bytes of storage. The very first version of DOS, version 1.0, which is seldom used, supported only this 160K format. You will rarely find this format being used today, although the newer 5.25-inch drives can read and write the older diskettes. This format is not addressed in the exercises in this book.

360K: Double-Sided Double-Density

DOS 2.0 included support for diskette drives that can read and write both sides of a 5.25-inch floppy diskette. This format provides for 360K capacity. To be used in this format, a diskette must have been manufactured to meet the specifications that support it. Most 5.25-inch diskettes that you buy today support the 360K format.

1.2MB: High-Density

When the IBM AT was introduced, a new format for diskettes came with it—the high-density 1.2MB drive. To use a 1.2MB drive in its high-density mode, you must use diskettes that are rated for high-density storage.

If you do not know whether your 5.25-inch drive is rated for 1.2MB or only 360K, you must find out. There are no external identifying marks on a typical 5.25-inch disk drive. If you have a high-density diskette, and your drive will read and write it, then you have a high-density drive. Without that clue, you will have to ask someone.

The 3.5-Inch Diskettes

The 3.5-inch diskettes come in two sizes: 720K and 1.44MB. You can tell the diskettes apart. The 1.44MB diskette has a small square hole in the upper right corner. Both formats have a similar hole in the upper right corner with a small plastic slider that opens and closes the hole. When the hole is open, the diskette is write-protected—the computer cannot write to it.

720K

DOS 3.2 offered support for the 720K 3.5-inch diskette although many laptop computers support this format with earlier DOS versions.

1.44K

DOS 3.3 added support for the 1.44MB 3.5-inch diskette format. As with the 1.2 MB 5.25-inch drive, the only way to know if your PC's disk drive supports the larger format is to try it.

Diskette Compatibility

There are compatibility concerns with the various disk formats. Since the purpose of this book is to allow you to teach yourself enough DOS 6.0 to get some work done, the advice here is to find a format that works for you and get on with it. Later, when you become a power user, you can try mixing and matching disks with the drives. To guide you, here are the basic rules of compatibility (and incompatibility) among the disk formats:

- You cannot put a 3.5-inch diskette into a 5.25-inch drive.
- You cannot put a 5.25-inch diskette into a 3.5-inch drive.
- You can read and write 720K diskettes in both formats of 3.5-inch disk drives.
- You can read and write a 1.44MB diskette only in a 3.5-inch drive that is rated for 1.44MB diskettes.
- You can read and write 360K diskettes in both formats of 5.25-inch disk drives.
- 360K diskettes that have been written on a 1.2MB disk drive might not be readable on 360K disk drives. This is not a fixed rule, but it happens often enough that you should never depend on being able to freely move data between the two drive formats without some difficulty.
- You can read and write a 1.2MB diskette only in a 5.25-inch drive that is rated for 1.2MB diskettes.

Figure 3.1 illustrates the operational relationships between the different formats of disk drives and diskettes.

DISKETTE		Disk Drive Type							
		5.25 "				3.5 "			
		360KB		1.2MB		720KB		1.44MB	
		Read	Write	Read	Write	Read	Write	Read	Write
5.25"	360KB	√	√	√	√*				
	1.2MB			√	√				
3.5"	720KB					√	√	√	√
	1.44MB							√	√

* 360KB diskettes written by 1.2MB drives might not be readable by 360KB drives.

Figure 3.1 *Diskettes' relationships*

Preparing a Diskette for Operation (FORMAT Command)

When you buy a box of diskettes, unless they are preformatted, they are not ready to use. You must prepare them for use by formatting them. The DOS FORMAT command manages this. First, you must know which diskette format you have. Then you must run the DOS FORMAT command, which is described in an exercise in Chapter 5. There are a number of ways to format a diskette, but for these lessons, you will use the FORMAT command that formats the diskette in its default configuration.

The FORMAT command is different among versions of DOS. When you get to the FORMAT exercise in Chapter 5, be sure you know the kind of disk drive you have and the version of DOS you are running. Be sure, also, to have a blank diskette of the proper type for the exercise.

Summary

This chapter introduced you to diskettes. You learned about the history of the diskette, the file diskette capacities, the compatibility issues, and the importance of knowing what kind of diskettes to buy.

Chapter 4

Installing DOS 6.0

This chapter teaches you how to install DOS 6.0 on your computer. The purpose is to address some aspects of installation that you will not find in the manual that was packaged with DOS 6.0. You will learn about:

- Running the SETUP program to install DOS 6.0
- Using the EXPAND program to modify a previous installation
- Modifying your AUTOEXEC.BAT and CONFIG.SYS files with SETUP
- Using the Uninstall diskette
- Using the DELOLDOS program to delete your previous DOS version.

Installations Not Covered

You will not learn how to install DOS 6.0 onto floppy disks here. While some users might want to do so, the PC that has no hard disk gains little from the benefits of DOS 6.0. An exception to this opinion is found in the workstations of networks where the file server provides the mass storage for users and the workstations have floppy disks from which to boot DOS 6.0. Such users can use the DOS *Getting Started* manual to learn how to install DOS 6.0 on a floppy disk.

The SETUP Program

The installation of DOS 6.0 is an automatic process that is performed for you by the SETUP program that comes with DOS 6.0. As distributed by Microsoft, DOS 6.0 can be installed only on a computer that is already running DOS 2.11 or later. Those versions of DOS were distributed on diskettes from which you could boot DOS to install onto your hard disk. This is not true with DOS 6.0.

You might ask why Microsoft chose to distribute a version of DOS that you cannot install on a bare-bones PC. Virtually every PC in use today already uses DOS 5.0 or earlier. Users who already have Unix, Xenix, OS/2, and other operating systems are not likely to install DOS 6.0. If they do, they must do so in a multi-operating system environment that entails technical problems too advanced for the first-time user. Get an expert to tackle such a weighty task for you. A PC that has never had DOS installed has several prerequisite steps to prepare the hard disk for the installation of DOS. This level of installation is beyond the scope of this book, which assumes that you have a PC with a hard disk and a diskette drive, and that DOS 5.0 or earlier is installed on the PC.

Installation Procedure

To install DOS 6.0 on your hard disk, you need the installation diskettes and one or two floppy diskettes that can be read and written by your A diskette drive. Review Chapter 3 for a discussion of diskette types. If you use 360K diskettes, you need two diskettes. Otherwise, you need only one. Follow these steps:

1. Put Disk 1 of the MS-DOS Upgrade Setup diskettes into either your A or B drive.
2. Depending on which drive you use, enter *one* of the following commands at the DOS command line prompt:

   ```
   a:setup
   b:setup
   ```

3. Press **Enter**.

   The SETUP program displays a screen, indicating that it is determining what kind of hardware you have. Then you receive a prompt about the diskettes you need.
4. Label the diskettes UNINSTALL #1 and—if needed-#2.

The SETUP program displays a screen that identifies the configuration into which DOS will install itself and allows you to change the items. Usually, you will leave them the way SETUP initially sets them.

Press **Enter** to continue the installation and respond to the questions asked by each subsequent screen. The SETUP program copies its files to your hard disk and installs DOS 6.0. When it is done, it boots the new operating system, and your installation is complete.

The EXPAND Program

The files on the DOS 6.0 distribution disks are compressed. SETUP uses a program named EXPAND to decompress and rename those files from the distribution disk to your hard disk. SETUP expands only those files that it needs to install to match your configuration.

You can use the EXPAND program to expand a DOS 6.0 file that has become corrupted or erased from your hard disk. If you know the name of the file you want to recover, you can find it on one of the installation diskettes by looking for a file with the same name and an extension that has the same first two characters and an underscore (_) as the third. For example, to recover the file named JOIN.EXE, you would find and expand a file named JOIN.EX_ from the distribution disks.

SETUP copies the EXPAND program into your DOS subdirectory. To run EXPAND, type its name on the command line followed by the file paths and names of the compressed file and the unexpanded file. This example shows the command for expanding the JOIN.EXE file. The example assumes that the DOS 6.0 distribution diskette is in the A: drive and that DOS 6.0 is installed in the \DOS subdirectory of the C: drive.

```
expand a:join.ex_ c:\dos\join.exe
```

You will learn about commands, file names, and paths in Chapters 5 and 6.

If you change hardware after you install DOS 6.0, you must use the EXPAND program to expand the files that match the new hardware.

The tough part is knowing what files to expand. The SETUP program has no mode for modifying an existing installation, so you have to use EXPAND. You can install DOS 6.0 a second time, or, if you know the files to expand, you can expand only the ones that relate to your new configuration.

The most common change to your configuration is the installation of a different video monitor or video adaptor card. This change will require different files from the DOS 6.0 distribution diskettes. Table 4.1 shows the video hardware you might install, the associated file names on the distribution disks, and the file names they should have after they are expanded. All files expand into the subdirectory where you installed DOS 6.0.

Table 4.1 *Video system distribution files*

Video system	Distributed file	Expanded file
EGA	EGA.SY_	EGA.SYS
	EGA.CP_	EGA.CPI
	EGA.GR_	DOSSHELL.GRB
	EGA.IN_	DOSSHELL.INI
	EGA.VI_	DOSSHELL.VID
EGA with monochrome monitor	EGAMONO.GR_	DOSSHELL.GRB
	EGA.IN_	DOSSHELL.INI
	EGA.VI_	DOSSHELL.VID
CGA	CGA.GR_	DOSSHELL.GRB
	CGA.IN_	DOSSHELL.INI
	CGA.VI_	DOSSHELL.VID
Hercules graphics adaptor	HERC.GR_	DOSSHELL.GRB
	MONO.IN_	DOSSHELL.INI
	HERC.VI_	DOSSHELL.VID
Monochrome display adaptor	MONO.GR_	DOSSHELL.GRB
	MONO.IN_	DOSSHELL.INI
VGA	VGA.GR_	DOSSHELL.GRB
	VGA.VI_	DOSSHELL.VID
	EGA.IN_	DOSSHELL.INI
VGA with monochrome monitor	VGAMONO.GR_	DOSSHELL.GRB
	VGA.VI_	DOSSHELL.VID
	EGA.IN_	DOSSHELL.INI

Do not attempt to use the EXPAND program with any other syntax. Do not, for example, assume that it will figure out the name of the file to be expanded. Some versions of the EXPAND program operate in an unpredictable manner, perhaps even erasing the unexpanded file if the command line syntax is not correct.

AUTOEXEC.BAT and CONFIG.SYS

DOS computers have files named AUTOEXEC.BAT and CONFIG.SYS in the root directory of the boot disk. These are ASCII text files. They contain startup configuration parameters that describe the characteristics of your hardware and software to DOS 6.0. Chapter 10 describes their contents in detail. Since you install DOS 6.0 from an earlier version of DOS, you probably already have these files. You should know that SETUP modifies them. SETUP adds the DOS subdirectory to the PATH statement in the AUTOEXEC.BAT file, and it adds several DEVICE statements to the CONFIG.SYS file so that the new drivers are resident. You will learn about these things in Chapters 5 and 10.

The UNINSTALL Disk(s)

When you run SETUP, it builds one or two UNINSTALL diskettes on the A drive. At the same time, it copies the files from the previous version of DOS to a subdirectory, which it names OLD_DOS.1. If such a subdirectory already exists, SETUP uses OLD_DOS.2, and so on. You can use the UNINSTALL disk to put the previous version of DOS back onto your computer. Put the UNINSTALL disk in the A: drive, boot the computer, and follow the instructions on the screen.

The DELOLDOS Command

If you are sure that you will never want to restore the previous version of DOS, execute the DELOLDOS command from the command line. Type its name, and press **Enter**. This command removes the OLD_DOS subdirectory from your hard disk, freeing the space it occupies. After you have used the DELOLDDOS command, you may not use the UNINSTALL diskette to return to the earlier version of DOS.

Summary

This chapter taught you how to use the SETUP program to install DOS 6.0. You learned how to use the EXPAND program to modify a previous installation. Additionally, the chapter explained how to use the uninstall diskette, and how to use the DELOLDOS program to delete your previous version of DOS.

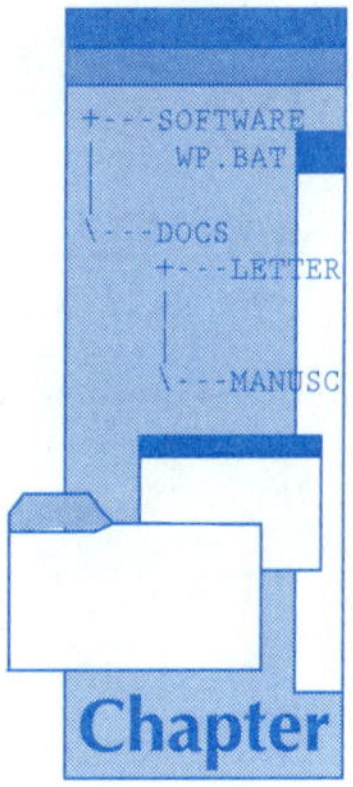

5

Introduction to DOS 6.0 Commands

This chapter is your first step in learning and using DOS 6.0. First, you will learn some basic DOS 6.0 commands. Then, to ease the process, you are going to make a special learning diskette. This diskette will figure prominently in the lessons that follow. As you get farther into the lessons, you will add features to the diskette. You will learn about:

- Using the DOS 6.0 command line edit keys
- Clearing the screen
- Viewing the DOS version
- Logging onto a different disk drive
- Setting the clock and calendar
- Formatting a floppy diskette
- Using file names and wild cards
- Displaying the disk directory
- Copying, moving, deleting, and renaming files
- Adding, deleting, renaming, and changing to a subdirectory
- Viewing the subdirectory tree
- The DOS 6.0 Help system
- Programming the keyboard.

Getting Started

You must start with a blank diskette and your PC with DOS 6.0 installed as described in Chapter 4. Turn on your PC now and allow it to load DOS 6.0. You are now looking at the DOS 6.0 prompt:

```
C>
```

From this point, you enter DOS 6.0 commands. The cursor is positioned to the right of the prompt, and DOS 6.0 is waiting for you to type a command. The area of the screen from where the cursor is to the right margin is the DOS command line. Actually, the command line is longer than that, but you will rarely if ever get much past the center of the screen.

The command line can be on any line of the screen, and its position is determined by where the prompt is displayed.

You learned about the DATE and TIME commands in Chapter 2. The format of a DOS 6.0 command is its name on the command line followed by any parameters that the command needs. A command can be up to 127 characters long. You can put spaces in front of the command and between parameters. It does not matter how many spaces you use as long as the command stays within 127 characters. Try this command now:

```
C>    dir
```

The DIR command executes even though you have preceded it with several space characters on the command line.

DOS 6.0 Edit Keys

To learn DOS 6.0 commands, you will try them on your PC. The exercise will tell you to type a command, and you will type it. You might make some mistakes, and DOS 6.0 has some ways to let you correct your mistakes. Certain keys have editing properties when you are typing onto the DOS 6.0 command line.

These edit keys are not only for correcting mistakes. You can use them to speed up certain repetitive operations that involve sequences of similar commands.

The Backspace Key and Left Arrow Key

Suppose you want to use the DIR command, but you have a typo and enter DOR instead of DIR. Type that error now, but do not press Enter.

```
C>dor
```

Either Backspace or Left Arrow on the numeric keypad moves the cursor back one position erasing the character it covers. You can press either of them twice and see this display:

```
C>d
```

Now type the *ir* and press **Enter**. The DIR command is executed. This method is more useful for longer commands. Many programs require sets of parameters on the command line following the command's name. Using Backspace is handy for correcting a keying error at the time you make it.

The Escape Key

Suppose you type in a command and realize that you do not want to execute it. If you realize that before you press Enter, you can press Esc to cancel the command. Try that now. Type the DIR command followed by Esc instead of Enter.

```
C>dir <press Esc here>
```

DOS 6.0 erases the command.

Now enter any other command you wish.

The F3 Key

Suppose you want to repeat a command. When you press F3, the program displays the most recent command on the command line. The cursor will be at the end of the command waiting for Enter. You can press Enter or you can use Backspace to edit and change the command. Try this now. Type the DIR command. Press **Enter** at the end of the command.

```
C>dir
```

You will see a file directory on the screen. Press **F3**. You will see the DIR command repeated as shown here:

```
C>dir_
```

(the cursor is at the end of the command)

Press **Enter**. The DIR command is repeated.

The F1 and Forward Arrow Keys

Just as F3 repeats the previous command, so do F1 and Forward Arrow on the numeric keypad, except these keys repeat the command one character at a time. Try this now. You just executed the DIR command in the last exercise. Press **F1** once. You will see the first letter (d) of the DIR command as shown here.

```
C>d_
```

(the cursor is just past the d)

Press **F1** a second time. Now the second letter (i) is displayed.

```
C>di_
```

Press **F1** a third time and the entire DIR command is displayed. Now press **Enter** to execute the command.

Any Displayable Key

While you are pressing F1 to space forward through the previous command, you can press any key that displays. The value of that key will replace the keystroke that was in the previous command. Try this after executing the DIR command. Press **F1** once. You will see the first letter (d) of the DIR command as shown here:

```
C>d_
```

(the cursor is just past the d)

Now press **E** and see this display:

```
C>de_
```

Press **F1** again, and the r from the DIR command is displayed as shown here:

```
C>der_
```

DER is not a command, and if you press Enter now, you will get this message:

```
Bad command or file name.
```

Instead, you can press **Esc** to ignore the command.

The Ins Key

While using F1, you can press Ins before typing other characters. Then the characters you type are inserted into the previous command rather than overwriting the character that was in the current position. Try this now. First execute the DIR command to get a command to repeat. Then press **F1** once. You will see the first letter (d) of the DIR command.

```
C>d_
```

(the cursor is just past the d)

Now press **Ins** and type *espa* like this:

```
C>despa_
```

Now press **F1** twice and see this word:

```
C>despair_
```

The first *d* and the last *ir* are from the previous DIR command. The others were typed by you. DESPAIR is not a DOS 6.0 command, but do not despair. Press **Esc** to reject it. Press **Enter** to get the DOS 6.0 prompt back.

The Del Key

While pressing F1, you can press **Del** to delete characters from the previous command. This requires that you remember what the previous command is. Try this: Press **F1** once. You will see the first letter (d) of the DIR command.

```
C>d_
```

(the cursor is just past the d)

Now press **Del** followed by **F1**. Del deletes the *i* of the DIR command, so you will see this display:

```
C>dr_
```

Press **Esc** to delete the invalid DR command.

Mixing the Keys

You can mix all of these keys in building a new command from the old one. Do not expect to fully understand how you will use these features until you are into the more complex DOS 6.0 commands and those of your applications programs. However, put a marker in this page of the book and return to this discussion after a while. The study of DOS 6.0 often requires that you learn a subject to get to the next plateau, yet the full power of the subject is not apparent until several plateaus later. Chapter 11 is dedicated to the DOSKEY program, which extends the keyboard functions of the DOS 6.0 command line.

Clearing the Screen

Enter this command:

```
C>cls
```

The screen goes blank, and the DOS 6.0 prompt and cursor are in the upperleft corner of the screen.

The CLS command is the second of the internal DOS 6.0 commands that you have now learned. Remember from Chapter 2 that internal DOS 6.0 commands are ones that are built into DOS 6.0. You do not need a program file to execute them.

Why would you clear the screen? Sometimes it just gets cluttered. Other times you do not want anyone to see what you have been doing. You may want to display something—a directory perhaps—so you can print the screen, and you do not want the residue of earlier operations to be on the screen print. Chapter 7 discusses screen printing.

The DOS Version

There are 11 versions of DOS: 2.0, 2.1, 2.11, 3.0, 3.1, 3.2, 3.3, 4.0, 4.1, 5.0, and 6.0. When the PC was first introduced, there was a DOS version 1.0. Version 1.0 is incompatible in many ways with the versions that followed, and is rarely used.

You can see what version you have by entering the VER command like this:

```
C>ver
```

The VER command tells you the DOS version with a message like this:

```
MS-DOS Version 6.00
```

The message may vary depending on where you got the particular version of DOS. The message might include the name of a particular computer manufacturer. However, the relevant information is the DOS version number. Regardless of the other information, all versions 2.0 are functionally identical, all versions 2.1 are identical, and so on.

Why should you care about the version? Often an applications program specifies that it runs with a particular version of DOS or higher. You need to know if you have a compatible DOS version so that you know if you can run that program.

Some applications specify that they only run with a particular version or subset of versions. This is because they rely on certain DOS features introduced in version 3, and the developers have not released programs that run correctly under version 4. Some applications run under DOS versions 3, 5, and 6 but not under version 4. However, the programs terminate if they are running under anything but version 3. Later in this chapter, you will learn about the SETVER command, which makes an applications program behave as if it is running under a different version of DOS. This command allows you to use applications that are supposed to run only with a certain DOS version other than version 6.0.

The Calendar and Clock

DOS 6.0 keeps track of the current date and time. When first loaded, DOS 6.0 does not have the correct date and time. If you have an AT-class machine or if your PC/XT has a clock/calendar card installed, there is hardware that remembers the date and time in your PC, and the startup procedures set the current date and time into DOS 6.0's clock and calendar. If, however, you are using a PC/XT without a clock/calendar board, then you must set the date and time each time DOS 6.0 is reloaded. If you do not, DOS 6.0 assumes it is midnight on January 1, 1980 every time you reload.

If you do not keep your date and time set properly, DOS 6.0 will associate incorrect dates and times with the files that it creates for you.

Not only will this cause confusion when you attempt to manage your own files, but the DOS 6.0 procedures for backing up and restoring files will not always work properly. The MSBACKUP command is discussed in Chapter 15.

DOS 6.0 has user commands to read and set the date and time. They are named, naturally enough, DATE and TIME. Try these commands now. Type this command:

```
C>time
```

DOS 6.0 displays the time like this:

```
Current time is 7:30:22.75p
Enter new time:
```

If you do not want to change the clock, press **Enter**. To change the time, you must use military time where the hour is 0 to 23. Just enter the time in minutes and seconds as follows:

```
19:30
```

To view the date, type this command

```
C>date
```

DOS 6.0 displays the date like this:

```
Current date is Wed 03-27-1991
Enter new date (mm-dd-yy):
```

If you do not want to change the date, press **Enter**. To change the date, enter it in the format shown here:

```
06-24-93
```

You can use a shorthand version of either command to set the date or time without the prompting displays. Simply include the new date or time on the command line as shown here:

```
C>date 06-24-93
C>time 19:30
```

If the date and the time in your hardware clock are wrong, the DATE and TIME commands do not reset them in all computers. In some PCs, the DATE and TIME commands only modify DOS's copies of the date and time. These are not permanent copies, but they remain in effect only until the next reload of DOS.

The procedures for resetting the hardware date and time vary from machine to machine. Some computers come with a program called SETUP that includes a procedure to reset the clock and calendar hardware. Others allow you to run a setup program that is always available. You press a sequence of keys, and the setup program pops up. Still others give you the option to execute the program when you first turn the computer on. Clock/calendar add-on boards for the PC/XT use other programs to change the settings, and there is no standard.

You will need to change the clock at least twice a year when Daylight Savings Time comes and goes.

Logging onto a Different Disk Drive

Up until now, you have used the C> prompt in all of the examples and exercises. The C is the standard designation for the default hard disk on most PCs.

When you issue commands, the commands are usually effective relative to the drive that is shown in the prompt. This drive is called the currently logged-on drive. For example, when you issue the DIR command from the C> prompt, you will see a directory of files that are stored on the C: drive. If you were to issue that command from the A> prompt, you would see a directory of the files on the A: drive.

You can change the currently logged-on drive with a simple DOS 6.0 command. For now, put any diskette you might have handy into the A: drive and enter this command:

```
C>a:
```

You will now see this prompt:

```
A>
```

Issue the DIR command now, and you will see a directory of the files on the diskette that you inserted in the A: drive. Put a different diskette in the A: drive and enter the DIR command, and you will see a different directory. To return to the C: drive, issue this command:

```
A>c:
```

You will see this prompt once again:

```
C>
```

This is an important lesson. Unless something in the command explicitly refers to a different drive, the command is generally assumed to be directed to files on the currently logged-on drive.

There are exceptions and other ways to override this rule, and you will learn them in time, but for now make sure you understand this concept. Unless you are told otherwise, all commands relate to the currently logged-on disk drive.

Formatting a Diskette (FORMAT)

Chapter 3 discussed the differences between the various kinds of diskettes and disk drives, and you learned that you must use the DOS 6.0 FORMAT command to prepare a diskette for use. Now, you will build your learning diskette by using the FORMAT command. Enter the following command at the DOS 6.0 command line to format a diskette in the A: drive and to write a copy of DOS 6.0 on the diskette:

```
C>format a: /s
```

When this operation is complete, you can initialize your PC with the diskette in the A: drive. DOS 6.0 will be on the diskette, and the system can boot itself from that DOS 6.0 image

When you issue the FORMAT command as shown above, DOS 6.0 responds with this message:

```
Insert new diskette for drive A:
and strike ENTER when ready...
```

While DOS 6.0 is formatting the disk, it gives you a running status. DOS 6.0 shows this message:

```
Checking existing disk format.
```

If the diskette has never been formatted, there could be a long wait while the FORMAT command figures out what kind of disk is in the disk drive. This characteristic was new in DOS 5.0. Earlier versions did not do it. The peculiar thing is that if you try to format a 360K diskette in a 1.2 MB drive, FORMAT thinks that it is a 1.2 MB diskette, and tries to format it accordingly. The results are rarely satisfactory. See Chapter 10 to learn the correct way to format a 360K diskette in a 1.2 MB drive.

If you format a diskette that was previously formatted, the FORMAT command displays this information:

```
Saving UNFORMAT information.
```

While FORMAT is formatting the diskette, it displays this information:

```
Verifying 1.44M
5 percent completed.
```

The percent completed value changes to show you how far the FORMAT command has progressed.

When the FORMAT command is done, the program displays this information:

```
Format complete.
System transferred
Volume label (11 characters, ENTER for none)?
```

You may enter a label for the diskette or press **Enter** for no label.

The FORMAT program now displays this information:

```
Volume Serial Number is 3437-15EE
Format another (Y/N)?
```

Type **N** followed by **Enter**.

The serial number in the display will be different.

To format a diskette without transferring a copy of DOS 6.0, omit the optional /s parameter in the FORMAT command. This is the usual way to format a diskette. You do not often need a copy of DOS 6.0 on your diskettes if you have a hard disk.

Chapter 10 has exercises to teach you the advanced FORMAT options. For now, you know all that new users need to know about the FORMAT command.

Some Lesson Review

You have just built your learning diskette by running the FORMAT command. That's a big step. You have actually made your PC do something meaningful. Put a label on the diskette that says *TYD Learning Diskette* so you will be able to find it next time you want it. Put it back into the A: drive. Now you can run some exercises that review some of the earlier lessons you learned.

Reloading DOS 6.0

Remember that DOS 6.0 reloads itself from the diskette in the A: drive if one is there. You have one there now, so try it. Hold down **Ctrl** and **Alt** at the same time that you press **Del**. This is the famous DOS three-fingered salute. You'll use it a lot.

The PC will emit a beep and a grinding sound, and will eventually read DOS 6.0 from the diskette you just built. Every PC is set up differently, so this new boot operation might differ from the one you are accustomed to seeing. However, you know what to expect now. First the computer displays this message:

```
Starting MS-DOS....
```

Next, DOS 6.0 loads and automatically runs the DATE command and the TIME command. Press **Enter** for each one as shown here:

```
Current date is Wed 03-27-1991
Enter new date (mm-dd-yy):
```

Press **Enter**.

```
Current time is 8:30:22.75p
Enter new time:
```

Press **Enter** again.

Now DOS 6.0 displays its copyright message followed by its prompt like this:

```
Microsoft(R) MS-DOS(R) Version 6.00
                (C)Copyright Microsoft Corp 1981-1991
A>
```

Since you loaded DOS 6.0 from the A: drive, A is automatically the currently logged-on drive. None of the startup options that were installed in your computer are in effect because you are booting from a sterile, unprepared system diskette, the one you just built. Gradually, you will build up that diskette's functionality. For now, it will serve your purposes just as it is.

The DIR Command

The DIR command shows you what is in the root directory of your TYD Learning Diskette. Type this command now:

```
A>dir
```

DOS 6.0 displays this information:

```
 Volume in drive A has no label
 Volume Serial Number is 3437-15EE
 Directory of A:\
COMMAND   COM  53022 10-26-92    6:00a
         1 file(s)    53022 bytes
                    1326592 bytes free
```

This display indicates that the diskette has no label (more about labels later), and has one visible file in its root directory, a file named COMMAND.COM. The size of the file and the date and time of its creation follow. The next line tells the total number of files in the directory and the total number of bytes used by those files. The last line tells how many bytes are free on the diskette.

The sum of the number of bytes free and the size of COMMAND.COM do not equal the 1.44MB capacity of the diskette. This is because DOS 6.0 includes two other files that are hidden from you. A hidden file is not shown by the DIR command.

```
A>c:
```

Now you are logged onto C:, and the prompt is displayed like this:

```
C>
```

If you use the DIR command, you will see the files in the root directory of the C: drive. That may or may not be what you saw earlier when you used the DIR command for the C: drive. What you saw then depended on how your boot procedures were installed. You might have been looking at the contents of a subdirectory. You will soon learn what that means.

While you are logged onto the C: drive, you can still look at a directory of the A drive if you want. Try this now. Enter this command:

```
C>dir a:
```

You will see the same directory you saw when you were logged onto the A: drive. The DIR command allows you to specify a different drive on the command line.

This is an important addition to your knowledge. The DIR command can be expanded by the use of command line parameters. You will soon learn more of them.

An Introduction to AUTOEXEC.BAT

Why did DOS 6.0 ask for the date and time when you loaded it from your TYD Learning Diskette? DOS 6.0 probably does not do that when you load it the way it was installed on your hard disk.

When DOS 6.0 is loaded, it looks for a file named AUTOEXEC.BAT on the boot disk. If it does not find that file, DOS 6.0 assumes that you need to set the date and time. If it does find the AUTOEXEC.BAT file, DOS 6.0 assumes that if you need to manually set the date and time, the AUTOEXEC.BAT file will take care of it.

The AUTOEXEC.BAT file is a file of text that contains DOS 6.0 commands. These commands are automatically executed every time DOS 6.0 is loaded. That's how the file got its name. There is a lot more to know about AUTOEXEC.BAT, but you do not need to know it just yet. You will learn more about AUTOEXEC.BAT in later chapters.

For now, you will build yourself an AUTOEXEC.BAT file on the TYD Learning Diskette so that DOS 6.0 will load without troubling you about the date and time ever again. You are learning AUTOEXEC.BAT here for the reason just given and also to show you how to add a file to the diskette. You need some files on the diskette so that you can run some more exercises.

Using COPY To Build a File

The simplest way to get a file onto the TYD Learning Diskette is with the DOS 6.0 COPY command. This is a housekeeping chore that supports the lessons.

COPY is the DOS 6.0 command that lets you copy files. COPY has many variations on its command format, and you will address them soon enough. Right now, you will learn what is needed to add a file to the TYD Learning Diskette. The COPY command format follows this pattern:

```
COPY <source> <destination>
```

Generally, you use file names and/or disk drives for the source and destination of the COPY command. However, you can also use fixed device names to copy from the keyboard or to the screen or printer. When you address the COPY command in detail, you will see how that works. For now, you will copy some text from the keyboard to a file on the TYD Learning Diskette. Specifically, you will build the first version of the AUTOEXEC.BAT file. Log onto the A drive with this command:

```
C>a:
```

Next, enter the command shown here:

```
A>copy con autoexec.bat
```

With that command, you said, effectively, "copy *con*, the source, to *autoexec.bat*, the destination."

You have told DOS 6.0 that you want to copy whatever is typed at the console keyboard (*con* means *console* to DOS 6.0) into a file named AUTOEXEC.BAT.

Using COPY to build a file from the keyboard is not the way COPY is normally used. COPY is usually for copying disk files from one place to another, perhaps to write a file that is on a hard disk to a diskette. This unconventional introduction to COPY is for convenience so that you can build files to use in the lessons. The COPY command gets a more comprehensive treatment later in the chapter.

Because you are logged onto the A: drive, the AUTOEXEC.BAT file will be written to the A: drive by the COPY command. After you enter the COPY command shown above, the cursor moves to the screen line below the command and DOS 6.0 waits for you to type something. Type the following lines very carefully. Press Enter at the end of each line. Before you press Enter, you can use Backspace to correct characters on the line.

```
echo off
cls
echo Teach Yourself DOS 6.0 Learning Diskette
ver
```

After the last line is typed, press F6 and then press Enter. Using F6 tells DOS 6.0 that you are done typing. The diskette drive makes a grinding sound as the file is written, and then you will see the DOS 6.0 A> prompt once more.

The AUTOEXEC.BAT file you just created contains two commands you already learned, CLS and VER. The other command, ECHO, is unfamiliar. ECHO is a special DOS 6.0 batch command. You never use it anywhere except in a batch (.BAT) file. The first use of ECHO, the one that says "echo off," tells DOS 6.0 not to display the other commands in the batch file while they are being executed. The second ECHO command tells DOS 6.0 to display the text on the command line when the ECHO command is encountered. This command provides a way for you to display meaningful messages while a batch file is processed. Chapter 13 describes batch files and their use.

Give the three-fingered salute (**Ctrl+Alt+Del**). After the disk drive makes some wheezing and grinding sounds, your screen will contain this display.

```
Teach Yourself DOS 6.0 Learning Diskette
MS-DOS Version 6.00
A>
```

Note that you have now loaded DOS 6.0 without being pestered to enter the date and time. The mere presence of the AUTOEXEC.BAT suppresses those prompts. If your PC has no hardware clock/calendar, you can include the DATE and TIME commands in the AUTOEXEC.BAT file. These commands can then at least ensure that you do not ignore the need for the correct date and time when DOS 6.0 is loaded. Now try the DIR command:

```
A>dir
```

You will see the display shown here. Note that the AUTOEXEC.BAT file is now on the diskette.

```
 Volume in drive A has no label
 Volume Serial Number is 3437-15EE
 Directory of A:\
COMMAND  COM      53022 10-26-92   6:00a
AUTOEXEC BAT         67 01-09-93   2:54p
        2 file(s)       53089 bytes
                      1326080 bytes free
```

With the addition of AUTOEXEC.BAT, the number of bytes free on the diskette has been reduced. Oddly, the reduction is greater than the size of AUTOEXEC.BAT. In fact, although AUTOEXEC.BAT is only 67 bytes long, the number of bytes free is now 512 bytes less than it was before AUTOEXEC.BAT was added to the diskette. This is because DOS 6.0 allocates disk storage space in even blocks. On 1.2MB and 1.44MB diskettes, the blocks are 512 bytes each. A 360K diskette uses 1024-byte blocks. Most hard disks use blocks of 2048 bytes.

The blocks that DOS 6.0 allocates to files are called *clusters*. On the 1.44MB diskette, files with lengths from 1 to 512 bytes use one cluster, files from 513 to 1024 bytes use two clusters, and so on in increments of 512.

Typing a File

DOS 6.0 has an internal command named TYPE that lets you display the contents of a text file. You can use this command to view the AUTOEXEC.BAT file that you just created. Enter this command:

```
A>type autoexec.bat
```

DOS 6.0 will now "type" the contents of the file on the screen. This is what you will see:

```
echo off
cls
echo Teach Yourself DOS 6.0 Learning Diskette
ver
```

Does this look familiar? It's what you built earlier with the COPY command. The TYPE command is an example of a command that requires a command line parameter, in this case, the name of the file to be typed.

Many DOS 6.0 and applications program commands require file names on the command line, and there are different ways that you can specify them, depending upon the command's requirements. Some commands operate on one or more files, and there are ways to use the DOS 6.0 file name convention to specify a group of files rather than just one. In addition, you can specify files that are on other disk drives. The next exercise shows how.

Files on Other Drives

Remember how you used the DIR command to look at the directory of a different drive. You issued the following command to view the A: drive's directory while you were logged onto the C: drive.

```
C>dir a:
```

Commands that take file names as parameters can also have disk drive designators that tell DOS 6.0 to look somewhere other than the currently logged-on drive. To illustrate that concept, log onto the C: drive like this:

```
A>c:
```

Then use the TYPE command that you just learned to type the AUTOEXEC.BAT file, which you know to be on the A: drive, like this:

```
C>type a:autoexec.bat
```

The display is the same as shown in the previous exercise because the AUTOEXEC.BAT file is the same one. Even though you are logged onto the C: drive, you can access files on other drives. Notice the a: before the file name. That is a drive designator, and it tells DOS 6.0 to find the file on the A: drive.

Remember that unless told otherwise, DOS 6.0 expects files named on the command line to be in the default drive. This exercise shows how DOS 6.0 is told otherwise. If you leave out the optional disk drive designator, DOS 6.0 looks to the default drive. If you include it, DOS 6.0 looks to the drive that it specifies.

Now log onto A: once more to learn about file names that specify groups of files rather than just one.

```
C>a:
```

File Names and Wild Cards

Until now, you have used simple file names, or file names that completely specify the file in question. When you specified AUTOEXEC.BAT, you gave the full name of the file, and there was no question about what file you meant. There are occasions where you want to name a group of files. The most frequent use of this is in the COPY command, which you will learn more about later. However, it is used in the DIR command, too. Now you will learn about how to specify an ambiguous file name.

First, however, for these exercises you will need more files on the TYD Learning Diskette, and so some housekeeping is in order. Build the first of the example files with this command:

```
A>copy con autotype.bat
```

Type the following lines:

```
cls
echo Running AUTOTYPE.BAT
```

Press **F6** and **Enter**. DOS 6.0 will tell you that one file was copied. This file is a batch file that you could run by entering the command AUTOTYPE. You do not need to do that just yet. Build the next file with this command:

```
A>copy con charley.001
```

Type the following line:

```
This is CHARLEY.001
```

Press **F6** and **Enter**. DOS 6.0 will tell you that one file was copied. This file is just a file of text. Build the last file with this command:

```
A>copy con charley.002
```

(A hint: Save keystrokes. Type **F3**, **Backspace**, **2**.)

Type the following line:

```
This is CHARLEY.002
```

Press **F6** and **Enter**. DOS 6.0 will tell you that one file was copied. You have just added three files named AUTOTYPE.BAT, CHARLEY.001, and

CHARLEY.002 to the TYD Learning Diskette. Use the DIR command to verify that the files were added.

```
A>dir
```

You will see this display:

```
COMMAND  COM      53022 10-26-92   6:00a
AUTOEXEC BAT         67 01-09-93   2:54p
AUTOTYPE BAT         32 01-09-93   3:04p
CHARLIE  001         21 01-09-93   3:05p
CHARLIE  002         21 01-09-93   3:06p
        5 file(s)       53163 bytes
                      1324544 bytes free
```

The dates and times will be different, of course, and the bytes free will be different if you are using other than a 1.44MB diskette.

Now that you have that housekeeping chore out of the way, you can learn about wild cards.

When you specify a file name on the command line, you can specify a set of files rather than just one. You do this by inserting wild cards in the file name. Following is a discussion of the simplest variation of this concept.

The Asterisk (*) Wild Card

The asterisk character in a file name is a *wild card*. The asterisk by itself represents all occurrences of file names. For example if you use *.BAT, you are requesting all files that have the extension .BAT, regardless of their names. Try it now.

```
A>dir *.bat
```

This is what you will see:

```
AUTOEXEC BAT        67 01-09-93   2:54p
AUTOTYPE BAT        32 01-09-93   3:04p
        2 file(s)         99 bytes
                     1324544 bytes free
```

The asterisk wild card works in file name extensions as well. Enter this command:

```
A>dir charley.*
```

This is what you will see:

```
CHARLIE  001        21 01-09-93   3:05p
CHARLIE  002        21 01-09-93   3:06p
        2 file(s)         42 bytes
                     1324544 bytes free
```

You asked for a directory of all files that were named CHARLEY, regardless of their extensions, and that is what you got.

You can use the asterisk on both sides of the period. For the DIR command, using *.* delivers the same directory as specifying no file name at all. This is because *.* means all file names, regardless of extension and all extensions, regardless of file names, and that specification specifies all file names.

You can also use the asterisk to specify part of a file name. You can give the part of the file name you know and use the asterisk to select the rest of it. For example, try any of these commands:

```
A>dir a*.*
A>dir au*.*
A>dir aut*.*
A>dir auto*.*
```

This is what you will see:

```
AUTOEXEC BAT          67 01-09-93    2:54p
AUTOTYPE BAT          32 01-09-93    3:04p
        2 file(s)           99 bytes
                       1324544 bytes free
```

Try this command:

```
A>dir c*.*
```

You will see this display showing all the files that begin with the letter C:

```
COMMAND  COM     53022 10-26-92    6:00a
CHARLIE  001        21 01-09-93    3:05p
CHARLIE  002        21 01-09-93    3:06p
        3 file(s)        53064 bytes
                       1324544 bytes free
```

You can use the asterisk the same way in the file name extension.

The Question Mark (?) Wild Card

The question mark is a wild card specifier that you substitute for a single character of the file name. For example, to see all the files that have a zero as the second character of the file name extension, enter this command:

```
A>dir *.?0?
```

This is what you will see:

```
CHARLIE  001        21 01-09-93    3:05p
CHARLIE  002        21 01-09-93    3:06p
          2 file(s)           42 bytes
                       1324544 bytes free
```

The asterisk matches all file names, and the ?0? mask matches the extensions that have any character as the first character, a zero as the second, and any character as the third.

Not all commands work with wild cards. Some commands, by virtue of what they do, operate with only one file. TYPE is an example of such a command. If you use a wild card in the file name for TYPE, the program displays an error message. Many applications programs do not work with wild cards in their file specifications. You must determine from the program's instructions whether wild cards are allowed.

Deleting a File (DEL)

Sometimes you want to delete a file. The file might be an old one, an earlier version of something you have updated, or just something you want to discard to make room on the disk. The DEL command serves that purpose. You can use wild cards in the DEL command. The AUTOTYPE.BAT, CHARLEY.001 and CHARLEY.002 files on the TYD Learning Diskette have served their purpose, so you can delete them. Enter these commands:

```
A>del autotype.bat
A>del charley.*
```

Use the DIR command to see that the files have been deleted. You will revisit the DEL command when you have learned more about subdirectories.

Subdirectories

Chapter 2 introduced the concept of subdirectories. The DOS 6.0 file system can be organized into a hierarchy of such subdirectories. Figure 5.1 is the structure you will build on the TYD Learning Diskette. Each subdirectory has a name. The directory at the top of the hierarchy is called the *root* directory, and has the peculiar name of "\" (backslash). That is the only directory in the hierarchy that has a fixed name. You name all of the subdirectories below the root when you create them.

A subdirectory can contain files, and it can contain other subdirectories. In Figure 5.1, the root directory contains the files named

COMMAND.COM and AUTOEXEC.BAT and the subdirectories named WORDPROC, SPRDSHT, and DOS. WORDPROC has the subdirectories named SOFTWARE and DOCS. SPRDSHT has SOFTWARE and SHEETS. The DOCS subdirectory under WORDPROC has LETTERS and MANUSCRP subdirectories. For clarity, the names of subdirectories are in capital letters in the figure and the names of files are in lowercase. That convention continues throughout these discussions.

```
\ .................................. (Root Directory)
├── command.com
├── autoexec.bat
├── WORDPROC ....................... (Word Processing)
│     ├── SOFTWARE ................. (Word Processing Software)
│     └── DOCS ..................... (Word Processing Documents)
│           ├── LETTERS ............ (Letters)
│           └── MANUSCRP ........... (Manuscripts)
├── SPRDSHT ........................ (Spreadsheets)
│     ├── SOFTWARE ................. (Spreadsheet Software)
│     └── SHEETS ................... (Spreadsheet data files)
└── DOS ............................ (DOS Utility Programs)
```

Figure 5.1 *The TYD Learning Diskette directory structure*

Consider the words *directory* and *subdirectory*. The root directory, WORDPROC, SPRDSHT, and DOS 6.0 are all directories. So are the subdirectories under WORDPROC and SPRDSHT. The root directory, however, is not a subdirectory because it is not subordinate to a higher directory. All other directories are subdirectories, being subordinate either to the root or to another subdirectory. The generic term *subdirectory* applies unless you are talking about the root directory, in which case you would use root *directory*.

The display from the DIR command is a *directory*, too. So, when you use the DIR command, you are getting a directory of a directory—or of a subdirectory. Try not to let it get to you. That's how they set it up when they designed DOS 6.0. Eventually, these apparent ambiguities will become part of your vocabulary, and they will seem natural.

There are four subdirectory operations to learn. You can make a new subdirectory, remove an existing subdirectory, change to an existing subdirectory, and rename a subdirectory.

The Currently Logged-on Subdirectory

Up until now, you have stayed in the root directory of the TYD Learning Diskette and the C: drive. You have logged onto first one drive and then the other, but you have ignored subdirectories because you have not learned them yet.

Look again at Figure 5.1. Just as you can be logged onto a drive, you can be logged onto one of the subdirectories of the currently logged-on drive. When you start out you are logged onto the root directory, which is named \ (backslash). You can change the logged-on directory with the CD command, soon to be discussed. What are the implications?

When you change disk drives, all commands refer to the new logged-on disk unless you specify otherwise. The same rule applies to subdirectories. When you change subdirectories, your commands apply to the new current subdirectory unless you specify otherwise.

Before you can play with subdirectories, you must create some on the TYD Learning Diskette. To do that, you use the MD command.

Making a Subdirectory (MD)

You make a subdirectory with the MD command, which has this format:

```
A>md <subdirectory path>
```

The <subdirectory path> parameter specifies the subdirectory. The parameter consists of the names of the subdirectories separated by backslashes. The root directory is named backslash, too, which may confuse the learning process, but can also be positive—it makes things easier after you get used to it. Make some subdirectories now. You will use the structure shown in Figure 5.1 for the exercise. Begin with this command:

```
A>md \wordproc
```

You have told DOS 6.0 to make a subdirectory named WORDPROC underneath (subordinate to) the root directory. Subdirectory paths are specified with the topmost directory at the beginning, and the root directory (\) is the topmost directory. You can verify that the subdirectory was made by using the DIR command:

```
A>dir
```

In addition to the other files on the TYD Learning Diskette, you will see this entry:

```
WORDPROC      <DIR>  01-09-93   3:24p
```

The <DIR> token tells us that WORDPROC is a subdirectory file.

Notice that there are two more subdirectories immediately under the root directory in Figure 5.1. These are named SPRDSHT and DOS. Make those subdirectories now.

```
A>md \sprdsht
A>md \dos
```

Use the DIR command to see that the subdirectories were made.

The WORDPROC subdirectory has two subdirectories named SOFTWARE and DOCS. You can make those subdirectories by specifying their full path. Enter these commands:

```
A>md \wordproc\software
A>md \wordproc\docs
```

Notice that the path specification uses the backslash to separate the names of subdirectories. The first backslash is, however, the name of the root directory and, since it is a backslash, does not need another separator. This makes more sense when you look at a path specification.

The \WORDPROC\DOCS subdirectory has two subdirectories named LETTERS and MANUSCRP. Make them now with these commands:

```
A>md \wordproc\docs\letters
A>md \wordproc\docs\manuscrp
```

The SPRDSHT subdirectory has two subdirectories named SOFTWARE and SHEETS. Make those subdirectories by specifying the full path to them. Enter these commands:

```
A>md \sprdsht\software
A>md \sprdsht\sheets
```

The TYD Learning Diskette is now complete as far as its directory structure is concerned. This diskette will be the basis for the exercises throughout most of Section I of this book. You will add and remove subdirectories and files as you need them to make the point under discussion. The diskette, as it is now, is the foundation.

Using a Subdirectory Path in a Command

As a preliminary exercise in the use of subdirectories, look at how they might affect the DIR command. Enter this command:

```
A>dir \wordproc
```

You will see this display:

```
  Directory of A:\WORDPROC
.               <DIR>     01-09-93    3:24p
..              <DIR>     01-09-93    3:24p
SOFTWARE        <DIR>     01-09-93    3:27p
DOCS            <DIR>     01-09-93    3:27p
        4 file(s)             0 bytes
                        1321472 bytes free
```

This is the directory display of the WORDPROC subdirectory. Notice that the drive and subdirectory name are shown above the directory display.

The two peculiar files named "." and ".." (dot and dot-dot) are always seen at the top of any subdirectory. Their purpose is to provide internal linkage to the parent directory of the subdirectory, which, in this case is the root directory. There is no reason that you should see these files other than that a DOS designer decided you should. You can generally ignore these entries in a directory.

The other two files are the SOFTWARE and DOCS subdirectories that you built above. Enter this command:

```
A>dir \wordproc\docs
```

You will see this display:

```
  Directory of A:\WORDPROC\DOCS
.             <DIR>     01-09-93   3:27p
..            <DIR>     01-09-93   3:27p
LETTERS       <DIR>     01-09-93   3:28p
MANUSCRP      <DIR>     01-09-93   3:28p
        4 file(s)           0 bytes
                      1321472 bytes free
```

Finally, enter this command:

```
A>dir \wordproc\docs\letters
```

You will see this display:

```
  Directory of A:\WORDPROC\DOCS\LETTERS
.             <DIR>      01-09-93   3:28p
..            <DIR>      01-09-93   3:28p
         2 file(s)           0 bytes
                      1321472 bytes free
```

This is a display of a subdirectory that has no files (other than dot and dot-dot).

Removing a Subdirectory (RD)

You can remove a subdirectory from a disk if it is empty, that is, if it has no files. First, make a dummy subdirectory to use in the exercise. Enter this command:

```
A>md \dummy
```

Next, add a subdirectory to the dummy subdirectory. Enter this command:

```
A>md \dummy\dummy01
```

Now put a file in the \DUMMY\DUMMY01 subdirectory. This is a further example of using subdirectories in the file names of commands. Enter this command:

```
A>copy con \dummy\dummy01\test.txt
```

Note that the path, \DUMMY\DUMMY01, is separated from the file name, TEXT.TXT, with a backslash. That is the convention for naming files with their subdirectory names. You will soon do more of this. Type some lines of text:

```
abcdefg
now is the time
whatever you like
```

Press **F6** followed by **Enter**.

To verify that the file got built, enter this command:

```
A>dir \dummy\dummy01
```

You will see this display:

```
  Directory of A:\DUMMY\DUMMY01
.              <DIR>      01-09-93    4:36p
..             <DIR>      01-09-93    4:36p
TEST       TXT         45 01-09-93 4:36p
         3 file(s)          45 bytes
                       1319936 bytes free
```

Now you have a subdirectory with a file in it. Try to remove the lowest subdirectory. Enter this command:

```
A>rd \dummy\dummy01
```

You will see this display:

```
Invalid path, not directory,
or directory not empty
```

That display is the catch-all error message for any reason why you cannot remove a subdirectory. In this case, the subdirectory is not empty. The subdirectory has the TEST.TXT file in it. Before you can remove the subdirectory, you must delete the files in it. Enter this command:

```
A>del \dummy\dummy01\test.txt
```

Now the subdirectory is empty and you can remove it. However, before you try to remove \DUMMY\DUMMY01, try to remove \DUMMY. Dummy is a subdirectory, and you should be able to remove it. Enter this command:

```
A>rd \dummy
```

You will get the same catch-all error message. Why? The \DUMMY subdirectory is not empty. It still has the DUMMY01 subdirectory in it, which must be removed before the \DUMMY subdirectory can be removed. Enter this command:

```
A>rd \dummy\dummy01
```

That command worked. Now try the one that did not work before:

```
A>rd \dummy
```

This time, the command worked and the TYD Learning Diskette is back to the subdirectory structure shown in Figure 5.1.

Removing a Subdirectory Tree (DELTREE)

The DELTREE command deletes a subdirectory and all of its files and lower subdirectories. Enter the command this way:

```
a>deltree \wordproc
```

You will see this message:

```
Delete directory "wordproc" and all its subdirectories? [yn]
```

If you enter *y* (do not do that now), the WORDPROC subdirectory and everything below it is deleted. Enter *n* at this time to preserve the subdirectory for subsequent exercises.

Changing to a Subdirectory (CD)

When you first start these sessions, you are logged onto the root directory of the TYD Learning Diskette. Figure 5.2 shows this relationship. You are logged onto the directory named "\" and can view and otherwise access the files named COMMAND.COM, AUTOEXEC.BAT, WORDPROC, SPRDSHT, and DOS. The last three of these files are subdirectories. Notice that even though there is nothing in the DOS 6.0 subdirectory, it is still a subdirectory.

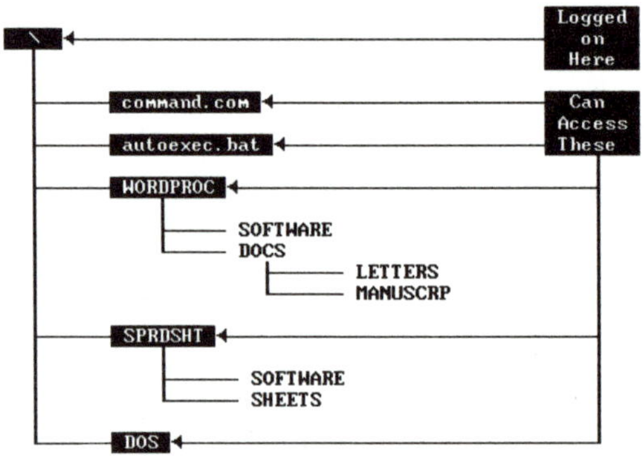

Figure 5.2 *Logged onto the root directory*

Suppose you want access to the files that are in the WORDPROC subdirectory, and you do not want to explicitly identify the subdirectory path every time you name a file. You need to log onto the WORDPROC subdirectory with the CD (Change Directory) command. Enter this command:

```
A>cd \wordproc
```

Figure 5.3 shows how the parameters in the CD command just executed relate to the subdirectory structure. The backslash in the command points to the root directory, and the named subdirectory is WORDPROC.

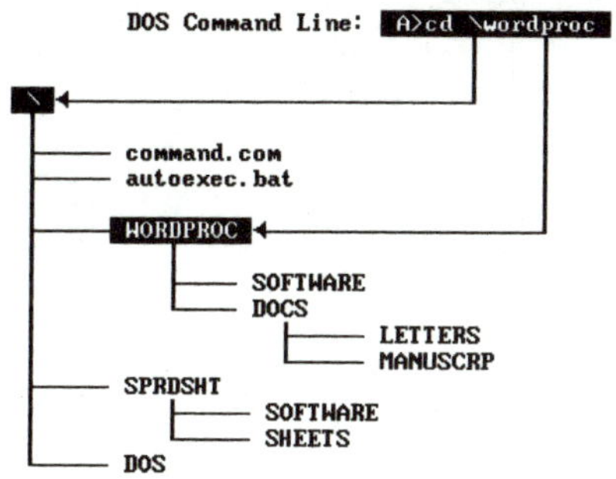

Figure 5.3 *Logging onto WORDPROC*

Figure 5.4 shows the effect of the CD command just executed. You are now logged into the WORDPROC subdirectory and have access to the files named SOFTWARE and DOCS. These files are also subdirectories. Because you have logged into WORDPROC, you no longer have implicit access to the COMMAND.COM and AUTOEXEC.BAT files in the root directory. You can still get at them by including an explicit path with the file name on the command line, but if you just give the file names, DOS 6.0 will not know where those files are.

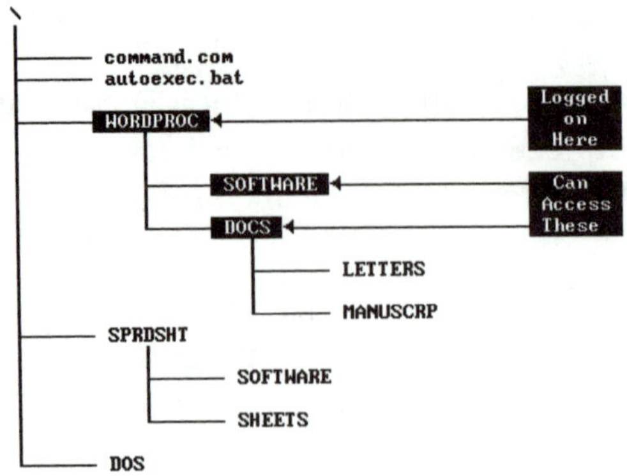

Figure 5.4 Logged onto WORDPROC

Suppose you want to be in the LETTERS subdirectory below the DOCS subdirectory. You can begin by moving to the DOCS subdirectory as shown in Figure 5.5, but that would be an unnecessary extra step.

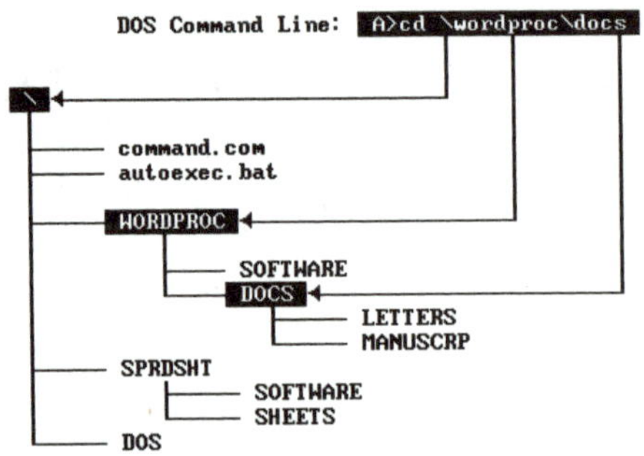

Figure 5.5 Logging onto DOCS

Instead of logging onto DOCS to get to LETTERS, you can log directly onto letters by naming the full path to the subdirectory. Enter this command:

```
A>cd \wordproc\docs\letters
```

Figure 5.6 shows the relationship between the parts of the command line parameter just used and the TYD Learning Diskette subdirectory structure.

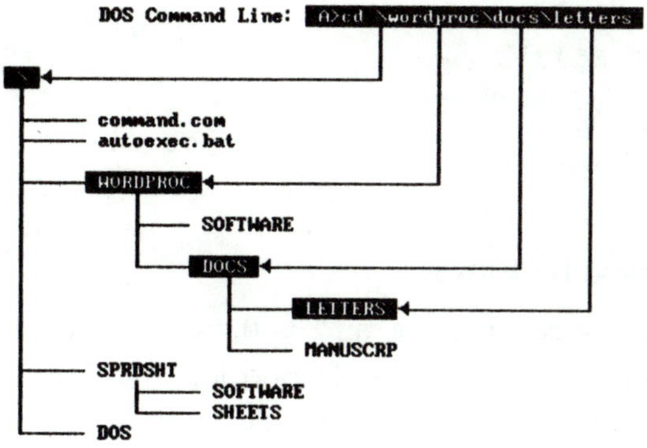

Figure 5.6 *Logging onto LETTERS*

Figure 5.7 shows the effect of the CD command just executed. You are logged into the LETTERS subdirectory and have access to any files that might be stored there.

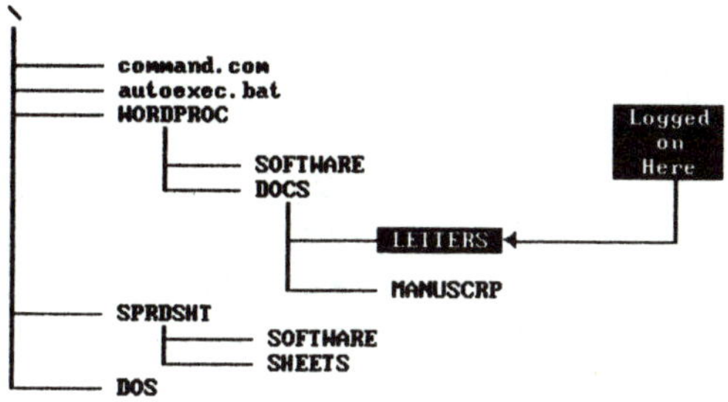

Figure 5.7 *Logged onto LETTERS*

Now that you are there, you cannot do much because the LETTERS subdirectory is empty. You need some files in this subdirectory to play with. Just as before, you will use COPY to build a file. Enter this command:

```
A>copy con milly01.ltr
```

This is your first letter to Aunt Milly. If you had word processing software on this computer, you could use it to write the letter. However, you have not gotten that far yet. Type some text in the letter to Milly. The text does not have to be exactly like this. Anything will do.

```
April 22, 1993
Dear Aunt Milly,
How are you? Wish you were here.
                    Sincerely yours,
                    Kilgore
```

Press **F6** followed by **Enter**.

You need a second letter, and you can use the same technique to write it. Put different text in the second letter so you can tell them apart later. Name the file that contains this letter MILLY02.LTR.

Use the DIR command to see that the two letters are indeed in the \WORDPROC\DOCS\LETTERS subdirectory. Figure 5.8 shows the TYD Learning Diskette subdirectories and the two files you just added. The figure shows that you are logged into LETTERS and that you can access MILLY01.LTR and MILLY02.LTR.

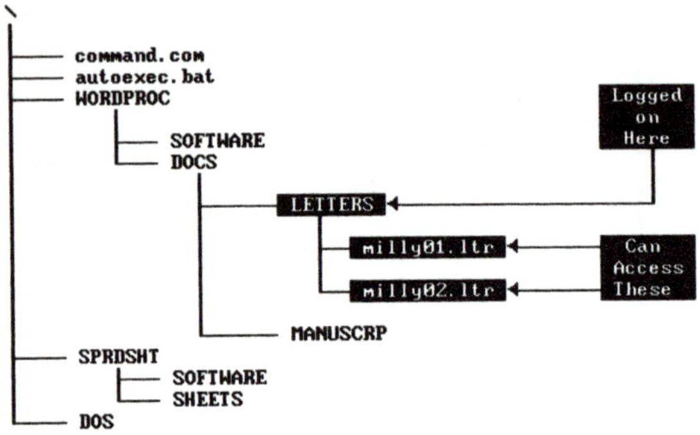

Figure 5.8 Accessing files in LETTERS

Subdirectory Shortcuts

Earlier you learned that the dot-dot (..) file in every subdirectory is used by DOS 6.0 to support linkage to the subdirectory's parent directory. That is why the root directory has no dot-dot file: the root has no parent. You can use the dot-dot file as a shortcut to change to the parent of the subdirectory where you are currently logged on. As of the most recent exercise, you are logged onto the subdirectory of the TYD Learning Diskette called \WORDPROC\DOCS\LETTERS. Enter this command:

```
A>cd ..
```

By changing to the dot-dot subdirectory, you automatically change to the parent of the current subdirectory without needing to remember its name. This last command has logged you onto the \WORDPROC\DOCS subdirectory.

Changing to an Immediately Subordinate Subdirectory

You can change to a subdirectory that is immediately subordinate to the one you are logged onto by specifying its name alone. You are currently at the \WORDPROC\DOCS subdirectory. Enter this command:

```
A>cd manuscrp
```

Note that there are no backslashes or prefix subdirectory names. This command moves you down to the \WORDPROC\DOCS\MANUSCRP subdirectory from the \WORDPROC\DOCS subdirectory. This technique works at any level. You can also use it with additional levels of subdirectories. To see how that works, change to the \WORDPROC subdirectory now with this command:

```
A>cd \wordproc
```

Now enter the following command to move down to the MANUSCRP subdirectory at the lowest level in the hierarchy.

```
A>cd docs\manuscrp
```

Moving Laterally to Another Subdirectory

You can also use the dot-dot shortcut to move laterally to another subdirectory that is at the same level below the parent as the one where you are logged now. From the \WORDPROC\DOCS\MANUSCRP subdirectory, enter this command:

```
A>cd ..\letters
```

This command changes to the \WORDPROC\DOCS\LETTERS subdirectory because \WORDPROC\DOCS is the parent of where you were and LETTERS is a subdirectory under DOCS.

Changing to a Remote Subdirectory

No matter where you are logged, you can change to a completely different subdirectory, unrelated to the current one, by using its fully qualified, unambiguous DOS 6.0 path. Currently you are logged onto the \WORDPROC\DOCS\LETTERS subdirectory. Enter this command:

```
A>cd \sprdsht\sheets
```

This command changes you to the \SPRDSHT\SHEETS subdirectory. By specifying the backslash, you have fully qualified the subdirectory name.

Changing to the Root Directory

You can change to the root directory while logged anywhere. Enter this command:

```
A>cd \
```

This command logs you onto the root directory of the TYD Learning Diskette.

Displaying the Currently Logged-on Subdirectory

From time to time, you will want to know where you are logged. The CD command, issued with no parameters, will tell you where you are. Try it now.

```
A>cd
```

Because you are logged onto the root directory of the A drive, you will see this display:

```
A:\
```

Change to a lower subdirectory and try the CD command without parameters again.

```
A>cd \wordproc\docs\letters
A>cd
```

You will see this display:

```
A:\WORDPROC\DOCS\LETTERS
```

Renaming a Subdirectory

The DOS 6.0 MOVE command renames subdirectories. Later you will learn that its primary function is to move files among subirectories. To rename a subdirectory, enter this command:

```
a>move \wordproc \wp
```

You will see this display:

```
a:\wordproc => a:\wp [ok]
```

Use the DIR command to see that the WORDPROC subdirectory is now names WP. Use the MOVE command now to change the name from WP back to WORDPROC so that your diskette matches subsequent exercises.

The PROMPT Command

Some users prefer to see the currently logged subdirectory all the time without having to ask for it. You can tell DOS 6.0 to include the subdirectory as a part of the prompt by issuing the PROMPT command.

```
A>prompt $p$g
```

The prompt will take this form:

```
A:\WORDPROC\DOCS\LETTERS>
```

The $p puts the path into the prompt, and the $g puts in the greater than (>) sign.

Return to the beginning of the CD exercises, and repeat them with the prompt so configured. You will not need to rebuild the letters to Aunt Milly. Decide from these exercises whether you prefer the prompt to include the subdirectory path or not. If you do not want to continue with it, you can turn it off by using the PROMPT command with no parameters.

```
A>prompt
```

There are other uses for the PROMPT command. You can make the prompt to be anything you like. Try this:

```
A>prompt [HERMAN'S SPIFFY COMPUTER CO]:
```

Your prompt will be whatever you tell it to be. One caution: you cannot use some special characters explicitly in the prompt. Those characters have special meanings on a command line. Examples are the greater than (>), less than (<), and vertical bar (|) characters. Chapter 9 discusses them. The PROMPT command allows you to use the dollar sign as a prefix to special switches that put special things in the prompting string.

Table 5.1 is a table of characters that, when prefixed with the dollar sign in a PROMPT command's parameters, will make special substitittions.

Table 5.1 *Prompt Command Parameter Characters*

<table>
<tr><th>The $ Character</th><th>The Substitution</th></tr>
<tr><td>$</td><td>$</td></tr>
<tr><td>_</td><td>Carriage return, line feed</td></tr>
<tr><td>B</td><td>|</td></tr>
<tr><td>D</td><td>The date (example: Mon 4-24-1989)</td></tr>
<tr><td>E</td><td>The ASCII Escape Character</td></tr>
<tr><td>G</td><td>></td></tr>
<tr><td>H</td><td>Backspace</td></tr>
<tr><td>L</td><td><</td></tr>
<tr><td>N</td><td>The Current Drive</td></tr>
<tr><td>P</td><td>The Current Drive and Path</td></tr>
<tr><td>Q</td><td>=</td></tr>
<tr><td>T</td><td>The time (example: 11:40:25.41)</td></tr>
<tr><td>V</td><td>DOS Version</td></tr>
</table>

You can use combinations of these switches to make all kinds of interesting prompts that can clutter your command line. If you come up with a prompt display that you want to install permanently, you can put the PROMPT command in the AUTOEXEC.BAT file. Then, whenever DOS 6.0 is reloaded, your customized DOS 6.0 prompt will take effect.

To continue with the exercises in this book, you will continue to use the unadorned DOS 6.0 prompt that all the examples so far have used. To reconfigure your prompt to the default after playing with it, issue the PROMPT command with no parameters.

Chapter 10 discusses the ANSI.SYS console device driver program. There you will learn special PROMPT command effects that you can use to control screen colors and other effects.

File Name Path Specifications

You have learned how to create and move among subdirectories and how to put files in them. Next, you will see how commands can cross subdirectory boundaries so that your software can be in one subdirectory and your data files can be in another.

The TYD Learning Diskette is organized so that you can have things related to word processing in the WORDPROC subdirectory. Under the WORDPROC subdirectory the word processing software is in the SOFTWARE subdirectory, and documents are in the DOCS subdirectory. The DOCS subdirectory is further divided into the LETTERS and MANUSCRP subdirectories. This subdirectory organization is typical. With such an organization, the software is isolated from your work, and the different aspects of your work—in this case, letters and manuscripts—are isolated from one another.

To see how this organization is put into use, you will simulate the presence of some word processing software. First, change into the SOFTWARE subdirectory with this command.

```
A>cd \wordproc\software
```

Next, you will create a file that simulates a word processor. The file will be named WP.BAT and will be a DOS 6.0 batch file. All this file will do is use the TYPE command to type a document that you specify on the command line. Enter this command:

```
A>copy con wp.bat
```

Now type these lines into WP.BAT:

```
echo off
cls
echo WP: — The Simulated TYD Word Processor —
type %1
```

Press **F6** followed by **Enter** to complete the file. Now you are ready to use the simulated word processor. WP.BAT is a batch command file, and, by adding it to the disk, you have effectively added a command to DOS 6.0. That command is named WP. The %1 string in the TYPE command inside the WP.BAT file is what is known as a *command line substitution.* When you execute the new WP command, DOS 6.0 substitutes whatever you put on the command line for the %1. You will learn more about command line substitutions in Chapter 13. Execute the WP command now, telling it to type the first letter to Aunt Milly.

```
A>wp \wordproc\docs\letters\milly01.ltr
```

This is an example of how you tell a command to access a file that is stored in a different subdirectory. The WP.BAT file substitutes the entire path and file name for its %1 parameter in its TYPE command, and you will see this display:

```
WP: — The Simulated TYD Word Processor —
April 22, 1993
Dear Aunt Milly,
How are you? Wish you were here.
                 Sincerely yours,
                 Kilgore
```

Command Path Prefixes

Sometimes when you are in a subdirectory, you will want to execute a command that is represented by a .COM, .EXE, or .BAT file in another subdirectory. One method for doing this is to use the DOS 6.0 PATH command, and that technique is discussed in Chapter 6. However, there is another way. When you issue the command, you can specify the subdirectory where the command file is stored. The subdirectory is prefixed to the command name just as a subdirectory can be prefixed to a file name.

Suppose you are logged into the LETTERS subdirectory and want to use the new WP command that is in the SOFTWARE subdirectory in

WP.BAT. To see how that works, first log onto the LETTERS subdirectory with this command:

```
A>cd \wordproc\docs\letters
```

If you were to try the WP command the same way you did in the previous exercise, DOS 6.0 would display this message:

```
Bad command or file name
```

This message means that DOS 6.0 cannot find the WP.BAT file because you are logged onto the LETTERS subdirectory, and WP.BAT is in the SOFTWARE subdirectory. Instead, you can specify where the command is when you issue the command. Enter this version of the command:

```
A>\wordproc\software\wp milly01.ltr
```

This command works and gives the same display you saw earlier. Notice that you did not have to specify the subdirectory where the MILLY01.LTR file is located. You are logged into that subdirectory, and so DOS 6.0 has no trouble finding that file. If you were logged into some other subdirectory where neither the software nor the document is located, you would need to specify paths for the WP.BAT software and the MILLY01.LTR data file. That command would look like this:

```
A>\wordproc\software\wp \wordproc\docs\letters\milly01.ltr
```

The command just shown is verbose and would be difficult to remember. Since the command is so long, it is conducive to keying errors as well. You are well advised not to use this kind of command entry on a routine basis. How you set up your PC is up to you. Chapter 6 eases this problem considerably. The chapter describes the DOS 6.0 PATH command, which lets DOS 6.0 find software in other subdirectories without you specifying the pertinent subdirectory whenever you run the software.

File Name Specifications

Now that you have used file names in a number of exercises, you can review the many ways to specify a file on the DOS 6.0 command line.

Disk File Names

The fully qualified, unambiguous DOS 6.0 file name follows this format:

```
<drive>:<dos path>\<file name>.<extension>
```

The <drive> designator is the drive letter where the file is to be found. Drive letters are A, B, C, and so on, through the highest drive letter installed on your computer. A colon must follow the drive letter if the letter is included. The drive letter is optional. If you leave it out, DOS 6.0 and most programs assume that the file being specified is on the currently logged-on drive.

The <dos path> designator specifies the path through the subdirectories where the file is located. Each lower subdirectory name is prefixed with a backslash character to separate it from its parent. If the path does not begin with a backslash, DOS 6.0 assumes that the first named subdirectory is subordinate to the currently logged-on directory. The path is optional. If you leave it out, DOS 6.0 and most programs assume that the file being specified is in the currently logged-on subdirectory for the drive. If the path is given, there must be a backslash character to separate it from the file name.

The <file name> is from one to eight characters, and can consist of letters, numbers and some special symbols. The file name can include the asterisk and/or the question mark wild cards.

Most file names include an extension as shown in the <extension> designator above. However, the extension is not mandatory. You can omit the extension when you create the file, and subsequent references to that file must be made without the extension. When an extension is used, it must be separated from the file name by a period. The extension can include the asterisk and/or the question mark wild cards.

Many applications programs allow you to specify file names from within the program rather than on the command line, and these programs usually use the same conventions for file names that DOS 6.0 uses. Many applications programs will, however, append default extensions to files you name. You will need to be aware of any such extensions if you are going to use a DOS 6.0 command to view or otherwise process the file from outside the program.

For example, your word processor software might allow you to identify your documents with the file name only, while the software appends something like .WP or .DOC to the name. Later, when you want to delete, copy, or view a directory of those files, you will need to know about the .WP extension you did not specify. The program documentation should tell you if the program does that. When in doubt, use the DIR command after a session with the program to see what has been added or changed in your data file subdirectory.

Device Names

File names in a DOS 6.0 command can be PC device specifiers. The effect is that the data content comes from or goes to the device rather than a file. You have already seen that you can copy the CON device to a file. You can specify printers and communications devices as well. Table 5.2 contains a list of all device names.

Figure 5.2 *Descriptions of devices*

Device Name	Description
CON	An input file is the keyboard, output is the screen
PRN	The default printer, usually LPT1
LPT1	The printer connected to physical printer port 1
LPT2	The printer connected to physical printer port 2;
(some PCs have LPT3, LPT4, and so on.)	
COM1	The device connected to communications port 1
COM2	The device connected to communications port 2;
(some PCs have COM3, COM4, and so on.)	
AUX	The default communications port, usually COM1
NUL	The null device. There is no input. Output goes nowhere.

The NUL device is special. If you specify it where a command expects an output file, the output goes nowhere and is effectively suppressed. If you specify the NUL device where a command expects an input file, the command behaves as if the input file exists but is empty.

There are not many occasions where you will use device names instead of files, but consider this example. Enter the following command. (It is assumed that you have a printer connected and turned on.)

```
A>copy con prn
```

Type as many lines of text on the screen as you want. When you are done, press **F6** followed by **Enter**. The text you typed is printed on the printer.

Most printers need a terminating form feed character to allow them to print a page immediately. Without one, they will wait a given length of time before printing the page. Since there is a time-out when absolutely nothing happens, you might conclude that your printer is not working properly. Try this: Before pressing F6, press **Ctrl+L**. The symbol ^L is displayed following the characters you have typed, and the Ctrl+L character, which is the form feed control character, is sent to the printer. That procedure tells the printer to print the page immediately.

Copying Files (COPY)

You have been using the COPY command to build test files by copying from the console keyboard to the files named on the command line. However, the COPY command has much more utility than that. COPY is the vehicle with which you copy files to diskettes to safe-store them or to move them to another subdirectory. COPY is the vehicle you use to import and install software from other sites. You will use the COPY command a lot. The format of the copy command is shown here:

```
copy <source> <destination>
```

The <source> and <destination> designators are usually file name specifications with the optional drive, path, file names, wild cards, and extensions as described above. They can also be device file names.

Copying Individual Files

Begin by logging onto the \WORDPROC\DOCS\LETTERS subdirectory where you have some text files to play with. Enter this command:

```
A>cd \wordproc\docs\letters
```

If you want, use the DIR command to see that the MILLY??.LTR files are still there.

Suppose you want to send the same letter to Uncle George that you sent to Aunt Milly. Rather than type the entire letter into a new file, you could make a copy of Milly's letter and use your word processor to change the salutation. This is a handy way to handle invitations, announcements, and other kinds of broadcast communications.

Make a copy of the MILLY01.LTR file, giving it another name. Enter this command:

```
A>copy milly01.ltr george.ltr
```

Use the DIR command to see that the copy has been made. You can now use your word processor to modify the letter for Uncle George.

Copying a File to Another Disk Drive

The COPY command has variations. For example, you can copy a file to another disk drive. Enter this command:

```
A>copy george.ltr c:
```

This command copies the GEORGE.LTR file from the A: drive where you are logged on to the C: drive as specified on the command line. Because you did not give a file name in the destination, the new file on the C: drive will also be named GEORGE.LTR. The file is copied to whichever C: drive subdirectory is currently logged on.

Copying to a Specified Subdirectory

If you want to copy the file to a particular subdirectory on the C: drive, you can name that subdirectory in the copy command as shown in the following example. Do not do this example as an exercise; it is merely an example. The example subdirectory probably does not exist on your C: drive, and you do not want to modify your hard disk's subdirectory structure just for these lessons.

```
A>copy george.ltr c:\wordproc\savearea
```

Copying with Wild Cards

You can use wild cards in the file name. To copy all your letters to the C: drive, enter this command:

```
A>copy *.* c:
```

Remember how wild cards work. The *.* specification calls out all file names and all extensions or, in other words, all files. This command says to copy all files in the current disk and subdirectory to the C: drive. You will see this display:

```
MILLY01.LTR
MILLY02.LTR
GEORGE.LTR
            3 File(s) copied
```

You do not want to leave those files on the C: drive, so use the DEL command to delete them. Enter this command:

```
A>del c:*.ltr
```

Copying into the Current Subdirectory

So far, the COPY exercises have all had source and destination specifiers. However, if you leave out the destination, you tell DOS 6.0 that the destination is the currently logged on disk and subdirectory, and that the file names are to be the same as those in the source. For example, suppose you want to copy the letters from the LETTERS subdirectory to the MANUSCRP subdirectory. First, change to the MANUSCRP subdirectory with this command:

```
A>cd ..\manuscrp
```

Now copy the files by specifying the source parameter only. Since you are no longer logged into the LETTERS subdirectory, you must specify the path to the files you want to copy. Enter this command:

```
A>copy ..\letters\*.*
```

To review: the dot-dot specifies the parent subdirectory of where you are logged. The LETTERS subdirectory is below the same parent, so its name is displayed next and is separated from the dot-dot parent with a backslash. The next backslash separates the path from the file name. The *.* is the wild card specification that specifies all files in the subdirectory. There is no destination file specification in the command. Therefore, this command says to copy of all the files from the LETTERS subdirectory that are on the same level under the same parent as the current subdirectory, and to copy those files into the current subdirectory. You will see this display:

```
..\LETTERS\MILLY01.LTR
..\LETTERS\MILLY02.LTR
..\LETTERS\GEORGE.LTR
              3 file(s) copied
```

In this kind of copy, where no destination is specified, the source file specification cannot point to the currently logged-on disk and path combination. Otherwise, you would be telling DOS 6.0 to copy a file on top of itself, which DOS 6.0 cannot do.

Copying Subdirectories

You can use the COPY command to copy entire subdirectories into the current one. You are currently logged into \WORDPROC\DOCS\MANUSCRP. Enter this command:

```
A>copy ..\letters
```

That file specification has no file name. The file ends with the name of the LETTERS subdirectory, and so it tells the COPY command to copy all the files in the LETTERS subdirectory. You will see this display:

```
..\LETTERS\MILLY01.LTR
..\LETTERS\MILLY02.LTR
..\LETTERS\GEORGE.LTR
              3 File(s) copied
```

Once again, use the DIR command to see that all three letters have been copied into the MANUSCRP subdirectory.

Copying Several Files into One File

The COPY command can be used to copy several files into one file, concatenating the source files so that the destination file is the combination of the source files. While still in the MANUSCRP subdirectory, enter this command:

```
A>copy milly01.ltr+milly02.ltr millies.ltr
```

You will see this display:

```
MILLY01.LTR
MILLY02.LTR
                1 File(s) copied
```

Note that although the copy command has listed two files, it says at the bottom that only one file was copied. Use the DIR command to see that you built a new file named MILLIES.LTR. The file's size is approximately the sum of the two files that were copied into it.

You can use wild cards to copy several files into one. Enter this command:

```
A>copy *.ltr letters.all
```

You will see this display:

```
MILLY01.LTR
MILLY02.LTR
GEORGE.LTR
MILLIES.LTR
                1 File(s) copied
```

Once again, only one file was copied, but this time, four were listed. This count is an important clue to a common user mistake. Suppose you want to copy all the files in the current subdirectory to a different subdirectory. However, you misspell the name of the destination subdirectory. Here is an example of such a mistake. Enter this command:

```
A>copy *.* \sprdsht\sheet
```

The mistake is in the spelling of the SHEETS subdirectory name. What you expect is to see a list of all of the files followed by a count of files copied. There are five files in the current subdirectory. However, this is what would be displayed if you executed that erroneous command:

```
MILLY01.LTR
MILLY02.LTR
GEORGE.LTR
MILLIES.LTR
LETTERS.ALL
            1 File(s) copied
```

Since you misspelled SHEETS as SHEET, DOS 6.0 thinks you mean to copy the files into one file named SHEET in the SPRDSHT subdirectory. Your clue that the copy did not work the way you expected it to is in the count of files copied. Since the count is one, you can tell that the files were copied to only one file instead of the five you expected. Run the DIR command against the SPRDSHT subdirectory now, and you will verify the error.

```
A>dir \sprdsht
```

You will see this display:

```
     Directory of A:\SPRDSHT
   .             <DIR>      01-09-93   3:26p
   ..            <DIR>      01-09-93   3:26p
   SOFTWARE      <DIR>      01-09-93   3:28p
   SHEETS        <DIR>      01-09-93   3:28p
   SHEET                859 03-28-91   4:56p
           5 file(s)          859 bytes
                        1315840 bytes free
```

(The size of the file might be different. The dates and times surely will.)

The SHEET file is a combination of the files you really wanted to copy into the SHEETS subdirectory. This circumstance results from the way the COPY command works. No doubt you will have this problem at some time, and no doubt you will not notice it. Copying will have become routine, and as long as you see no error message, you will seldom notice the little clue given by the file count. You can only hope that it does not cause too much inconvenience.

Moving Files (MOVE)

The MOVE command works exactly like the COPY command except that the file is moved rather than copied. A move removes (deletes) the file from its current location and moves it into its new location. The MOVE command is the equivalent of doing a COPY command followed by a DEL command of the original file.

To move groups of files, you must specify wildcards or a comma-separated file list in the source and a subdirectory name as the destination.

If you move a file and specify a different name for the destination with no change in subdirectory, the command is the same as the REN command.

The Delete (DEL) Command Revisited

These last exercises have left some debris in the TYD Learning Diskette. You will use the DEL command to clear it up. You can use DEL command to delete all of the files in a subdirectory.

```
A>del *.*
```

DOS 6.0 recognizes that this command has serious implications. You have just said that you want to delete everything in the current subdirectory. DOS 6.0 displays the following statement and question:

```
All files in directory will be deleted!
Are you sure (Y/N)?
```

Press **Y** and DOS 6.0 deletes the files.

If you use the DEL command on a subdirectory file, you are telling DOS 6.0 to delete all the files in the subdirectory. The SPRDSHT subdirectory has one data file and two subdirectories. The DEL command does not extend below the specified subdirectory, so you can use this command to delete the erroneous SHEET file from the SPRDSHT subdirectory.

```
A>del \sprdsht
```

The command just shown is the equivalent of this next command:

```
A>del \sprdsht\*.*
```

DOS 6.0 asks you to press Y followed by Enter to verify the deletion.

Renaming Files (REN)

There will be times when you will want to rename a file. The DOS 6.0 REN command is used to rename files. This is the general format of the REN command:

```
ren <oldname> <newname>
```

Change now to the root directory for the next exercise. Enter this command:

```
A>cd \
```

Renaming Single Files

Suppose you want to make a new version of your AUTOEXEC.BAT file, but you do not want to lose the old one. You can rename the old file to something else and then create the new one. To rename AUTOEXEC.BAT to AUTOEXEC.SAV, enter this command:

```
A>ren autoexec.bat autoexec.sav
```

Now use the DIR command to see that the file still exists, but with the new name

If you do not change the name back and do not build a new AUTOEXEC.BAT file to replace the renamed one, your next reload of DOS 6.0 will be just like it was just after you formatted the TYD Learning Diskette. Use this command to reset the name:

```
A>ren autoexec.sav autoexec.bat
```

Renaming Groups of Files

You can rename groups of files with one command by using wild cards. Change to the LETTERS subdirectory with this command:

```
A>cd \wordproc\docs\letters
```

Rename all of the letters files so that the extension changes from .LTR to .TXT. Enter this command:

```
A>ren *.ltr *.txt
```

Use the DIR command to see that the file name extensions have changed.

Renaming Files in Other Places

You can rename files on other disk drives or in other subdirectories by specifying the drive and path in the first (old name) parameter. The second (new name) parameter does not need to be qualified.

You are logged into the \WORDPROC\DOCS\LETTERS subdirectory. To change the name of the WP.BAT, which is in \WORDPROC\SOFTWARE file to EDIT.BAT, enter this command:

```
A>ren \wordproc\software\wp.bat edit.bat
```

Use the DIR command to see that the WP.BAT file is now named EDIT.BAT

Put Everything Back

Try some file housekeeping. First, use REN to give the word processor batch file its original name. Enter this command:

```
A>ren \wordproc\software\edit.bat wp.bat
```

Next, delete the GEORGE.TXT file from the LETTERS subdirectory with this command:

```
A>del george.txt
```

Finally, rename the letters files so that they have the .LTR extensions again.

```
A>ren *.txt *.ltr
```

Building the DOS 6.0 Subdirectory

For the next series of exercises in this and the chapters that follow, you will need a number of the DOS 6.0 utility programs on the TYD Learning Diskette. The exercises cannot know for sure where those programs are on your system. The DOS 6.0 SETUP program places them on the C: drive in a subdirectory named DOS 6.0 unless you override the default, and the exercises will assume that you installed your system by using the SETUP program's default.

If the following procedure gives you trouble, use the CD and DIR commands to poke around in your hard disk until you find the files in question. You must copy the files you need to the TYD Learning Diskette with the following commands. (Hint: use F1, F3, Ins, and Del to copy duplicated keystrokes in the commands that are similar to the previous command.)

```
A>cd \dos
A>copy c:\dos\chkdsk.exe
A>copy c:\dos\diskcopy.com
A>copy c:\dos\format.com
A>copy c:\dos\label.exe
A>copy c:\dos\mode.com
A>copy c:\dos\more.com
A>copy c:\dos\tree.com
A>copy c:\dos\find.exe
A>copy c:\dos\sort.exe
A>copy c:\dos\xcopy.exe
A>copy c:\dos\ansi.sys
A>copy c:\dos\print.exe
A>copy c:\dos\setver.exe
A>copy c:\dos\choice.com
```

Displaying the DOS 6.0 File Tree (TREE)

You learned earlier about the DOS 6.0 file hierarchy. DOS 6.0 stores files in a hierarchy of subdirectories. The TREE command allows you to view that subdirectory. Remain in the \DOS subdirectory of your TYD Learning Diskette and type the TREE command as shown here:

```
A>tree \
```

You will see the display shown in Figure 5.9.

```
Directory PATH listing
Volume Serial Number is 3446-16F0
A:.
├───WORDPROC
│   ├───SOFTWARE
│   └───DOCS
│       ├───LETTERS
│       └───MANUSCRP
├───SPRDSHT
│   ├───SOFTWARE
│   └───SHEETS
└───DOS
```

Figure 5.9 *The directory tree*

The TREE command begins displaying from the currently logged-on subdirectory unless you provide a path on the command line. The backslash on the command just issued tells the TREE command to build the tree beginning from the root directory.

The TREE command has two other command line option switches. The /f switch tells the command to list files as well as subdirectories. The /a switch tells the command to use ASCII characters instead of the PC's graphics characters. The following display shows a tree command that uses all three command line parameters.

```
A>tree \wordproc /a /f
Directory PATH listing
Volume Serial Number is 3437-15EE
A:\WORDPROC
+--SOFTWARE
|       WP.BAT
|
\--DOCS
   +--LETTERS
   |       MILLY01.LTR
   |       MILLY02.LTR
   |
   \--MANUSCRP
```

The DOS 6.0 Help System

DOS 6.0 introduces an improved help system. You can display the syntax, notes, and examples of any DOS 6.0 command in a full-screen HELP application, or you can view an abbreviated help message directly on the command line.

The HELP Command

Your TYD Learning Diskette does not have the HELP command installed, so you will need to log onto your hard drive for these exercises.

The HELP command displays a full-screen list of all of the DOS 6.0 commands as shown in Figure 5.10.

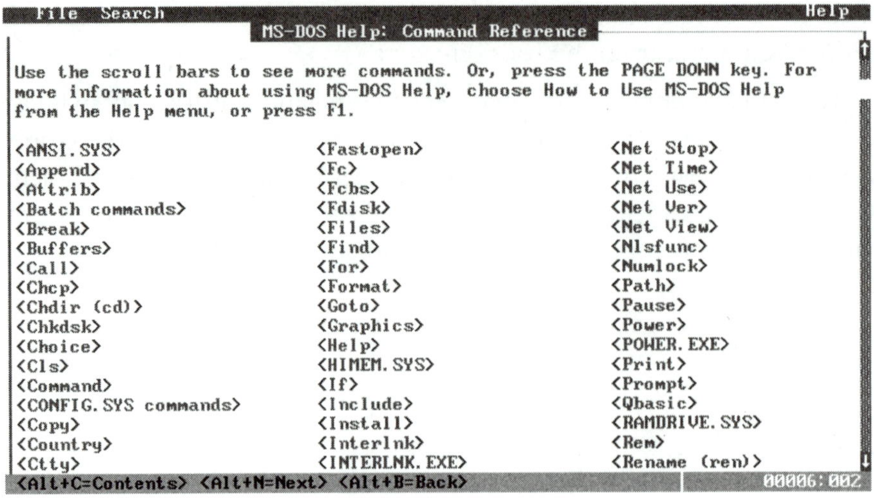

Figure 5.10 *The HELP application*

Selecting a Command for Help

The screen cursor is initially positioned on the first of the command selections. To get help for the command, move the cursor to it and press Enter. If you are using a mouse, you can click the command as well. If you choose to see the help information for the COPY command, for example, you will see the screen shown in Figure 5.11.

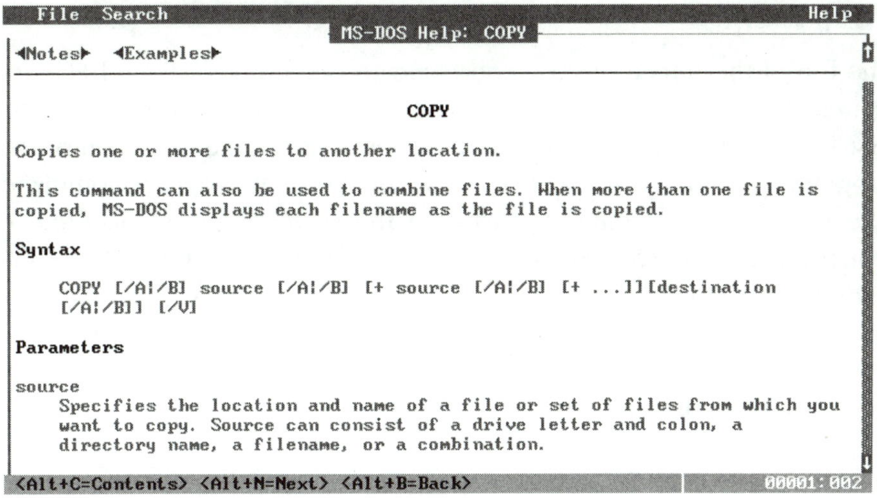

Figure 5.11 *Help for the COPY command*

Help's Syntax, Notes, and Examples

Most Help displays consist of three parts, Syntax, Notes, and Examples.

The top part of the Help display shows two control buttons, which change depending on which of the three parts you are viewing. Initially, you will be viewing the Syntax part of the Help display, and the two buttons are labeled <Notes> and <Examples>. You can select a different part by tabbing to the button and pressing Enter or by clicking the button with the mouse.

Navigating the Help System

The Help display has three buttons at the bottom of the screen, labeled <Alt+C=Contents>, <Alt+N=Next>, and <Alt+B=Back>. You select the buttons by clicking them with the mouse or by pressing their Alt+letter combination. The Contents button redisplays HELP's initial screen, which lists all the DOS 6.0 commands. The other two buttons move forward and backward through the Help displays for all the DOS 6.0 commands.

Help Menus

The top of the screen has a menu bar with two entries, labeled File and Search. You select a menu bar entry by clicking it or pressing Alt+ the first letter of the menu, F or S. When you select a menu bar entry, the program pops down a menu from which you can select a command. The File menu has commands to Print the current Help display and to exit the program. The Search menu has a Find command that lets you search the Help database by specifying a string of text. You can also select a Find Next command that will continue a previous search past the point of the last Find. Figure 5.12 shows the Find dialog box that the Find command displays.

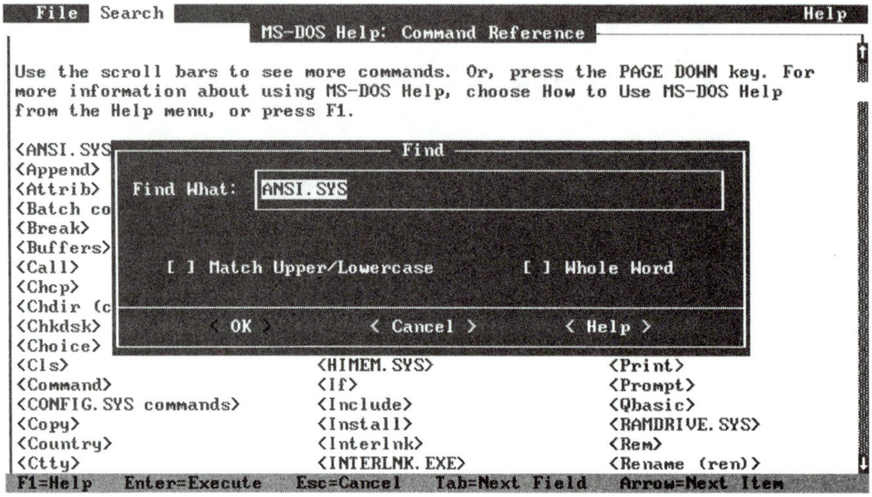

Figure 5.12 *The Find dialog box*

After entering a text string into the Find What: field, you choose the OK command by clicking it or by pressing **Enter**. The program searches the database for a match on the text and displays the first topic it finds that contains the matching text. You can specify that the search be done by matching the upper/lower case of the text you enter by selecting the Match Upper/Lowercase check box on the Find dialog box. You can specify that the search look for matches on whole only by selecting the Whole Word check box on the Find dialog box.

Help for a Specific Command

You can use the HELP command to go directly to the Help display for a specific command as well. Type HELP followed by the name of the command for which you need help as show here.

```
C>help tree
```

The HELP application goes directly to the display for the command you included on the command line, in this case the TREE command.

Command Line Help (/?)

You can an abbreviated help display by typing the command followed by the /? command line switch as shown here for the TREE command:

```
A>tree /?
```

You will see this display.

```
Graphically displays the directory structure of a drive or path
TREE [drive:][path] [/F] [/A]
  /F Displays the names of the files in each directory.
  /A Uses ASCII instead of extended characters.
```

The DOS 6.0 HELP facility works with all DOS 6.0 commands, whether they are internal commands (such as TYPE, COPY, DIR) or external commands implemented with a .COM or .EXE file. More and more programs are implementing the same help facility to be compatible with the DOS 6.0 convention.

The Keyboard Typematic Rate

The keyboard on the typical PC repeats at the rate of 10 characters per second (CPS). When you hold down a key, the key repeats at that rate. Ten CPS might seem fast when you first think about it, but at that rate, it takes a word processor eight seconds to move the cursor from the left margin to the right margin of the screen.

The DOS 6.0 MODE command allows you to change the keyboard's typematic rate. The typematic rate consists of two values, the delay period after you first press the key until repeating begins, and the rate at which the key repeats. To set the keyboard's typematic rate enter this command:

```
mode con: rate=32 delay=1
```

The rate parameter is expressed in the values 1-32 and represent from 2 to 30 CPS. The delay parameter is 1 to 4 representing 1/4, 1/2, 3/4, and 1 second, respectively. The command in the example above sets the delay to 1/4 second and the repeat rate to 30 CPS. Most users prefer these values.

You can put the typematic MODE command in your AUTOEXEC.BAT file so that it is executed whenever you boot DOS 6.0.

Some programs change the typematic rate. You might find that the keyboard feels differently after you exit from an application. Use the MODE command to set it to the values you prefer when that happens. Chapter 11 shows how you can use the DOSKEY macro facility to define a shortcut command that reprograms the typematic rate.

Some older keyboards and some keyboards on contemporary laptop computers do not respond to the MODE typematic command.

Summary

You have taken in a lot of knowledge in this chapter. These exercises have prepared you to use as much of DOS 6.0's power as most users will ever need. Certainly you are now ready to use the PC in the manner prescribed by whomever installed the system. If nothing else has been accomplished, you can now find your data files and copy them to a safe place for backup.

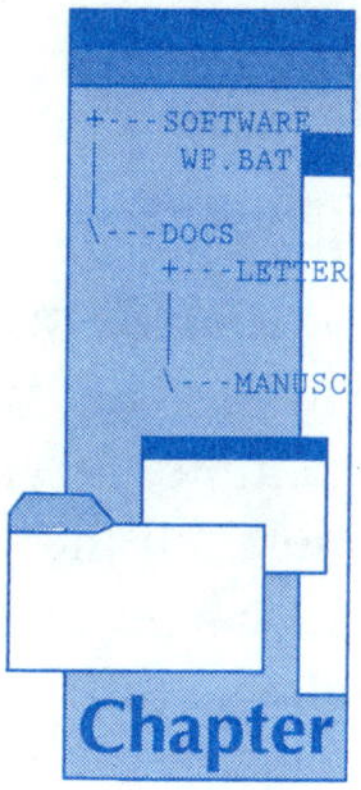

Chapter 6

The DOS 6.0 Path

This chapter describes the DOS 6.0 PATH variable, a mechanism that allows DOS 6.0 to find command files that are in remote drives and subdirectories. You will learn about the:

- DOS 6.0 path
- PATH environment variable
- PATH command.

File Organization

If you organize your data files in one subdirectory and your software in another, as you did on the TYD Learning Diskette, you must specify where one or the other is located. Since you can be logged onto only one place at a time, if you are logged onto where the software is located, you must tell the programs where to find the data files. If you are logged onto where the data files are located, you must tell DOS 6.0 where to find the software.

Simulate a Spreadsheet

In Chapter 5, you built a simulated word processor called WP.BAT. You will use that software in this chapter, too, but you need another software file to show the versatility of the PATH, so you will simulate a spreadsheet program as well.

You will use the COPY command as before to build the spreadsheet data and command files. Build the command file by entering this command:

```
A>copy con \sprdsht\software\ss.bat
```

Now enter these lines of text:

```
echo off
cls
echo SS: - The Simulated TYD Spreadsheet -
type %1
```

Press **F6** followed by **Enter**. This batch command file displays the file you name on the command line. The file is functionally equivalent to the WP.BAT file, except that it has its own program title so you can tell them apart.

Next, build a simulated spreadsheet data file with this command:

```
A>copy con \sprdsht\sheets\taxes92.sps
```

Type some lines of spreadsheet data like this:

```
Gross Income:              25000.00
Bracket:                        .10
Taxes:                      2500.00
```

Press **F6** and **Enter**.

Finally, build a manuscript file for the WP simulated word processor by entering this command.

```
A>copy con \wordproc\docs\manuscrp\novel.doc
```

Type some deathless lines of prose the likes of which follow.

```
Illusions on the Moors - Chapter 1.

It was a cold and stormy night.
Tiffany pulled her lace shawl about her
bare shoulders and shuddered in the cold air.
The count smiled at her and beckoned for
her to follow him down the corridor and
into the bedchambers.
```

Press **F6** and **Enter**. That concludes the immortal test data.

How DOS 6.0 Finds the Commands

When you organize a subdirectory hierarchy, you almost always have one copy of each software package and then several categories of data files that the software package processes. That is the situation simulated on the TYD Learning Diskette. You have one word processor and two different kinds of documents: letters and manuscripts.

The usual way to access your data files with your programs is to log onto where the data files are kept and run the software from where you keep the program. Up until now, you have done that, but you have always specified the path to the program when you issued its command.

In Chapter 5, you ran the word processor while logged onto where the letters are kept by entering this command:

```
A>\wordproc\software\wp milly01.ltr
```

This will always work, but it has disadvantages. You are required to remember where everything is stored and you must type the path whenever you want to use a command.

The PATH Variable

DOS 6.0 has a mechanism called the *DOS PATH variable* that provides a shortcut to locating your software. The PATH specifies a subdirectory path that DOS 6.0 will search when it is looking for a .BAT, .COM, or .EXE file that you have issued as a command. The PATH consists of one or more drives and subdirectory paths. You call the PATH a variable because you can change its value with the DOS PATH command.

If a PATH has been specified, DOS 6.0 looks first in the currently logged-on drive and subdirectory, and, if the command file is not there, DOS 6.0 searches the specified path for it. If no PATH has been specified, DOS 6.0 looks for the command file only in the currently logged-on drive and subdirectory. Up until now, no PATH has been specified in your exercises.

The PATH Command

You set the PATH variable with the PATH command. You can also view the current path by issuing the PATH command with no parameters. Enter this command:

```
A>path
```

You will see this display:

```
No Path
```

That message means that no PATH has been established. Now review what happens when you try to run software that DOS 6.0 cannot find. First, log onto the MANUSCRP subdirectory where you put that great American novel. Enter this command:

```
A>cd \wordproc\docs\manuscrp
```

Figure 6.1 shows where you are logged and that DOS 6.0 can find no software. There are no command files in the MANUSCRP subdirectory and DOS 6.0 has no PATH to search.

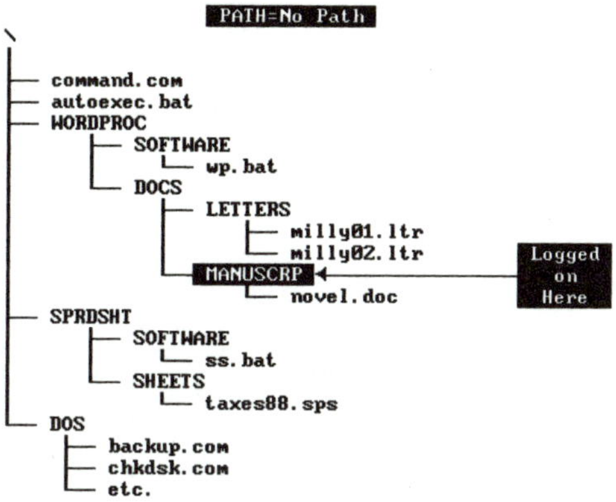

Figure 6.1 *No path, no software*

To prove this situation, try to use the WP command to display the novel without specifying the software's path.

```
A>wp novel.doc
```

DOS 6.0 responds with this error message:

```
Bad command or file name.
```

This message means that DOS 6.0 cannot find the WP.BAT file because you are logged onto the LETTERS subdirectory, and WP.BAT is in the SOFTWARE subdirectory.

Setting the PATH

Earlier, you had to specify where the command was stored when you issued the command. However, now you know that if you can specify the path to the software in the DOS 6.0 PATH variable, DOS 6.0 will be able to find the software. Do so with the following command:

```
A>path=a:\wordproc\software
```

Viewing the PATH

Now use the PATH command with no parameters to see that the PATH variable has been set. Enter this command:

```
A>path
```

You will see this display:

```
PATH=A:\WORDPROC\SOFTWARE
```

Figure 6.2 shows that even though you are logged onto MANUSCRP, DOS 6.0 can find the command file that is stored in SOFTWARE.

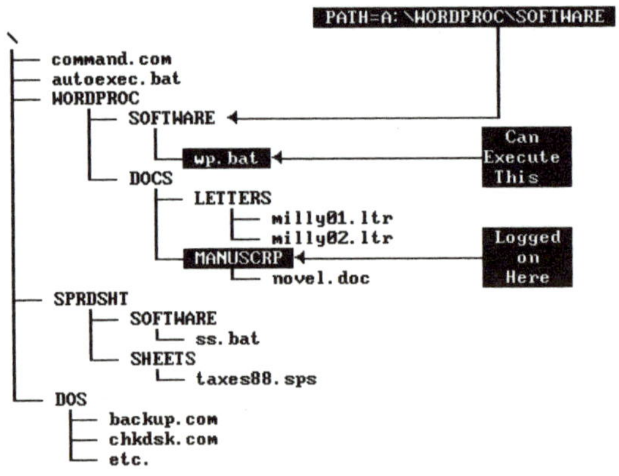

Figure 6.2 *A Path to WP.BAT*

Using the PATH

Try again to use the WP command to display the novel without specifying the software's path.

```
A>wp novel.doc
```

The command works because DOS 6.0 found the WP.BAT file by searching the PATH you established. You will see this display:

```
WP: — The Simulated TYD Word Processor —
Illusions on the Moors - Chapter 1.

It was a cold and stormy night.
Tiffany pulled her lace shawl about her
bare shoulders and shuddered in the cold air.
The count smiled at her and beckoned for
her to follow him down the corridor and
into the bedchambers.
```

Multiple Paths

As you saw in Figure 6.2, the PATH you have used so far leads to only one subdirectory. If word processing was all you ever needed to do, that would be enough. However, most users use the PC for several tasks, and every user needs to use the DOS 6.0 utility programs once in a while. A single path is not enough.

The TYD Learning Diskette includes the SS.BAT simulated spreadsheet in the SPRDSHT subdirectory, and it is presumed that you would want to run spreadsheets too. You could issue the PATH command every time you wanted to change from word processing to spreadsheet processing. However, that would be less efficient than simply typing the path on the command line when you issue the commands that run your programs. You are looking for a better way, not a less efficient way.

As you might expect, the PATH command allows you to identify several paths for DOS 6.0 to search. To see how that works, enter the following command:

```
A>path=a:\wordproc\software;a:\sprdsht\software
```

Notice that there are two distinct paths in this command, and they are separated by a semicolon. When you issue a command, DOS 6.0 searches using this sequence. First, the currently logged-on subdirectory is searched. If the command file is not found, the \WORDPROC\SOFTWARE subdirectory is searched. If the command file is still not found, the \SPRDSHT\SOFTWARE subdirectory is searched.

Figure 6.3 shows the effect of the command just issued. You can now execute WP.BAT and SS.BAT regardless of where you are logged.

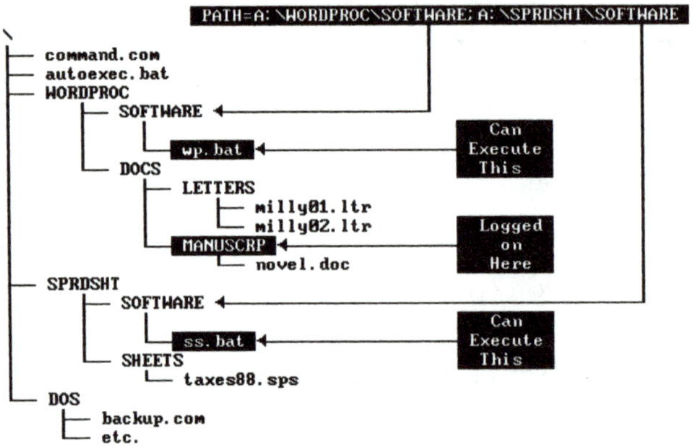

Figure 6.3 *Multiple paths*

Run the Spreadsheet

Issue this command to change to the SHEETS subdirectory:

```
A>cd \SPRDSHT\SHEETS
```

Now run the SS.BAT command against the TAXES92.SPS file with this command:

```
A>ss taxes92.sps
```

You have successfully run the simulated spreadsheet, and you will see this display:

```
SS: — The Simulated TYD Spreadsheet —
Gross Income:              25000.00
Bracket:                        .10
Taxes:                      2500.00
```

A PATH to DOS 6.0

No matter what your programs, whether they are word processing, spreadsheets, desktop publishing, databases, CAD/CAM, software development, or custom applications, you will frequently use the DOS 6.0 utility programs. In anticipation of the advanced exercises in later chapters, you have already copied some of these programs into the DOS 6.0 subdirectory on the TYD Learning Diskette. You will want a PATH to these programs as well. Enter this command:

```
A>path=a:\wordproc\software;a:\sprdsht\software;a:\dos
```

This command adds the DOS 6.0 subdirectory to the DOS 6.0 PATH. Figure 6.4 shows the effect of this path.

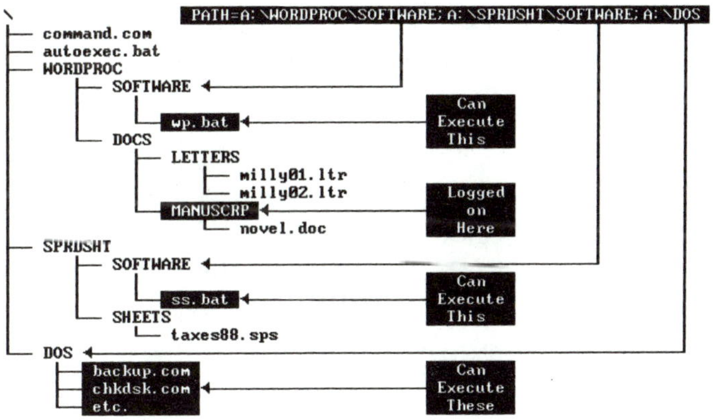

Figure 6.4 *Paths to DOS 6.0 utility programs*

The PATH Command in AUTOEXEC.BAT

You do not want to type in a long PATH command every time you load DOS 6.0. Why not add it to your AUTOEXEC.BAT file? Then it will be automatically executed whenever you reload DOS 6.0, and your path will be established. Log onto the root directory and enter this command:

```
A>copy con autoexec.bat
```

Then type these lines:

```
echo off
cls
echo Teach Yourself DOS 6.0 Learning Diskette
ver
path=a:\wordproc\software;a:\sprdsht\software;a:\dos
```

Press **F6** and **Enter**, and your new AUTOEXEC.BAT file will be built.

Commands with the Same Name

You might have guessed that it is possible to have command files in different subdirectories with the same name. For example, you could build another subdirectory and put a file named WP.BAT in it. This is a perfectly legitimate DOS 6.0 construction. If you logged onto that new subdirectory and issued the WP command, the new WP.BAT command would be executed because DOS 6.0 looks in the currently logged-on subdirectory first for command files. If you logged onto a different subdirectory and issued the command, the old WP.BAT command would be executed because that is the one DOS 6.0 would find as it searched the paths.

Suppose both subdirectories with WP.BAT files were in the DOS 6.0 PATH. Then DOS 6.0 executes the first one it finds. DOS 6.0 searches the paths in the sequence in which they are specified in the PATH command beginning with the leftmost path.

It is not a good idea to have different programs on your system with the same name, however, sometimes it is hard to avoid. For example, many applications software systems include command files named INSTALL and README. When you run into these conflicts, it is best to keep a keen watch on what you are doing and make sure you are running the correct command file.

Invalid Subdirectories in the PATH

DOS 6.0 does not complain if you specify a path that does not exist. DOS 6.0 sets it up and waits to register its objection until the first time you try to use it. Enter this command:

```
A>path=\nonsense
```

Now issue the path command to see that DOS 6.0 thinks there is a path to a subdirectory called NONSENSE.

```
A>path
```

You will see this display:

```
PATH=NONSENSE
```

DOS 6.0 has not displayed an error message yet. Now try to execute the WP command.

```
A>wp
```

DOS 6.0 cannot find WP.BAT, and displays this error message, which looks just like the one you got when there was no path.

```
Bad command or file name
```

DOS 6.0 will let you know if the path contains an invalid disk drive. Enter this command:

```
A>path=g:\nonsense
```

(This assumes that your PC has no G drive. Most do not, but some networked PCs will have drives well up into the alphabet.)

Now try the WP command again.

```
A>wp
```

Now you not only get the earlier error message, you also get a clue as to what is wrong.

```
Invalid drive in search path
Bad command or file name
```

Summary

This chapter taught you about the DOS 6.0 path. You learned how DOS 6.0 finds the commands. You also learned about the PATH variable that provides a shortcut to locating your software. Finally, the chapter taught you about the PATH command.

Chapter 7

Printing

This chapter is about printing with your PC and DOS 6.0. Programs such as the word processor or spreadsheet perform most of your printing. However, there are some print tasks that DOS 6.0 can do for you. You will learn about printing:

- Files from the command line
- Files while you do other tasks
- Screens

Using DOS 6.0 To Print

If you have an ASCII text file that you generated with a text editor program, such as EDIT (Chapter 12), you can use DOS 6.0 to print the file without going through an applications program. Sometimes the effort required to import and convert a simple text file into a word processor is not worth the trouble when all you want to do is print the file. DOS 6.0 can do it for you an easier way. In another case, if your application can send print files to an ASCII text file instead of to the printer, DOS 6.0 can print those files for you while you do something else.

The Standard Print Device

You learned about the PRN device in Chapter 5. If you use that device name on the command line where DOS 6.0 expects an output file name, then DOS 6.0 writes the data to the printer instead of to a file.

Printing from the Command Line

Using your TYD Learning Diskette, enter the following command to get to the novel that you wrote in Chapter 5.

```
A>cd \wordproc\docs\manuscrp
```

To print the file named NOVEL.DOC, enter this command:

```
copy novel.doc prn
```

Depending on your printer, you might not see any activity after DOS 6.0 displays the A prompt. Your printer might need a form feed character to tell it to print the page. Your novel does not have a form feed character embedded in its text, so you must either send it one or wait for the printer to time out. Most dot matrix printers print right away. Most laser printers do not. To send a form feed character to the printer, enter the following command. The ^L is a result of holding down Ctrl while you press L.

```
A>echo ^L >prn
```

Chapter 8 will teach you how to use the DOSKEY macro facility to automate the printer form feed process.

You can cause DOS 6.0 to print whatever it is displaying on the console screen. Press **Ctrl+P**, and all subsequent command line input and output are written to the printer and to the screen. You can print the NOVEL.DOC file in the example just given by entering this command. (Do not press Enter at the end of the command.)

```
A>type novel.doc
```

Press **Ctrl+P**. Then press **Enter**. The file is displayed on the screen and sent to the printer. When the file is fully printed, press **Ctrl+P** again to turn off the printing of console input/output.

The technique just shown is handy if the file has tab characters in it. The COPY command does not expand the tabs into spaces. Many printers do not either. The TYPE command expands tab characters into spaces as if there were tab stops every eight positions.

You can use output redirection to cause filters to send their standard output to the printer. (Chapter 9 describes input/output redirection in detail.) For example, the command just used can be entered this way to get the tab expansion of the TYPE command, but without displaying the file on the screen. By suppressing screen output this way, you speed up the printout.

```
A>type novel.doc >prn
```

The DOS 6.0 Print Spooler (PRINT)

When you used the COPY or TYPE commands to print in the examples given above, you had to wait until the file was printed before you could use the PC for anything else. DOS 6.0 has a command called PRINT. With this command, you can send text files to the printer. While the files are being printed, you can do other work at the PC.

If you have a long document to print from your word processor, you can tell the word processor software to send the printout to a file rather than to the printer. (Many word processor programs have that feature.) Then you can exit the word processor and use the PRINT command to print the file. As soon as it starts printing, you can return to the word processor or any other program. Printing goes on while you use the PC for other jobs.

Some word processor programs have their own background printing operations. You can continue to do word processing while they run, but you cannot exit the word processor to run other jobs until printing is complete.

Loading the PRINT Command

The PRINT command loads a memory-resident program the first time you use it. You can load the program into memory without telling it to do anything by entering the PRINT command at the command line. If you intend to use the DOS 6.0 Shell's PRINT command, described in Chapter 8, you will need to have the PRINT command loaded. If you load the Shell program with the DOSSHELL command in your AUTOEXEC.BAT file, you will want to load the PRINT command first.

Queuing a File To Print

To print a file, enter this command:

```
A>print novel.doc
```

The PRINT command displays this message:

```
Name of list device [PRN]:
```

You can press Enter to queue for printing on the standard print device, or you can enter the name of a different printer device, such as LPT1. The PRINT command loads its program into memory and remains there until you reboot DOS 6.0. You will see these messages:

```
Resident part of PRINT installed
A:\WORDPROC\DOCS\MANUSCRP\NOVEL.DOC is currently being
printed
```

You do not need to worry about sending form feed characters to the printer like you did when you used TYPE or COPY. The PRINT command takes care of it for you.

Queuing Several Files To Print

You can build up a queue of files to be printed by issuing several successive PRINT commands or by specifying multiple files on the command line, either with wild cards or by entering more than one file name. Enter the following command to change to the subdirectory where you stored the letters to Aunt Milly.

```
A>cd \wordproc\docs\letters
```

Any of these commands would queue both letters for printing:

```
A>print milly01.ltr milly02.ltr
A>print *.ltr
A>print *.*
```

The PRINT command displays these messages:

```
A:\WORDPROC\DOCS\LETTERS\MILLY01.LTR is currently being
printed
A:\WORDPROC\DOCS\LETTERS\MILLY02.LTR is in queue
```

The example files you are using here are small, and they go to the printer before you can catch them. For the next several exercises, take your printer off line. Most printers have a button labelled "On Line" and a light that goes on and off when you press that button. Turn off that light. This means that the printer will not accept data from the computer. Now re-enter one of the commands from the exercise above that queues the two letters to be printed. Follow that command with this command to add a third file to the print queue:

```
A>print ..\manuscrp\novel.doc
```

You will see the same series of messages with this line added:

```
A:\WORDPROC\DOCS\MANUSCRP\NOVEL.DOC is in queue
```

Viewing the Print Queue Contents

To see what files are in the print queue, enter the PRINT command with no parameters. If everything is working according to plan, you will see these messages:

```
Errors on list device indicate that it
may be off-line. Please check it.
A:\WORDPROC\DOCS\LETTERS\MILLY01.LTR is currently being
printed
A:\WORDPROC\DOCS\LETTERS\MILLY02.LTR is in queue
A:\WORDPROC\DOCS\MANUSCRP\NOVEL.DOC is in queue
```

Even though the messages tell you that MILLY01.LTR is currently being printed, it is not because the printer is off-line.

Canceling a File from the Print Queue

To cancel a file from the print queue, enter this command:

```
A>print milly02.ltr /c
```

You will see the print queue displayed without the file you canceled. Observe that this command format works only if you are logged into the subdirectory where the named file exists. Try this command:

```
A>print novel.doc /c
```

The PRINT command will display this message:

```
File not in PRINT queue -
A:\WORDPROC\DOCS\LETTERS\NOVEL.DOC
```

The PRINT command thought that you were specifying a file in the current subdirectory. You must specify the path if it is not current as shown in this example:

```
A>print \wordproc\docs\manuscrp\novel.doc /c
```

This may seem like a bother, but it has a purpose. You could very well have several files queued that have the same name, but are in different subdirectories.

PRINT Command Line Options

There are several PRINT command line options. Some are related to buffer sizes and internal timing operations. The DOS 6.0 user's manual attempts to explain them, but it is difficult to understand them unless you are a computer programmer. If the PRINT command either slows down your other jobs or prints the files too slowly, then changing the options might help. Table 7.1 is a summary of the PRINT command options.

Table 7.1 *PRINT command options*

Option	Description
/b:nnn	Set the buffer size (nnn, 512-16384 characters)
/c	Cancel the named print file from the queue
/d:dev	Name the print device (prn, lpt1-3, com1-4)
/m:n	Set the number of ticks to print characters (1-255)
/p	Adds the named print file to the queue
/q:n	Set thc queue size from 4 to 32 print files
/u:n	Set the number of ticks to wait for the printer (1-255)
/s:n	Set the time slice to n (1-255)
/t	Cancel all jobs in the print queue

The /c and /p options apply to the file names that the option switches follow. You can combine these on a single command line.

The /m option specifies the number of ticks that PRINT can use to print a single character. A tick is approximately 1/18 of a second. The default value is one tick.

The /u option specifies the number of ticks that PRINT waits before deciding that the printer is not operating. The default value is one tick.

The /s option is the time slice. It specifies how many ticks that PRINT will use while it is printing before it allows the foreground task—whatever else you are doing while PRINT is printing in the background—to operate. The default value is eight ticks. The higher this number, the slower your foreground task will seem to be.

The PRINT command loads a memory-resident program. Once loaded, the program remains in memory. The /d, /b, /u, /m, /s, and /q switches apply the first time you execute the PRINT command and remain in effect until you reboot DOS 6.0. You should not execute PRINT the first time from inside an applications program, that is, when you have "shelled out" to DOS 6.0 while an applications program is still running. You should run it the first time from the DOS 6.0 command line with nothing else going on. Once you have started it, you can make subsequent calls to it from anywhere.

Screen Prints

You can print the contents of the screen with a keyboard keypress. If you have an extended keyboard, the key to press is labeled Print Screen. This is the key you see throughout this book. If you have an older keyboard, the key is labeled PrtSc, and you must press the Shift key and hold it down while you press the PrtSc key. You can use Shift with Print Screen on an extended keyboard, too because it works the same as not using it. In any case, the contents of the screen are printed on the standard print device.

A PC displays images on the screen either as text or as graphics. The DOS 6.0 command line is usually displayed as a text screen. Programs such as Windows display all of their screens in graphics. The DOSSHELL program described in Chapter 8 can display its screens in either mode.

Printing Text Screens

When DOS 6.0 is initially loaded, it can print any text screen when you press Print Screen. DOS 6.0 prints the screen as 25 lines of 80-column text. Not all printers will properly display the PC's graphics characters, which are the ones that form the frames around screen windows and symbols such as the smiling faces or playing card symbols. Others will display the symbols correctly only if you have certain printer fonts selected.

The screen print process does not automatically send a form feed to the printer. You must do that yourself as described above if you need a form feed to make the page print immediately.

Printing Graphics Screens (GRAPHICS)

Before you can print a graphics screen, you must first use the DOS GRAPHICS command. This command loads a program into memory that remains resident until you reboot DOS 6.0. You can specify your printer type when you load the program with this command:

```
A>graphics 'printer type'
```

The valid printer type parameters are shown in Table 7.2.

Table 7.2 GRAPHICS command printer types

Parameter	Printer Type
color1	IBM PC Color Printer (black ribbon)
color4	IBM PC Color Printer (RGB ribbon)
color8	IBM PC Color Printer (CMY ribbon)
hpdefault	HP PCL Printer
deskjet	HP DeskJet
graphics	IBM Personal Graphics, Proprinter, Quietwriter
graphicswide	IBM Personal Graphics, Proprinter, or Quietwriter with wide carriage
laserjet	HP LaserJet
laserjetII	HP LaserJet II
paintjet	HP PaintJet
quietjet	HP QuietJet
quietjetplus	HP QuietJet Plus
ruggedwriter	HP RuggedWriter
ruggerwriterwide	HP RuggedWriterwide
thermal	IBM PC-convertible Thermal
thinkjet	HP ThinkJet

You can include the command line option switches shown in Table 7.3 when you run the GRAPHICS command. The switches follow the printer type parameter on the command line.

Table 7.3 *GRAPHICS command switches*

Switch	Description
/r	Prints white characters on a black background
/b	Prints color background for color4 and color8 printers
/lcd	Uses the LCD aspect ratio. Printer type must support LCD.

Changing the Print Configuration

If you have an IBM or Epson printer (or a compatible) connected to a parallel port, you can use the MODE command to set some of the printer's internal configuration parameters. This is the format for the command:

```
A>mode lpt1: 80,6,n
```

The first parameter is the LPT port. The second parameter is the number of columns on a line, which can be 80 or 132. The third parameter is the number of lines per inch, which can be 6 or 8.

The last parameter specifies what to do when the MODE command times out trying to print. The parameter can be e to return an error, b to return a busy signal, p to continue retrying, r to return a ready signal, and n to do nothing. The p parameter is the most common one and works for most printer setups.

An alternative format for the command is as follows:

```
A>mode lpt1: cols=80 lines=6 retry=n
```

With this format, the parameters may be in any sequence on the command line.

Redirecting Printer Output to a Serial Device

Unless you specify otherwise, the PRINT command prints to the DOS 6.0 standard print device. Commands that specify the PRN device also go to this device. Some programs direct their print output to this device. When DOS 6.0 boots, it directs all standard print device output to the LPT1 device output port by default. Some printers use a serial interface rather than the parallel interface of LPT1, and they must be connected to one of the serial ports, COM1 through COM4.

You can modify the standard print device by using the DOS MODE command to direct printing to a serial device as shown here:

```
A>mode lpt1 = com1
```

You can similarly redirect LPT2 or LPT3 output to a COM port.

Configuring the Serial Port for Printing

Usually, a serial port is connected to a modem for remote communications or to another computer for file transfers. The communications software that supports these connections manages the configuration of the serial port for you. However, when you use a serial port for printing, and redirect the output of the LPT port to the COM port, you must set up the configuration parameters of the COM port as well. The DOS MODE command handles this for you.

First, you must know how your serial printer is configured. You must know the baud rate, the parity, the number of data bits, the number of stop bits, and the kind of retry action to take when the MODE command times out trying to transmit a character to the printer through the serial port.

There is a lot to know about serial communications, and books have been written on the subject. You can read such books and learn all about what these configuration parameters mean, or you can take it on faith, find out how your printer is set up, put the proper MODE command into your AUTOEXEC.BAT file, and forget about it.

How do you find out how your printer is set up? Its operating manual should identify the location and setting of switches that set the various parameters. If not, ask someone who knows more about them.

This is the most typical format for the MODE command to set serial configuration parameters:

```
A>mode com1:1200,n,8,1,p
```

The first parameter is the COM port. The second parameter specifies the baud rate and can have these values: 110, 150, 300, 600, 1200, 2400, 4800, 9600, and 19200. You can abbreviate the values using their first two digits.

The third parameter can be n for no parity, e for even parity, and o for odd parity. The fourth parameter is the number of data bits in a character, usually 7 or 8. The fifth parameter is the number of stop bits in a character frame, usually 1 or 2.

The last parameter specifies what to do when the MODE command times out trying to print. The parameter can be e to return an error, b to return a busy signal, p to continue retrying, r to return a ready signal, and n to do nothing. The p parameter is the most common one and will work for most printer setups.

An alternative format for the command is as follows:

```
A>mode com1: baud=1200 parity=n data=8 stop=1 retry=p
```

With this format, the parameters may be in any sequence on the command line.

Summary

This chapter covered the details of printing from the DOS 6.0 command line and controlling the printer device. You learned about using the standard print device and the DOS 6.0 print spooler, queuing multiple files, viewing print queue contents, and canceling a file from the print queue. The chapter also taught you about PRINT command line option and printing screens. Finally, you learned how to change the print configuration and how to redirect print output to a serial device.

Chapter 8

The DOSSHELL Program

This chapter is about the DOS 6.0 Shell program, which is named DOSSHELL. The program uses the screen, mouse, and keyboard to provide a visual user interface to files and programs. You might like the Shell or you might prefer to stay with the DOS 6.0 command line. Each user develops his or her preferences. You will learn about:

- Using the Shell menu system
- Switching between several concurrently loaded tasks
- Managing programs in groups
- Running applications
- Managing files

The Shell in These Exercises

The Shell program and its related files are big. They occupy more space than is available on your TYD Learning Diskette. Therefore, the few exercises in this chapter use the copy of DOS 6.0 that you installed on your hard disk. However, they will use the diskette for directory and data displays. This chapter contains more explanation of the Shell than exercises that you run. You can load the Shell into your computer and follow along with the screens that the figures show.

Running the Shell

To run the Shell, type DOSSHELL on the command line. If you decide that you want to use the Shell for all of your DOS 6.0 operations, put the DOSSHELL command as the last entry in your AUTOEXEC.BAT file. When you run the Shell, you will see a display similar to Figure 8.1.

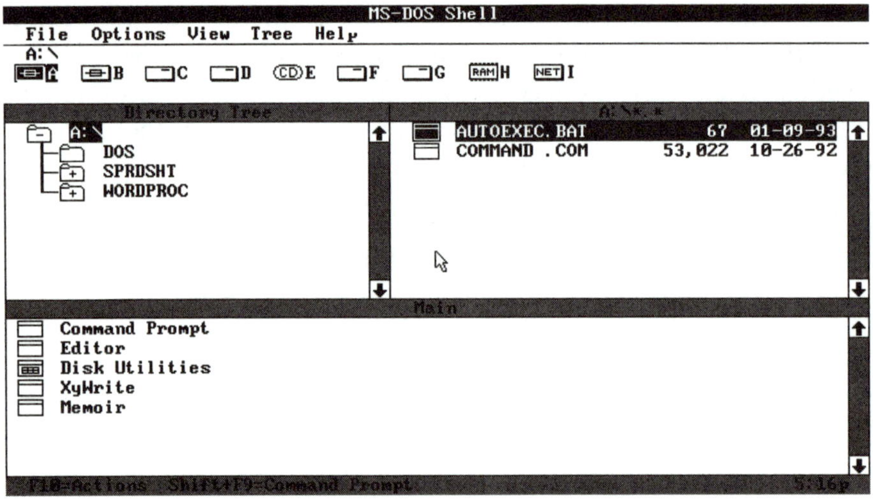

Figure 8.1 *The DOS 6.0 Shell screen*

The MOUSE Driver Program

The first time you run DOSSHELL, it might tell you that your mouse device driver program is an old version and possibly not compatible with DOS 6.0. DOSSHELL allows you to terminate or ignore the problem and continue.

If you elect to continue without correcting the problem, DOSSHELL will never warn you again, and assumes that what you are doing is correct. You will almost surely have problems. As soon as possible, replace the mouse device driver program, named MOUSE.COM or MOUSE.SYS with one that is compatible with DOS 6.0. Device driver programs that are version 7.0 or greater should work fine. The vendor who makes your mouse can supply an updated mouse driver program.

The Shell Screen

The Shell's screen configuration, shown in Figure 8.1 above conforms to a standard user interface called the *Common User Access* interface and is the model used by Microsoft Windows and many applications programs, including the EDIT program described in Chapter 12.

The Shell's display characteristics depend on what kind of monitor you have. The display can be graphics or text. If you have a monitor that displays graphics as well as text, you can switch between the two kinds of displays. You will learn how to do that in this chapter.

The Shell screen consists of a menu bar, the drive icon area, the directory tree, the file list, the program list, and the task list. The task list is not initially in view. You must enable task swapping, discussed later in this chapter, to view the task list.

Selecting Areas on the Shell Screen

You can select any of the five areas on the screen in which to work. When you are working in an area, it has what is called the input focus. Press the **Tab** key several times in succession. You will see the input focus move from area to area. Move the mouse cursor to an area and click the left button to select that area.

When you select the file icon area, the current drive changes its highlight to indicate that the file icon area has your attention. When you select one of the other three areas, its title becomes highlighted. If you are in the text display mode, A small arrow is displayed in the selected display area next to whichever item is currently selected as well. If you have a monochrome monitor, the highlight changes might not be visible, so the arrow is your indication that the area has the focus.

The Menu Bar

The Shell screen has a menu bar across the top of the screen and a pop-down menu associated with each selection on the menu bar. The menu bar selections are File, Options, View, and Help. When you have selected the drive icons, the directory tree, or the file list, the Tree selection is added to the menu bar.

Pop-down Menus

Pop-down menus are windows that are displayed when you select the menu's name on the menu bar. A pop-down menu shows a list of commands that you can execute when the menu is in view. There are several ways to select a pop-down menu so that you can execute one of its commands. You can:

- Move the mouse cursor to the menu bar selection and click the left button once. The menu pops down. Click an area outside the menu or press **Esc**. The menu will no longer be displayed.
- Hold down the **Alt** key and press the first letter of the selection's name to pop down the menu. For example, Alt+F pops down the File menu. Press **Esc**. The menu will no longer be displayed.
- Press and release either **Alt** or **F10**. The File menu bar selection will be highlighted. Use the **right** and **left arrow** keys to change the highlighting to the next right or left menu bar selection.

When the selection you want is highlighted, press **Enter** to pop down the menu. Press **Esc**. The menu will no longer be displayed.

- After pressing and releasing Alt or F10, press the letter that is underlined or highlighted in the menu bar selection that you want to pop down. For example, press **F** to pop down the File menu. Press **Esc**. The menu will no longer be displayed.

Figure 8.2 shows the File menu popped down.

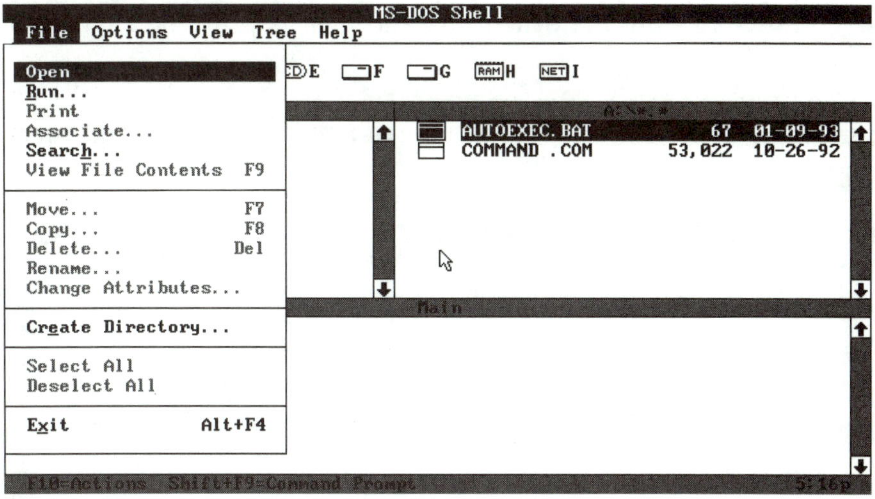

Figure 8.2 *The File menu*

Note that the selections on a particular popped-down menu will not always be the same as they were for an earlier pop-down of the same menu. Menu selections can vary depending on other conditions in the other windows of the Shell screen.

When a menu is popped down, you can move to other menus by pressing the Right and Left Arrow keys. The current pop-down menu will go away and the next right or left menu will pop down. As an exercise, pop down the File menu and use the arrow keys to move among menus.

Menu Selections

Each pop-down menu has a list of commands. Sometimes a command will be disabled. A disabled command displays with lesser intensity than the active commands. In some display configurations, the disabled commands are invisible.

Using the steps you just learned, pop down the Help menu. The About Shell command displays the dialog box shown in Figure 8.3. The next several exercises will display that dialog box by using the several menu command methods. Each time you display the dialog box, press **Esc** or **Enter** to close the dialog box and then pop up the Help menu again.

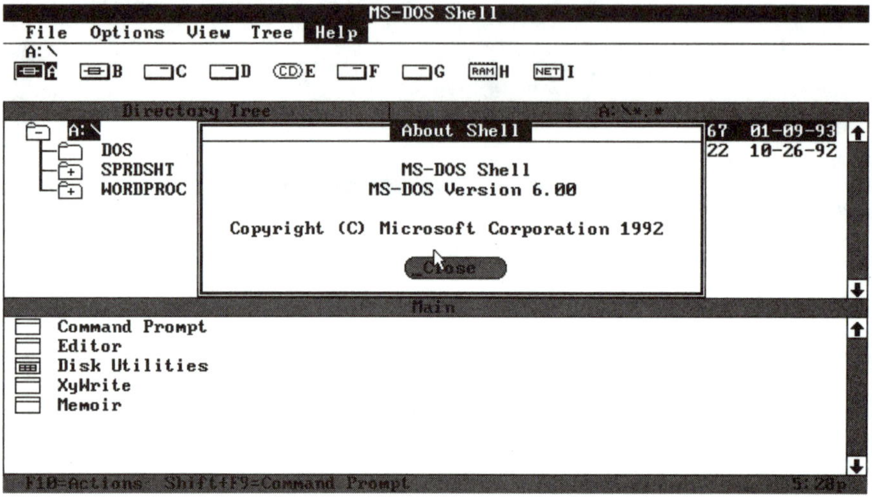

Figure 8.3 *The About Shell dialog box*

There are four ways to execute a pop-down menu command:

- Move the mouse cursor to the About Shell command and click the left button once.
- Use the Up and Down Arrow keys to highlight the About Shell command and then press **Enter**.

- Each command has one letter that is highlighted in a text display or underlined in a graphics display. You can press that letter while the menu is popped down to execute the command. Press **A** while the Help menu is popped down.

- Some commands have "shortcut" keys. These are key combinations that execute the command at any time whether the menu is popped down or not. These keys are shown on the menu to the right of the command. For example, the shortcut key for the Exit command on the File menu is Alt+F4. The About Shell command does not have a shortcut key.

The Disk Drive Icons

The disk drive icons are displayed immediately below the menu bar. There is one icon for each drive that is available in your PC. If you use the graphical Shell display, the icons resemble the disk drives they represent. Otherwise, they are in brackets as shown here:

```
[A:]  [B:]  [C:]
```

Observe the H: drive icon in Figure 8.1. The icon has the label, "RAM." This means that it is a RAM disk. You will learn how to install and use RAM disks in Chapter 14. The E: drive icon is labeled "CD" indicating that it is a CD-ROM drive. The I drive icon is labeled "NET" indicating that it is a network drive. A: and B: are diskette drive icons, and the rest are hard drive icons.

The highlighted drive icon is the currently logged on disk. You can log onto a different disk by holding down Ctrl and pressing the letter that corresponds with the drive. For example, Press **Ctrl+A** to log onto the A: drive.

You can press **Tab** to move to the drive icon area of the Shell display and use the Right and Left Arrow keys to select the other drives one at a time. Then you can press Enter to log onto the selected drive. You can move the mouse cursor to a drive and click the left button to log onto the drive.

When you change the logged on drive, the Shell takes some time to read in all of the directory information. Then it updates the displays in the directory tree and the file list areas to reflect what is stored on the new drive.

Put the Teach Yourself DOS 6.0 Learning Diskette into the A: drive. Select the A drive by clicking its icon or pressing **Ctrl+A**. After reading the diskette's directory information, the DOS 6.0 Shell will display the A: drive's directory.

The Directory Tree

The Directory Tree displays the directories and subdirectories of the currently logged on disk. Each subdirectory is represented by a folder icon in graphics display mode or within brackets in text display mode. The subdirectory tree structure is shown by the bars that connect the folder icons in a hierarchical representation. Observe in Figure 8.2 shown earlier, that the A:\ root directory has the three subdirectories, DOS, SPRDSHT, and WORDPROC. You built those subdirectories in the exercises in Chapter 5.

The root directory icon has a minus sign in it, the SPRDSHT and WORDPROC subdirectory icons have plus signs in them, and the DOS subdirectory icon is empty. The minus sign means that the directory has subdirectories that the Directory Tree is now displaying. The plus sign means that the directory has subdirectories which are not currently displayed. An empty directory icon means that the directory has no subdirectories.

Expanding a Directory

You can expand a directory that has a plus sign so that its subdirectories are in view. First, make sure that the Directory Tree window has the focus. Then select the WORDPROC subdirectory by using the Down Arrow key to move the highlight bar down to it. To select a subdirectory with the mouse, click its name. The WORDPROC subdirectory has a plus sign, so it can be expanded. Press the **Plus** key (+) or click the plus sign in the directory icon to expand the directory and see its subdirectories.

When you expand the WORDPROC directory, the plus sign in its icon changes to a minus sign and its subdirectories are displayed as icons below it. Figure 8.4 shows the Shell screen with the WORDPROC subdirectory expanded.

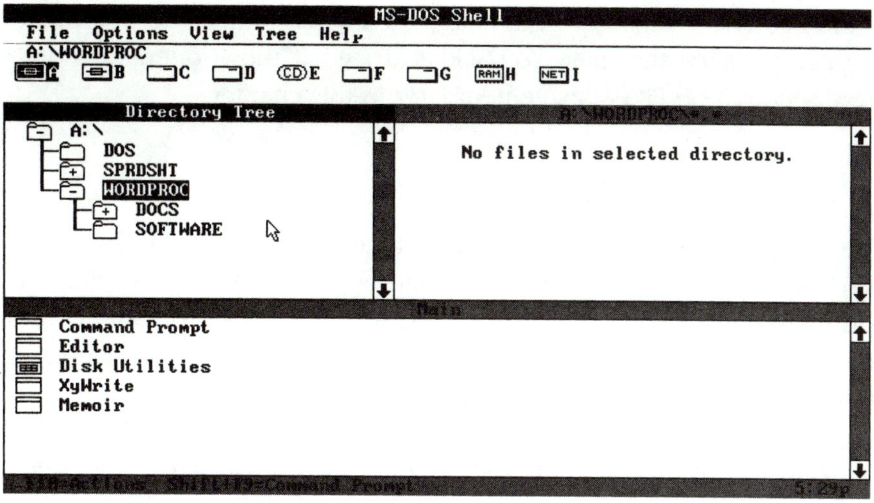

Figure 8.4 *An expanded subdirectory*

Collapsing a Directory

You can collapse an expanded directory the same way you expanded it, except that you press the **Minus** key (-) or click on the minus sign in its directory icon.

The Tree Menu

The Tree menu has commands that correspond to the expand and collapse shortcut keys. The Expand One Level command is the same as the plus key. The Collapse Branch command is the same as the minus key. The Expand Branch command, with asterisk (*) as its shortcut key expands all subdirectories below the current one. The Expand All command (Ctrl+Asterisk) expands all of the subdirectories in the drive.

The File List

The File List is to the right of the Directory Tree. The list shows all of the files that are in the directory that is selected in the Directory Tree. As you select different directories in the Directory Tree, the files displayed in the File List change. You can select the File List and perform a number of operations on the files. You will learn what those operations are in the discussion on File Management later in this chapter.

The Program List

The Program List is a list of programs that you can execute from within the Shell. The Program List in the figures above show how the list is configured when you first install DOS 6.0. Programs are organized into a hierarchy of Program Groups, and the Program List displays the programs in a selected group. When you first start the Shell, it displays the contents of the Main program group, which the figures above show. The title bar of the Program List window always displays the name of the current group.

You can add and delete programs and program groups to the Program List and execute programs directly from the Program List. These procedures are shown later in this chapter.

The Active Task List

You do not see the Active Task List in the figures above because the Shell is not set up to do task swapping. Execute the Enable Task Swapper command on the Options menu. The Shell screen will look like the one in Figure 8.5.

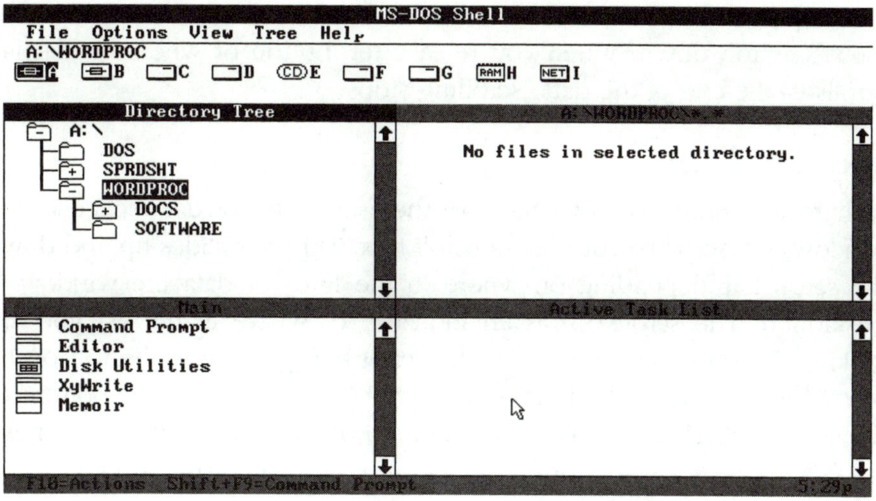

Figure 8.5 *The Active Task List*

Observe that the lower half of the screen has split into two windows. The Program List, which formerly occupied the entire lower half, now shares that space with the Active Task List. The Active Task List lists any tasks that are currently loaded. You will learn about task swapping later in this chapter.

Scroll Bars

Each window in the Shell has a scroll bar at the left end of the window. The scroll bar lets you scroll the display with the mouse when the length of the data exceeds the length of the window.

The Scroll Arrows

A scroll bar has two scroll arrows at its ends. When you click one of the scroll arrows, the window scrolls one line of data. The up arrow at the top of the bar scrolls the window down. The down arrow at the bottom of the bar scrolls the window up. If that sounds backwards, try it. The procedure is intuitive.

To perform a continuous scroll, click the scroll arrow and hold the mouse button down. When you release the button or when the display scrolls to the end of the data, scrolling stops.

The Scroll Box

If there are more lines of data than there are lines of data space in the window, the scroll bar displays a scroll box. This box slides up and down the scroll bar depending on where in the lines of data the window is positioned. The scroll box is an indicator of where in the list you are looking. When it is at the top of the scroll bar, you are at the top of the list. When it is at the bottom of the scroll bar, you are at the bottom of the list. The box's travel adjusts to the ratio of data lines to window lines.

You can drag the scroll box to a different position by clicking it and moving the mouse up and down without releasing the button. When you release the mouse button, the window display adjusts to the new position of the scroll box.

If you position the mouse cursor in the scroll bar and click, the scroll box jumps to that location, and the window display adjusts to the new position of the scroll box.

Horizontal Scroll Bars

Some displays have horizontal scroll bars at the bottom of the window. These work the same as the vertical scroll bars except that they scroll a text window horizontally. The EDIT program described in Chapter 12 uses horizontal scroll bars.

Dialog Boxes

The Shell communicates with you by opening special data entry windows called *dialog boxes.* The dialog box is a part of the Common User Access (CUA) interface standard. Other DOS 6.0 programs, such as the EDIT program described in Chapter 12, use similar dialog boxes. Figure 8.6 shows the Search File dialog box that the Search command on the File menu displays. (Note that the File menu includes this command when the Directory Tree or the File List has the focus.)

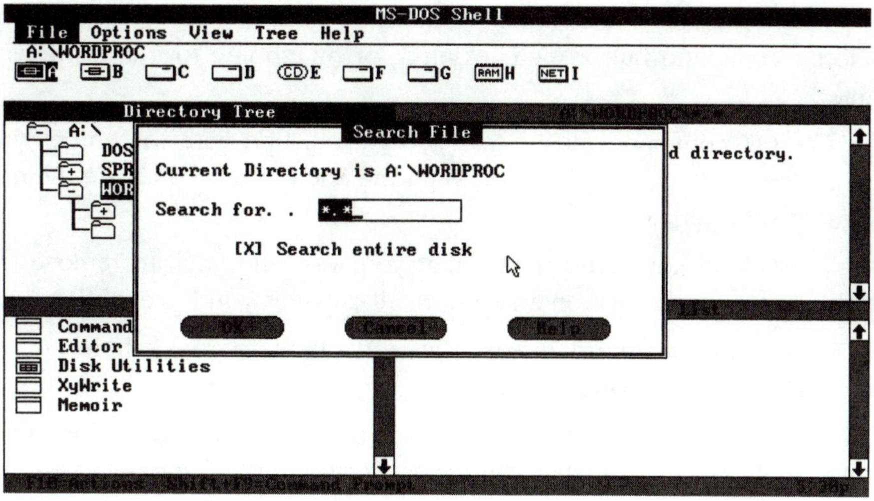

Figure 8.6 *The Search File dialog box*

The Search File dialog box is typical in that it contains several of the different kinds of data entry fields. You move from field to field by pressing Tab or by clicking the field with the mouse.

Text Boxes

The first field on the Search File dialog box is the Search For text box. You can type a file name into this text box.

Check Boxes

The second field on the Search File dialog box is the Search Entire Disk check box. If you click this box or tab to it and press the Spacebar, the X character will turn on and off. A check box is either selected or not. This is a way for the dialog box to control a yes/no optional condition.

Command Buttons

The bottom of the Search File dialog box has three command buttons, labeled OK, Cancel, and Help. These three command buttons are on most dialog boxes. Some dialog boxes have other command buttons.

When you select a command button, you execute its command. You select a command button by clicking it, or by tabbing to it and pressing Enter.

The OK command means that you are satisfied with the entries you have made to the dialog box and want the Shell to record or use them in subsequent operations.

The Cancel command means that you want the Shell to remove the dialog box from the screen and ignore all changes you have made to it.

The Help command means that you want to see a help screen related to the dialog box.

If you select a field that is not a command button and press Enter, the convention is that you have selected the OK command button. Pressing Esc at any time is the same as selecting the Cancel command button. Pressing F1 is the same as selecting the Help command button.

Option Buttons

Figure 8.7 is the File Display Options dialog box displayed by the File Display Options command on the Options menu.

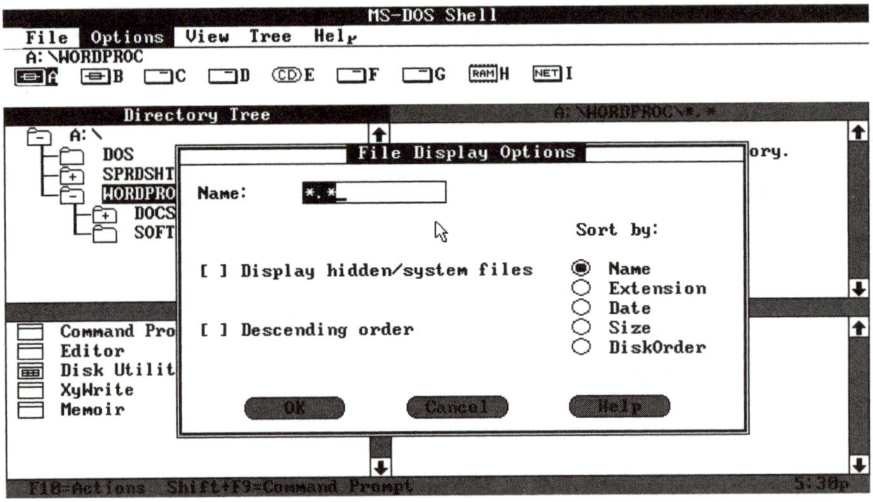

Figure 8.7 *The File Display Options dialog box*

The File Display Options dialog box includes a text box, two check boxes, and the usual three command buttons. The dialog box also includes a list of option buttons under the heading, Sort By. Option buttons are displayed in a group where only one of them can be selected. They are represented by circles, the currently selected option has a dot inside its circle, and the others in the group are empty. When the Shell is displayed in text mode, the circles are represented by parentheses.

When you select an option button, it gets a dot and the one that had a dot before it loses its dot. The appearance and behavior of option buttons cause them to be called "radio" buttons. They behave like the mechanical station selector push buttons on old car radios. Push a radio button in, and the current one pops out.

You can select an option button by clicking its circle. To select an option button with the keyboard, press **Tab** until the cursor is on the selected option button in the group. Then you can use the up and down arrow buttons to change the currently selected option button.

List Boxes

Figure 8.8 shows the Screen Display Mode dialog box displayed by the Display command on the Options menu.

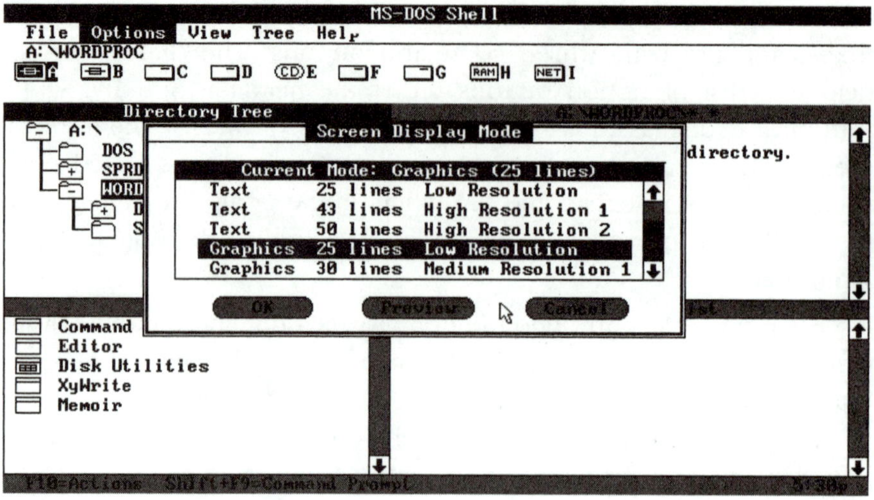

Figure 8.8 *The Screen Display Mode dialog box*

The first field in the Screen Display Mode dialog box is a list box. A list box is very much like the commands on a menu. The purpose of the list box is to allow you to select one item from a list. The box has a highlight bar that you can move up and down with the up and down arrow keys. You can also move the highlight bar by clicking the item that you want. A single click does not cause the item to be chosen; it moves the highlight bar to the item in the list. You choose an selected item by pressing Enter or by double-clicking the item.

When a list box contains more items than can be displayed within its space, you can scroll the display with the up and down arrow keys or by using the scroll bar that is to the right of the list.

Changing the Display

The Shell adapts to the display monitor you have when you first run it. You can change the characteristics of the Shell's display by using the Display and Colors commands from the Options menu.

Text and Graphics

The Display command on the Options menu displays the Screen Display Mode dialog box shown above in Figure 8.8. Depending on your display hardware, the list box will contain up to three text modes and five graphics modes for the display. The primary difference in the modes is the number of lines that the screen will display. These range from 25 to 60. The one you select depends on your own preference. Most users do not like the displays that conventional monitors render for modes greater than 43 lines.

The distinction between text and graphics display modes might seem confusing at first. After all, they both display the same information, which is mostly textual. The difference is that a text-mode display uses only the characters from the PC's ASCII and extended ASCII character set, while the graphics mode display can draw pictures on the screen. The text mode display cannot draw pictures. That is why the disk drive icons on a graphics display are pictures of disk drives while the same icons on a text display use square brackets. It is also why the graphics Directory Tree uses little pictures of folders for directory icons while the text Directory Tree uses square brackets.

Colors

You have a limited amount of control over the colors of the Shell's screen. The Colors command on the Options menu displays the Color Scheme dialog box. The list box in the Color Scheme dialog box allows you to select from a fixed set of color schemes. You should try different ones to see which one you prefer. The Preview command button gives you a chance to see what a color scheme looks like on your monitor. Select the color scheme from the list box by moving the highlight bar to it. Then click the Preview command button. The entire Shell screen including the dialog box will change to the selected color scheme. If you want to use that color scheme, click the OK command button. Otherwise, click the Cancel command button.

Program Groups

The Shell manages programs in program groups. The Main program group is the one that you see when you first run the Shell. As installed, the Shell has two program groups: the Main group and the Disk Utilities group. A program group displays the programs in that group, any other groups that are subordinate to the current group, and the group that is the parent of the current one, if any. The Main group is the top one, so it has no parent.

You can distinguish programs from groups by the way they are displayed. On a graphics screen, groups have a different icon than programs. On a text screen, the group names are surrounded by square brackets.

The Shell comes with several programs already installed in its two program groups. You can manage the configuration of programs you want to run by adding and deleting program groups and programs within a program group.

Changing to a Different Program Group

To change from the current program group to a different one, click the group name or select the Program List to be in focus, move the highlight cursor to the group name you want to select, and press **Enter**. The new group is displayed in the Program List.

To go directly to the parent program group of the current program group, press **Esc**.

Adding Program Groups

To add a program group, put the Program List into focus and select the New command on the File menu to see the New Program Object dialog box. Select the Program Group option button and press **Enter** or click the **OK** command button. You will see the Add Group dialog box.

Program Group Title

Enter the name of the new program group into the Title text box. If you want to add some help text to the group, enter it into the Help Text box. This text will display when you press F1 while your new program group is selected in the Program List.

Password

You can add a password to the new program group by entering it into the Password text box. This feature is of little use because nothing prevents someone else from deleting the group or running its programs from another place in the Shell or from the DOS 6.0 command line.

When you have the program defined the way you want it in the Add Group dialog box, choose the **OK** command button. Your new group will now be displayed in the Program List.

If you select the new group at this time, all you will see in it is the name of its parent group, the one that was active when you built the new program group. You must add programs or other groups to the group.

Adding Programs to a Group

To add a program to a group, put the Program List into focus and select the New command on the File menu to see the New Program Object dialog box. Select the Program Item option button and press **Enter** or click the **OK** command button. You will see the Add Program dialog box, which allows you to establish what are called the program's properties, which are parameters and configuration options that specify the way the program is known to the Shell and how it is to be run. You enter all the properties into the dialog box and its associated Advanced dialog box, and then execute the OK command button to add the program to the program group. The following discussions address each of the program's properties.

Program Title

Enter a title for the program in the Program Title field. This is the title that is displayed in the Program List and in the Active Task List when the program is running.

Program Command

The Commands field is where you put the command that runs the program. This is the same command that you type on the DOS 6.0 command line to run the program.

If the program is in the DOS 6.0 path, you do not need to specify where its executable file is located. Otherwise, you can specify the path ahead of the command just like you can when you run a program from the command line.

If the program uses variable parameters on the command line, you can enter them as %1 through %9 into the Command field on the Add Program dialog box. When you have finished filling in the Add Program dialog box, the Shell will display a dialog box that allows you to customize the dialog box that the Shell displays for each variable parameter when you run the program. The Window Title field identifies the title of the dialog box. The Program Information field is text that is displayed at the top of the dialog box window. The Prompt Message is displayed next to the field where you enter a value for the parameter.

The Default Parameter field specifies a default value for the parameter that will be filled in on the dialog box when you run the program. You will be allowed to change this parameter. If you enter %F as the default parameter, the Shell inserts the name of the file that is currently selected in the File List. If you enter %L as the default parameter, the Shell inserts the value used the last time you ran the program. Later, when you run the program, the Shell prompts you with the dialog box for each variable parameter in the command.

You can add a program to a program group that consists of more than one program running one after the other. Separate the commands with commas in the Command field. Put a space before and after each comma. The combined length of all the commands cannot exceed 255 characters.

If a command is the execution of a DOS 6.0 batch file, you must precede its name with the word *call.*

Startup Directory

The Startup Directory field on the Add Program dialog box specifies what drive and directory will be current when the program executes.

Application Shortcut Key

The Application Shortcut Key field allows you to assign a shortcut key to the program. When the task swapper is active, the shortcut key will call a program that is waiting in the background. The key will not, however, initially execute the program. The shortcut key works when you are running the Shell or another program that is on the Active Task List. You should assign a key that other programs do not use because this program's shortcut use of the key will take precedence over any other use.

The shortcut key that you assign must include Ctrl, Alt, or Shift or any combination of the three, plus a letter, number, or function key.

The Shell reserves some key combinations, but it does not prevent you from assigning an illogical shortcut key. You can, for example, assign Shift+S as a shortcut key. That means that whenever the program is loaded that uses that shortcut key, the Shift+S combination is not available to other programs. A word processor or text editor would not accept an uppercase S because when you pressed Shift+S, the Shell would run the program that is using Shift+S as a shortcut key.

Pause After Exit

The Pause After Exit check box specifies that you either want the program to return immediately to the Shell when the program exits or you want a pause to occur. This pause allows you to view the last screen that the program produces. Some programs perform some calculations, display their results, and exit. If you do not pause such a program, you will not have time to read the screen before the Shell is running again.

When the program pauses, the Shell displays a small window that prompts you to press any key to return to the Shell.

Program Password

The Password field on the Add Program dialog box allows you to specify a password that someone must enter before they can run the program. This is a mostly useless feature except that you must know the password to modify the program's properties.

Advanced Command

The Advanced command button displays the Advanced dialog box.

Help Text

You can enter some text into the Help Text field that the Shell will display when you select the program in the Program List, and press **F1**.

Conventional Memory

The Conventional Memory K Required field specifies the minimum amount of conventional memory that the program needs before it will run. This field has meaning only when task swapping is enabled.

You enter the amount in increments of 1024 bytes. In computer language, K means 1024. For example, you would enter the value for 8192 bytes as 8. If you do not enter an amount, the Shell assumes that it needs 128K to run the program. You will learn about memory management in Chapter 14, which addresses such terms as conventional memory. If you try to run the program and the available memory is less than what you specify here, the Shell displays a message and does not run the program.

How do you know how much memory the program really needs? Many programs publish their memory requirements, and you can use that value. What happens if you do not specify enough memory and the Shell tries to run the program? DOS 6.0 will not let the Shell run the program. What happens if the program tries to allocate more memory than you have specified? If the memory exists, the program runs properly. If not, the program will not run.

XMS Memory

The XMS Memory entry on the Advanced dialog box has two fields: the K Required field and the K Limit field. XMS memory is described in Chapter 14. You specify both fields in kilobytes. The fields have no meaning when the task swapper is not enabled. Some programs run differently when XMS memory is available. Some of those programs use all the XMS memory that they can get.

The K Required field specifies how much XMS memory must be free before the Shell can run the program. Most of the time, you can leave this field blank. A program's documentation will specify if it absolutely cannot run without some amount of XMS memory. Such programs are rare.

The K Limit field specifies the maximum amount of XMS memory that the Shell will allow the program to have. If you leave this setting blank, the program cannot have any XMS memory. If you set it to -1, the program can have all the XMS memory that is available. Setting it to a value tells the Shell to report that value as available XMS memory to the program and to allow it to have that much.

Video Mode

Some programs run in text mode, and some use video graphics. You can usually leave this field set to text mode. The program will usually turn on the video mode for itself, and the Shell can properly switch in and out of whatever mode the program uses. If swapping the program in and out causes video problems, try specifying the graphics mode option here.

Reserve Shortcut Keys

The task swapper uses the shortcut keys Alt+Tab, Alt+Esc, and Ctrl+Esc. If an applications program needs to use one or more of these keys, you must select the corresponding check boxes on the Advanced dialog box. Otherwise, the task swapper will preempt these keys, and the program will not be able to use them.

Prevent Program Switch

Select the Prevent Program Switch check box for a program that you do not want to be swapped out. Some programs cannot be interrupted that way because of their relationship with external hardware events. Communications programs that are reading streams of data from a modem are typical of such programs. If you were to swap out a communications program, its modem input stream would continue to come in without being read or processed, and the integrity of the communication with a remote computer would be damaged.

Changing a Program's Properties

You can change the properties of a program that is already installed in a program group. Select the group and the program that you want to change. Then execute the Properties command on the File menu. The Program Item Properties dialog box that you will see has the same format and works just like the Add Program dialog box that you just learned. The difference is that you will be changing the properties of an installed program rather than establishing the properties of a new one.

Deleting a Program from a Group

To delete a program from a group, select the program in the Program List and press **Del** or execute the Delete command on the File menu.

Copying a Program to a Different Group

To copy an installed program to a different group, first select the program in the Program List. Then execute the Copy command on the File menu. The menu will pop up and this message will be displayed in the status bar at the bottom of the screen:

```
Display the group the copy to, then press F2. Press Esc
to cancel.
```

Change to the program group where you want to copy the program. Press **F2**. The program is now installed in the group, and is still in the original group as well.

Deleting a Program Group

To delete a program group, select the group in the Program List and press **Del** or execute the Delete command on the File menu.

Running Programs

There are several ways to run programs from within the Shell. You just learned how to maintain your programs in program groups. You can run them from there, and if you have a number of programs that you routinely use, the program group is a handy way to get to them, particularly given the convenience of automatic subdirectory selection and default and replaceable command parameters.

Not all of the programs you run are going to be in program groups. Some of them are DOS 6.0 utilities that you use infrequently. The Disk Utilities program group has a few of the DOS 6.0 utility programs, but there are others that are not in any group. You might have programs that are on your disk but not in a group. The Shell provides ways to execute all such programs.

Running Programs from Program Groups

To run a program from a program group, select the Program List, move the highlight bar to the program, and press **Enter**. To run the program with the mouse, double-click the program title in the Program List.

If the program has command line parameters, you will see a dialog box for each one. The format of the dialog box will be the way you set it up when you installed the program into the group.

The Run Command

The Run command on the File menu allows you to run a program just as if you were at the DOS 6.0 command line. When you execute the Run command, you see the Run dialog box. Enter a command into the Command Line text box field and press **Enter**. The command is the same command that you would type on the DOS 6.0 command line to run the program.

Running Programs from the File List

As you navigate the Directory Tree, the File List displays the files that are in the current subdirectory on the current drive. Some of these files have the extensions .COM, .EXE, and .BAT. As you learned in Chapter 5, these files are executable command files. You can execute the programs that these files represent from the File List. First, select the file list itself. Then move the highlight bar to the command file you want to execute and press **Enter**. You can execute a command file from the File List by double-clicking its name.

Dragging a Data File to a Program

If a data file and the program command file that processes it are both in view in the File List, you can click on the data file, hold the mouse button down, and drag the mouse cursor to the command file. Release the mouse button when the mouse cursor is on the command file. You will see the Confirm Mouse Operation dialog box. Select **OK** to execute the program.

It is possible to drag a data file to a command file that is not visible. With the mouse button still held down, move the mouse cursor to one of the scroll arrows to scroll the window until the command file comes into view. Without releasing the mouse button, drag the mouse cursor to the command file. This is a tricky operation. Most users do not use it.

Associating Programs with Data Files

You can use the facilities of the Shell to associate data files with program command files. With this feature, you can run a program by selecting one of its associated data files from the File List. This feature works only with programs that expect a file name as the first parameter on the DOS 6.0 command line.

First, make sure that the Select Across Directories toggle option in the Options menu is off. When it is on, a small diamond is displayed to the left of the menu command name.

Next, select File List and select the command file with which you want to associate data files. For example, you might want to associate all .DOC files with your word processing program, which might be named WP.EXE. Execute the Associate command on the File menu. You will see an Associate dialog box, which displays the name of the command file with which you are going to associate data files. Enter the file extension without its period prefix into the Extensions field. If you want to associate several different extensions with the command file, enter them into the Extensions field and separate them with spaces. Execute the OK command button when you are done. The associations have been made.

To execute the program, select the File List. Move the highlight bar to a data file that has the file name extension you associated with the program, and press Enter. You can also double-click the file name. The program executes with the file name as the program's command line parameter.

If you select a file that is not an executable command file and then execute the Associate command on the File menu, the Shell will display the Associate File dialog box, which displays the command that is associated with the selected file's extension. You can change the name of the command by typing a new one into the dialog box and executing the OK command button.

The DOS 6.0 Command Line

The Main program group includes a program called Command Prompt. When you run it, the Shell displays the DOS 6.0 version screen and provides a DOS 6.0 command line prompt. You can do all the normal DOS 6.0 command line operations here. To terminate the Command Prompt process, return to the Shell, and type EXIT at the DOS 6.0 command line prompt.

The Task Swapper

The Enable Task Swapper command on the Options menu turns the DOS 6.0 Shell task swapper on and off. When it is on, the command has a small diamond next to it on the menu and the lower half of the Shell's screen includes the Active Task List.

Task swapping is a way to load more than one program into memory at one time and to rapidly switch among them. Only one of them is running at a time, but they are all loaded and ready to run, and when you switch from one to another, the swapped-out program remembers its condition. When you return to the interrupted program, it resumes running just as if it had never been interrupted.

Running Multiple Programs

To run multiple programs, you enable the task swapper and run the first program, using one of the techniques you learned in the discussion immediately preceding this one. While that program is running, you can return to the Shell by pressing Ctrl+Esc. You will see the program's name on the Active task list. You can now run another program. When you return to the Shell, both programs are on the Active Task List.

Adding Programs to the Active Task List

You can add a program to the Active Task List without entering it and having to return to the Shell. Select the program on the Program List or its command or data file name on the File List, and press **Shift-Enter**. You can add a program to the Active Task List with the mouse, too. Hold down **Shift** and double-click the program in the Program List or the program's command file or associated data file in the File List.

Switching to Programs on the Active Task List

There are three ways to resume a program from the Shell. You can double-click the program in the Active Task List. You can also select the Active Task List, move the highlight bar to the program, and press Enter. If the program has a shortcut key, you can press that key.

Choosing a program from the Program List that is already on the Active Task List does not resume the loaded copy of the program. The action starts a second copy of the same program.

Return to the Shell from a Running Program

Press **Ctrl+Esc**. The active program will swap out, and the Shell will be running.

Switch Among Active Programs

Hold down **Alt** and press **Tab**. Do not release Alt. The screen clears, and the name of the next program on the Active Task List is displayed at the top of the screen. Continue to press **Tab** until you see the name of the program you want to run. One of the programs in the cycle is the Shell itself. Release **Alt** to resume the program that is named at the top of the screen.

Terminating Programs on the Active Task List

Normally, you terminate a program by running it and executing its normal program termination procedures, whatever they are. However, there are times when that does not work. Perhaps the program has failed. To terminate such a program, select it on the Active Task List and press **Del** or execute the Delete command on the File menu. You will see a Warning dialog box.

Most dialog boxes have the OK command button as the default. The Warning dialog box has the Cancel command button as the default to prevent you from deleting the program too soon with a reflexive press of Enter. You must tab to the OK command button or select it with the mouse to execute it. When you do, the Shell terminates the program and removes it from the Active Task List.

File Management

The Shell provides tools to manage your disk file system. You can add, delete, rename, move, and copy files and work with their attributes. You can also view the contents of any file and create and remove subdirectories.

The Directory Tree

To work with files in the Shell, you must first select the drive and subdirectory where DOS 6.0 stored the files. You learned earlier how to select a drive from the drive icons. You select a subdirectory by first selecting the Directory Tree to have the focus, then moving the highlight bar to the directory where the files are. You can move the highlight bar with the arrow keys or by clicking the directory name with the mouse. You might need to expand a collapsed directory in order to view its subdirectories.

The Directory Tree also provides a way to add and delete subdirectories.

Adding a Subdirectory

To make a new subdirectory, select the Directory Tree to have the focus. Select the directory that will be the parent of the new subdirectory. Execute the Create Directory command on the File menu. You will see a Create Directory dialog box.

Enter the name of the new subdirectory into the New Directory Name field on the Create Directory dialog box. Press **Enter** or click the **OK** command button. The subdirectory is now displayed in the Directory Tree.

Deleting a Subdirectory

You can delete a subdirectory only when it has no files in it. If you wish to delete a subdirectory that has files, you must first delete or move the files. Those procedures are explained below.

To delete an empty subdirectory, select it in the Directory Tree. Press **Del** or execute the Delete command on the File menu. The Shell will ask you to confirm the delete by displaying a confirmation dialog box. If you confirm the delete, the subdirectory is deleted from the disk and removed from the Directory Tree display.

Selecting Files in the File List

Many of the file management operations—such as moving, copying, and deleting—deal with the file or group of files that you select. You will learn each of these operations later, but first you must learn how to select a file or a group of files.

Selecting a Single File

To select a single file, you select the File List to have the focus, and you put the highlight bar on the file you want to select, either by moving it down with the **Down Arrow** key or clicking it with the mouse. You can perform the operation on the file without changing the File List.

Selecting a Contiguous Group of Files

A contiguous group of files is a group of files that are displayed together in the File List. To select a contiguous group of files, put the highlight bar on the first one. Hold down **Shift** and move the highlight bar with the Up and Down Arrow keys. As you do, the files you pass over are selected and highlighted. To select the contiguous group with the mouse, put the mouse cursor on the first one. Hold down **Shift**, press the left mouse button, and drag the mouse cursor up or down to the last file in the group.

Selecting a Scattered Group of Files

To select files that are not contiguous, select the first file. Press **Shift+F8**. Move to subsequent files and press the **Spacebar** to select them one by one. Press **Shift+F8** when you are done.

To select a non-contiguous group of files with the mouse, hold **Ctrl** down while you individually click each file in the group.

Selecting Multiple Blocks of Files

You can select more than one group of files. To do so with the keyboard, select the first group with **Shift+Up Arrow** and **Shift+Down Arrow**. Press **Shift+F8**. Select the first file in the next group by moving to it and pressing the **Spacebar**. Use Shift+Up Arrow or Shift+Down Arrow to select the remaining files in the group. Select subsequent groups the same way. Press **Shift+F8** when you are done.

Canceling a Single Selection from a Group

To deselect individual files from a group, press **Shift+F8**, move to the files in turn and press the **Spacebar** to deselect them from the group. To deselect with the mouse, click the file while you hold down **Ctrl**.

Selecting Files Across Subdirectories

You can select a group of files that spans subdirectories by enabling the Select Across Directories option on the Options menu. Then move from directory to directory selecting groups of files and single files by using the methods you just learned. When you perform a file operation that works with selected files, all of the selected files in all of the directories are involved in the operation.

Selecting All Files

You can select all files in the current directory by executing the Select All command on the File menu or by pressing **Ctrl+/**. The Deselect All command on the File menu deselects any files that are currently selected.

Moving and Copying Files

To move or copy files, you must first select one or more files in the manner just described. Moving implies that the file or files will be copied to their new location and deleted from their original location. Copying does not include the implied delete.

Begin by selecting the drive and directory where the files to be moved or copied presently reside. Then select the file or group of files you want to move or copy.

Moving Files

To move files with the mouse, click a file in the group (or the single file you want to move) and drag the mouse cursor to a subdirectory in the Directory Tree.

If the destination subdirectory is not visible in the tree, you can use the Up and Down Arrow keys to scroll the tree until the subdirectory is visible. This procedure may not seem easy at first because the window scrolls quickly. However, you can stop the scrolling, by moving the mouse away from the scroll bar. You cannot release the mouse button or the move operation stops. When you can see the subdirectory where you want to move the files, drag the mouse cursor to it and release the mouse button.

A better way to move files to an out-of-sight directory is to execute the Dual File Lists command on the View menu. This command is discussed later. With the command, you can display a second Directory Tree and File List, which can display different part of the same subdirectory, a different subdirectory, or even a different drive. See "Moving and Copying to Other Disks" in this section for a discussion of the differences involved in moving files to a different disk.

After you complete the move procedure, the Shell displays a dialog box that asks you to confirm the move before it takes place.

To move files with the keyboard, press **F7** or execute the Move command on the File menu. If no files are selected, the Move command is disabled.

The Move File dialog box identifies the files you have selected and the current subdirectory as the destination for the move. If the subdirectory is the one where the file exists, you cannot simply execute OK because that would be telling the Shell to move the files to themselves. You must either enter new file names to move, change the subdirectory where the files are to go, or add a different file name to the destination subdirectory. You can do any or all of the above.

Copying Files

Copying files works the same as moving files with these exceptions:

- With the mouse, drag the mouse cursor from the files to the directory tree while holding down **Ctrl**.
- With the keyboard, use **F8** or execute the Copy command on the File menu.

Moving and Copying to Other Disks

You can move files to a disk drive icon by holding down **Alt** while you drag the mouse cursor from the selected file(s) to the icon. If you do not hold down **Alt**, you are doing a file copy to the drive. The files will move to the subdirectory that is current for the disk drive where you drag the files.

If you use the Dual File Lists view, and move or copy the files to a different drive, the mouse procedures reverse themselves. That is, you hold down **Ctrl** to move and do not hold it down to copy.

This feature is inherited from Windows, which does the same thing. The theory is that you will most often move files from one subdirectory on the same disk, and you will most often copy files from one disk to another. The differences may be confusing enough that they will not quickly become intuitive or second nature, and it may take a while to get used to them. The best rule to follow is to always carefully read the Confirmation dialog boxes to make sure that you are doing what you intend to do.

Deleting Files

You delete files by selecting them and pressing **Del**, or executing the Delete command on the File menu.

Renaming Files

You rename files by selecting them and selecting the Rename command on the File menu. You will see the Rename dialog box, which lists the first file you have selected and allows you to enter a new file name for it. If you have selected more than one file, the process will continue, letting you rename each selected file in turn.

File Attributes

Every file in a DOS 6.0 system has a set of five file attributes. DOS 6.0 and its utilities use these attributes to control how a file may be accessed. The five attributes are:

- Hidden
- System
- Directory
- Archive
- Read-only.

Each of these attributes is an indicator that is either on or off. If an attribute's indicator is on, the file is said to have that attribute.

Hidden files are the ones that you do not usually see when you display the disk directory, either with the command line DIR command or from the Shell. You will learn in Chapter 10 how to display hidden files with DIR. You will learn here how to display them in the Shell.

System files belong to DOS 6.0 itself. Programs and users should not delete or change these files.

Subdirectory files have the Directory attribute. When you see a subdirectory entry in a directory listing, the entry is really a DOS 6.0 file that has the directory attribute and contains a list of the files that are in the subdirectory. That is the mechanism DOS 6.0 uses to implement the hierarchical subdirectory structure.

Whenever any program modifies the contents of a file, DOS 6.0 sets the file's Archive attribute indicator. Programs that perform backup functions (an example is the DOS 6.0 MSBACKUP command, described in Chapter 15) test the Archive attribute and backup only those files that have it. Then the backup programs turn the attribute off. This procedure prevents unnecessary backups of files that have not changed since the last backup

You cannot delete or change files that have the read-only attribute. Your applications programs cannot delete or change them either, unless they take measures to remove the read-only attribute from the files first. Most programs do not do this, respecting the read-only attribute as your way to protect files from unintentional modification or deletion.

Changing a File's Attributes

To change a file's attributes, select the file and execute the Change Attributes command on the File menu. You will see the Change Attributes dialog box. The list of attributes on the dialog box does not include the Directory attribute. You cannot change that attribute. If a file is a directory, it is always a directory until you remove it. If a file is not a directory, you cannot turn it into one. To change the other attributes, move the highlight cursor to the attribute and press the spacebar or click the attribute. Execute the OK command button to put the changes into effect.

If you give a file the Hidden attribute, the file will no longer be on the File List. The file is not gone, it is simply hidden. See "Changing How Files Display" in this chapter to learn how to view hidden files.

Viewing a File's Contents

To view a file's contents, select the file and press **F9** or execute the View File Contents on the File menu. Depending on the format of the file, the Shell displays its contents in ASCII or hexadecimal character representations. ASCII is the mode for most text files. You can read the file in this mode. The .BAT, .LTR, and .DOC files you have built with the exercises in this book are ASCII files. The .COM and .EXE and most .SYS files are not text, so an ASCII display is not always meaningful. You will see the hexadecimal display for these files.

You can change the display mode by using the ASCII and Hex commands on the Display menu. The menu bar changes when you are viewing a file. The bar has a Display menu, a View menu, and a Help menu. The Help menu is the same as the Help menu when you are in the Shell.

To return to the Shell from viewing a file, press Esc or execute the Restore View command on the View menu.

Viewing Information About a File

The Show Information command on the View menu displays a window that has information about the current disk, subdirectory, and file.

Customizing the Shell

The Shell has a number of modes for changing the configuration of its screens and the way it displays directories.

Repainting and Refreshing the Screen

The Repaint Screen command on the View menu repaints the Shell's screen. This command is useful if you have a memory-resident program that pops up over the shell and fails to fully restore the screen when it pops down. As more video adapters become available, the number of video modes that they support increases, and more of the older pop-up programs do not correctly handle them. If you cannot see enough of the screen to get to the Repaint Screen command, you can press **Shift+F5** to execute it.

The Refresh command on the View menu reloads the information about the current disk and directory so that the screen display is current. This command is useful in environments where something external to the Shell has changed the contents of a directory. One such example is found in networks. You might be looking at the directory of a network file server while another user at another workstation adds a file or deletes one. Your Shell has no way to know that. The Refresh command, also available through F5 (shortcut key), refreshes the Shell's copy of the disk directory and repaint the screen.

Changing the Window Configurations

You can display the Shell's windows in several different configurations. The default display is the way you have been viewing the Shell with a Directory Tree and File List for a single drive on top and the Program List and Active Task List on the bottom. The Program/File Lists command on the View menu selects this default configuration.

The Single File List command on the View menu gives the entire screen to the Directory Tree and File List. The Program List and Active Task List do not display. You would use this view to see more of what the two windows display than what the half screen configuration affords.

You can view two different Directory Trees and File Lists by executing the Dual File List command on the View menu. This view is convenient when you are moving or copying files from one drive to another or to a different subdirectory.

The All Files command on the View menu displays all of the files on the currently logged on drive. The right half of the screen is a list of the files. The right half of the screen is a display of information about the currently selected file in the list.

The Program List command on the View menu dedicates the screen to the Program List and, if the task swapper is enabled, the Active Task List.

Changing How Files Display

The File Display Options command on the Options menu displays the File Display Options dialog box shown in Figure 8.7 earlier in the chapter. This dialog box controls how the files display in the File List. You can specify a file name with wild cards to select from the files to display by entering the file specification in the Name field. The Display Hidden/System Files check box specifies that hidden and system files will be displayed. Normally they are not.

The Sort By option buttons determine which field the File List will be sorted by: name, extension, date, size, or disk order. The disk order selection displays the files in the order in which they are stored on the disk, which has little meaning because DOS reuses deleted file directory entries when you add files. The Descending Order check box specifies that the sort is to be in descending order. This would be useful if you were sorting by date and wanted to see the newest files first or if you were sorting by size and wanted to see the biggest files first.

Confirmations

You have noticed by now that almost every time you take an action, the Shell displays a confirmation dialog box. The Confirmations command on the Options menu lets you control when the Shell will do this. The command displays the Confirmation dialog box, which has three check boxes labeled Confirm on Delete, Confirm on Replace, and Confirm on Mouse Operation. Turn the check boxes off for any confirmations that you do not want prompting you. This is a personal preference. Some users believe that once they take an action, the computer should obey without question. Others know that they can issue a command in error from time to time, and appreciate having the computer asking them to verify their requests, particularly when those requests could have far-reaching consequences, such as deleting all of the files in a subdirectory.

Printing

The Shell allows you to print text files or printer output files that your word processor creates, but only if you have loaded the PRINT command from the DOS command line. Chapter 7 describes the PRINT command.

To print a file or a group of files, you select them and execute the Print command on the File menu. The Shell sends the files to the PRINT command with no further interaction.

The Help System

Press **F1** at any time in the Shell to view a help text display that describes the current situation. Most dialog boxes have a Help command button that does the same thing. The Help menu includes commands to display an index of the help topics, explanations of the Shell's keyboard commands, and a tutorial introduction to the Shell and how it works. The menu also includes explanations of the Shell commands within each menu, procedures for using the Shell, and a tutorial on the use of the Help system. The About command on the Help menu displays a message with the MS-DOS version and the Microsoft copyright notice.

Exiting from the Shell

To exit from the Shell, press **Alt+F4** or execute the Exit command on the File menu. If any programs are still loaded by the task swapper, the Shell will not exit. You must swap those programs in and use their procedures to terminate the programs. Then you can exit from the Shell.

Summary

This chapter covered information about the Shell menu system and how to switch between several concurrently loaded tasks. You learned how to manage programs in groups, run applications, and manage files.

With this chapter under your belt, you are ready to use your PC and look almost like a master. You may not be a full-fledged power user yet, but your new knowledge of DOS 6.0 will serve you well for most of your PC usage.

Section II: The Power User

You have come a long way. You are now equipped to use DOS 6.0 in ways that support most of your work. However, DOS 6.0 has many fascinating and useful extensions. These are features that you could ignore and maybe never miss. If you have enough under your belt to get the job done, you can slow down now. However, you are encouraged to look through these next few chapters to get a glimpse at some of the potential that DOS 6.0 offers you, for these are the basic tools of the Power User.

If you do stop now, return here in a few weeks or months after you have more experience with DOS 6.0. By then, you will have better insight into the kinds of things you need to do.

This section is not a comprehensive treatment of Power User tools and techniques. Its purpose, now that you have learned the basic principles of DOS 6.0 operation, is to stir your imagination and introduce you to some of the advanced DOS 6.0 features. If it arouses your curiosity and gets you thinking, you will invent more uses of these tools than any book could possibly cover.

Chapter 9

Filters, Pipes, and Input/Output Redirection

This chapter is about a special kind of DOS 6.0 command called the *filter* command and about the DOS 6.0 pipes and I/O redirection that support filters. Not all commands are filters, but the ones that are can be executed in unique ways to achieve some interesting results. You will learn:

- What a filter is
- How to redirect a filter's input and output
- How to connect filters with a pipe
- Some practical applications for filters

The Filter

DOS 6.0 supports a category of command called the filter, which is a program that reads and writes text. More specifically, the filter reads text from what is called the *standard input* device and writes text to the *standard output* device. Some filters have no input. Unless you redirect the input and output devices, input comes from the keyboard and output goes to the screen.

Not all applications commands are filters, but many DOS 6.0 commands are. Word processors, spreadsheets, database programs, and other custom applications are not usually written to be filters even though they read from the keyboard and write to the screen. These programs have broader concerns than the translation of an input text stream to an output text stream, and their developers chose not to implement them as filters.

Figure 9.1 is a diagram of a filter program that has no input. You have already run several such filters in the exercises in the preceding chapters. The DOS 6.0 DIR and TYPE commands are examples of filters that have no input, except what is specified on the command line. When you issue the DIR command, DOS 6.0 writes the directory display to the standard output device. When you issue the TYPE command, DOS 6.0 writes the file display to the standard output device.

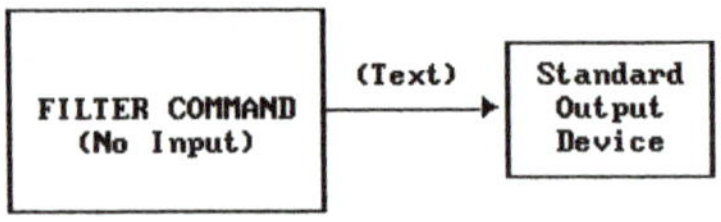

FILTER

Figure 9.1 *A simple filter command*

Figure 9.2 is a diagram of a filter program that has both input and output. The DATE and TIME commands are examples of filters with input and output. When you execute either command with no command line parameters, the date and time are written to the standard output device along with the prompts to enter a new date and time. The new date and time (or the single Enter key) are read from the standard input device.

Figure 9.2 *A filter with input/output*

Until now, the standard input device has always been the keyboard, and the standard output device has always been the screen. Later, you will see how the input to filters can come from other places and how the output from filters can be used in other ways.

The filter category of command is well named. A filter reads lines of text and filters them into modified lines of text. Filters that have no standard input get the data to modify from other places.

Input/Output Redirection

The power of using standard devices becomes apparent when you consider the ability to redirect the data. Any program that takes text input from the standard input device can get that text from any file or input device. The program does not know or care where the text comes from; it simply reads whatever text DOS 6.0 provides on the standard input device. Any program that writes text to the standard output device can write that text to a file or device.

When you run a filter from the command line, you can tell DOS 6.0 that the input is to come from somewhere other than the keyboard. For example, you can tell DOS 6.0 that the input is to be found in a disk file. Figure 9.3 shows input redirection. The filter command reads its text from the standard input device, but DOS 6.0 has substituted the contents of the disk input file for what you would normally type on the keyboard.

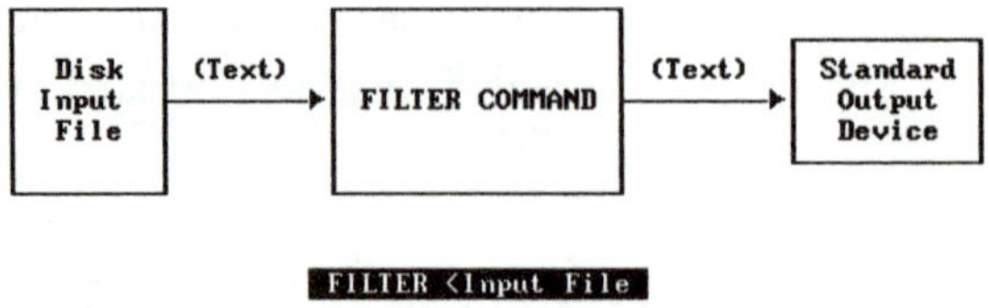

Figure 9.3 *Redirected input*

To redirect input from a file, you include the less than (<) character on the command line followed by the name of the file.

You can also tell DOS 6.0 that the output is to be written to a disk file. Figure 9.4 shows this relationship. The filter command writes its text to the standard output device, but DOS 6.0 has substituted the disk output file to receive what you would normally see on the screen.

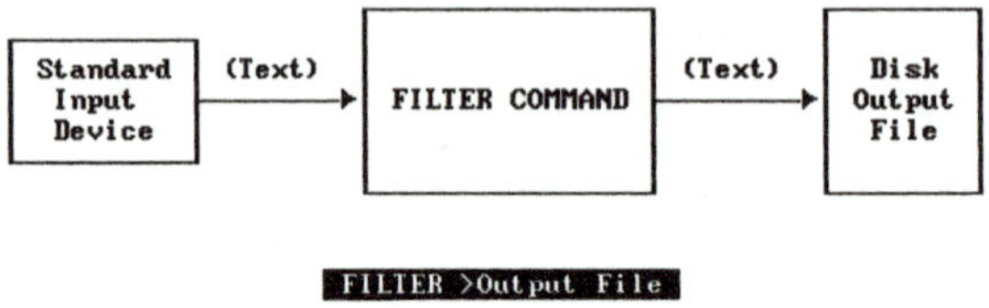

Figure 9.4 *Redirected output*

To redirect output to a file, you include the greater than (>) character on the command line followed by the name of the file to be created. If you name a file that already exists, DOS 6.0 replaces that file with the new one.

The SORT Filter

DOS 6.0 has a utility filter program called SORT. This program reads lines of text from the standard input device, sorts those lines of text, and writes the sorted output text to the standard output device. First, look at how SORT behaves when there is no input/output redirection. Enter this command:

```
A>sort
```

The cursor will wait at the left margin of the screen for you to type. Enter some lines of text that you want to have sorted:

```
There
was
a
young
man
from
Nantucket
```

Press **F6** and **Enter**. The SORT filter sorts your lines of text and display the sorted text on the screen.

```
a
from
man
Nantucket
there
was
young
```

This exercise demonstrates the function of a filter, but not its usefulness. To derive any benefit from the SORT filter, you would want to sort files. The silly limerick just used would have little meaning in its sorted version. However, there are occasions when you will want to sort some real data files.

To illustrate this point, build a file of names and birthdays. Build it in no sequence at all to begin. Use the COPY command to build the file.

```
A>copy con names.dat
```

Type some data records in a fixed format of columns as shown here.

```
Marvel, Captain  1950/01/01
Washington, Geo. 1732/02/22
Brown, Clifford  1956/06/26
Tatum, Art       1910/10/13
```

Press **F6** and **Enter** to store the file. Now you are ready to sort it. To test your sort, try it without redirecting the output. If what has been explained works, the file should be sorted and sent to the screen. Enter this command:

```
A>sort <names.dat
```

You will see the sorted data displayed on the screen like this.

```
Brown, Clifford  1956/06/26
Marvel, Captain  1950/01/01
Tatum, Art       1910/10/13
Washington, Geo. 1732/02/22
```

Sorting files to the screen can be useful. However, you will more often want to sort a file and write the sorted data to another file for processing by another program. Figure 9.5 shows how a filter can read one file and write another.

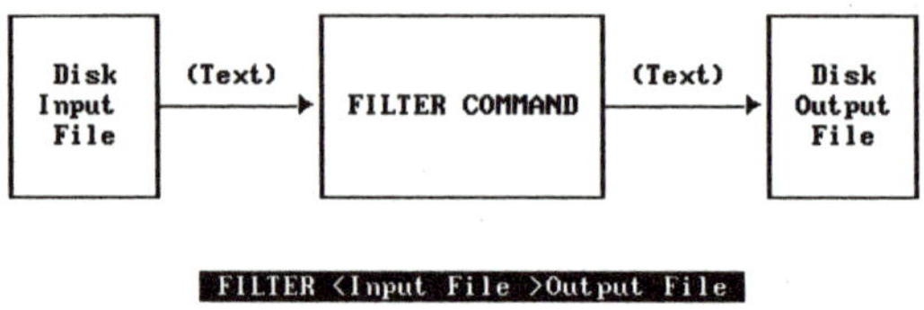

Figure 9.5 *Redirected input and output*

To sort the NAMES.DAT file and retain the results, enter this command:

```
A>sort <names.dat >names.srt
```

This command tells the SORT filter to read the file named NAMES.DAT, sort it, and write it to a file named NAMES.SRT. There is no screen display associated with this command. Use the DIR command to see that the NAMES.SRT file was created. Use the TYPE command to view the file.

The SORT command collates the text starting in the first column. However, you can tell it to start in a different column. The NAMES.DAT file includes dates that are in year/month/day sequence and that start in column 18. You can sort on these dates with this command:

```
A>sort <names.dat /+18
```

The output will be in this sequence:

```
Washington, Geo. 1732/02/22
Tatum, Art       1910/10/13
Marvel, Captain  1950/01/01
Brown, Clifford  1956/06/26
```

DIR and TYPE as Filters

The DIR and TYPE commands are each one-half of a filter because their displays are written to the standard output device. For example, enter this command:

```
A>dir >latest.dir
```

This command writes the directory to the file named LATEST.DIR. This feature is useful in preparing operating procedures for your system. The feature has even more utility when used with the DOS 6.0 Pipe described below.

The TYPE command sends its output to a file the same way. Try this command:

```
A>type latest.dir >typed.dir
```

This command types the LATEST.DIR file, sending the typed result to a new file named TYPED.DIR. Using the command has the same effect as copying one file to the other with the COPY command.

Much of this information will begin to take shape by the time you finish this chapter.

The FIND Filter

The FIND filter reads lines of text from the standard input device and writes selected lines of that text to the standard output device. The selection is a function of the arguments you include on the command line. Suppose you wanted to see all of the records in the NAMES.DAT file that had dates in the fifties. The FIND filter can find them for you. Enter this command:

```
A>find "195" <names.dat
```

This command says to read the file named NAMES.DAT and write out every line that contains the string value, "195." This is the criterion you chose for the selection of dates in the fifties. You would see this display.

```
Marvel, Captain  1950/01/01
Brown, Clifford  1956/06/26
```

If you want this subset of the original file to be written to another disk file, you can use output redirection on the command line as shown here.

```
A>find "195" <names.dat >names.195
```

This command writes the selected records to a new file named NAMES.195.

A variation of the FIND command allows you to select all the records that do not match the criterion. That variation is invoked by the /V command line switch as shown here.

```
A>find /V "195" <names.dat
```

This command would provide this display, which could have been sent to a file instead.

```
Washington, Geo. 1732/02/22
Tatum, Art       1910/10/13
```

The FIND filter has two other command line options. The first is the /C option which displays a count of the number of lines that match the criterion. Enter this command:

```
A>find /C "195" <names.dat
```

The FIND program returns the number 2 on the screen.

The other option is the /N option which displays the line number in the file where the matches occur. Enter this command:

```
A>find /N "195" <names.dat
```

You will see this display:

```
[1]Marvel, Captain  1950/01/01
[3]Brown, Clifford  1956/06/26
```

This feature is useful if you plan to use a text editor to work on the text file. Knowing the line numbers where the matching text lines are will help you in finding them.

The MORE Filter

The MORE filter is particularly handy when you are dealing with large text files that you want to display. You have no such file on the TYD Learning Diskette, but perhaps you know where there is one on another disk. Assume that it is named LONG.DOC and that it is on the C drive. Enter this command:

```
more <c:long.doc
```

The MORE filter reads the standard input and writes one screen full to the standard output device. Then it displays the "-- More --" message at the bottom of the screen and waits for a keystroke. The keystroke is taken from the keyboard, regardless of whether the standard input device is redirected (which it usually is).

This filter allows you to view long text files without worrying about them scrolling off the screen faster than you can read them.

Appending Text to a File

Output redirection normally creates a new file, replacing any existing file with the same name. A variation on output redirection allows you to append what is written to the standard output device to an existing file. You use the concatenation (>>) symbol on the command line to append to a file rather than the redirection (>) symbol. Figure 9.6 depicts this operation.

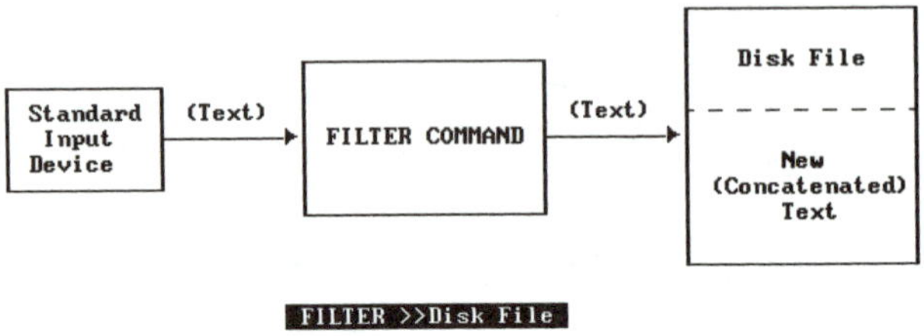

Figure 9.6 *Concatenating text*

For example, to add some lines to the NAMES.DAT file, enter these commands:

```
A>echo Armstrong, Louis 1900/07/04 >>names.dat
A>echo Stauffer, Judy   1941/11/17 >>names.dat
```

The ECHO command is a filter; its output is sent to the standard output device. In this case, you have used ECHO to append text to the NAMES.DAT file. Each execution of the command causes an additional append.

Redirecting Output to a Printer

The standard output device can be redirected to a DOS 6.0 device. The most common use of this feature is to print something. To redirect the standard output device to the printer, you use the PRN device name instead of a file name after the output redirection (>) symbol. Figure 9.7 shows this operation.

Figure 9.7 *Redirecting output to the printer*

Perhaps, for example, you want a hard copy of the directory of a diskette. Make sure your printer is connected and turned on, and enter this command.

```
A>dir >prn
```

The directory will be printed. You can also redirect output to the LPT1, LPT2, LPT3, COM1, COM2, COM3, and COM4 devices.

Redirecting Output to the NUL Device

When you redirect output to the NUL device, you effectively disable the output. This is most often used in batch files when you do not want to see a particular message. For example, if you routinely copy a file or files, perhaps as a backup procedure, you might have the COPY commands in a batch file. Normally, the COPY command displays the number of files copied. You might not want to see those messages.

Enter the following command to change to the WORDPROC \DOCS\LETTERS subdirectory:

```
cd\wordproc\docs\letters
```

Enter the following command to make backup copies of your letters:

```
A>copy *.ltr *.sav
```

The COPY command lists the files it is copying and a count of the files when it is done as shown here:

```
MILLY01.LTR
MILLY02.LTR
2 file(s) copied
```

To suppress the output displayed by the COPY command, use the following format, which redirects the COPY command's message output to the NUL device.

```
A>copy *.ltr *.sav >nul
```

You will not see the messages that would otherwise be displayed about the copy operation.

Redirecting the standard output device to the NUL device does not suppress the display of error messages. Error messages are typically sent to the standard error device, which is the screen, and which cannot be redirected. Try this command:

```
A>copy xxx yyy >nul
```

There is no file named XXX, and the COPY command displays this error message on the screen even though you have redirected its standard output device to the NUL device.

```
File not found - XXX
```

Pipes

The real power of input/output redirection is realized when you use DOS 6.0 pipes. A pipe is a DOS 6.0 mechanism that connects two filter programs. The standard output of the first filter becomes the standard input of the second filter. Both programs are named on the command line and are connected by the pipe (|) symbol. (See Figure 9.8.)

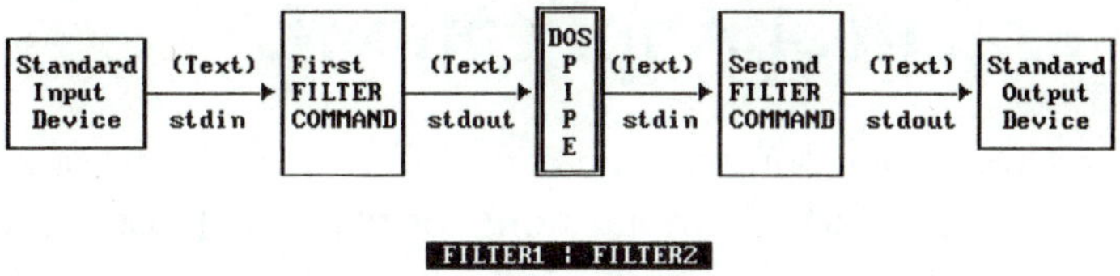

Figure 9.8 *The DOS 6.0 pipe*

Several filters can be strung together with pipes on the command line. For example, suppose you want a directory of all files that are subdirectories. Furthermore, since you expect a lot of files in the display, you want the display to pause at each screen full. Change to the root directory of your hard disk and type this command.

```
C>dir | find "<DIR>" | more
```

This command sequence executes the DIR command first. Since the DIR command is followed by the pipe (|) symbol, the entire directory is written to the DOS 6.0 pipe. Then the FIND filter is executed, and, since the command name follows a pipe symbol, FIND reads its input from the DOS 6.0 pipe. The next entry on the command line is the /V option, which tells FIND to select all lines from the pipe that do not match the “<DIR>” string. This will eliminate the subdirectories from the directory. The MORE filter reads the directory from the pipe and sends it a page at a time to the standard output device which is, finally, the screen.

Take a moment and consider what you have learned. Imagine how the command you just executed would have looked before you began this book—gobbledygook. You can see why well-meaning system designers and installers try to shield users from this cryptic command language with shells and menu programs. Yet, now that you understand as much as you do, you can begin to appreciate the concise elegance of command line control.

Some Practical Applications

Pipes, filters, and input/output redirection offer more than just a study in elegance. There are practical applications for filters that you can begin to use right away.

Remember that filters work with files of text. You will not run your spreadsheets, databases, or word processing documents through a filter. Certainly all of these files look like text as they are presented to you by their programs, but most such data files contain embedded non-text control fields that would confuse most filters.

The best test to see if a data file is acceptable to a filter is to use the TYPE command to display it on the screen. If the information displays cleanly, chances are other filters will be able to process it. If, however, you see a lot of strange characters and hear an occasional beep, forget using the file with filters because it contains non-textual data.

Chaining FIND Commands

Earlier, you used the FIND command to filter unwanted lines of text from a directory and to select specific lines from a data file. However, suppose you want the select criteria to be a complex set of selectors. Consider NAMES.DAT shown here again.

```
Marvel, Captain  1950/01/01
Washington, Geo. 1732/02/22
Brown, Clifford  1956/06/26
Tatum, Art       1910/10/13
```

Suppose you wanted to select those records with dates in the 1900s but nothing from the month of June. You could enter this command:

```
A>find " 19" <names.dat | find /V "/06/"
```

This command tells the FIND filter to select all of the records from NAMES.DAT that have the value " 19." (The leading space prevents the selection of records that might have "19" as the day. None do, but you might not know that when you run the command.) The filtered records are then piped through a second execution of FIND, which filters out all records with the value "/06/." The result is this display:

```
Marvel, Captain  1950/01/01
Tatum, Art       1910/10/13
```

Filtering Directly to the Printer

Suppose you routinely print your return address onto envelopes, and you do not want to load your word processor every time to do it. You can build this batch file, which you might name ADDRESS.BAT.

```
echo Barbara's Jazz Lounge >prn
echo 535 Bebop Blvd. >prn
echo New York City, NY >prn
```

Insert an envelope in the printer and enter the ADDRESS command. For each additional envelope, press **F3** to save keystrokes. You are on your way to becoming a Power User. Chapter 9 has more detail about batch files.

Many printers are programmable. You send them what are called setup strings to set their character size, pitch, underlining, boldface, fonts, and many other controls. Most users do not concern themselves with these matters, allowing their applications programs to control printing. It is possible, however, to use the ECHO filter to send simple command strings to the printer. This method is for those times when you want to print something a certain way and your word processor and spreadsheet programs are not involved.

First, you must know the command strings that your printer uses. Many of these are what are called *escape sequences,* strings that begin with the ASCII ESC character. For example, the EPSON FX80 series of printers uses this sequence of characters to turn on boldface printing:

```
<esc>E
```

The <esc> token represents the ASCII Escape character. You cannot enter this character into a file with the COPY CON <filename> method used so far in this book. You must use a text editor program, and that program must allow the entry of the Escape character. The EDIT text editor included with DOS 6.0 and described in Chapter 12 allows it, and you must use an editor that does.

To enter the Escape character into a text file with most editors, hold down **Alt+Shift** with the Num Lock toggle off and press **2** followed by **7** on the numeric keypad. If a small arrow pointing to the left is displayed, the ASCII Escape character (1Bh) is inserted into the text.

To change an EPSON FX80 printer to boldface, put this command into a batch file named BOLD.BAT. You must use a cooperating text editor program to build this file.

```
echo ↔E >prn
```

To put your printer into boldface mode enter the BOLD command.

A Directory of Today's Updates

You can use the FIND filter to control the DIR command. Suppose you have a subdirectory with a large number of files, and you are interested in those files with a certain date, perhaps today's. Enter this command:

```
A>dir | find " 4-28-93"
```

This command displays a directory of only those files with a date of April 28, 1993.

Timing an Operation

Some PC processes take a while. You might be posting your month's accounting journals or doing a cyclic database backup operation. Perhaps you would like a record of how long one of these extended, unattended operations takes so that you will know how much time to set aside the next time. Maybe you do not want to hang around with a stop watch waiting for the run to complete. You would rather go to lunch.

One way to time an operation is to allow DOS 6.0 to do it for you. As an example, suppose your extended program is called DOIT. You can build the following batch file to record the start time in a file, execute your DOIT program, and record the stop time. When you get back from lunch, you can use the TYPE command to see the two times.

Since the TIME command expects a keyboard entry, and will wait for one, you must use input redirection to give it one. Build a file named ENTER with this command:

```
A>copy con enter
```

Now press **Enter**, **F6**, and **Enter**. You have just built a file with an Enter keystroke in it. This file can be read by the DATE and TIME commands.

Now build the batch file named TIMEIT.BAT with this command:

```
A>copy con timeit.bat
```

Enter these lines:

```
echo — START TIME —
date <enter >elapsed
time <enter >>elapsed
doit
echo — STOP TIME —
date <enter >>elapsed
time <enter >>elapsed
type elapsed
```

Run your timed operation by entering the TIMEIT command. When you return, and when the job is done, the start and stop times are on the screen in this format.

```
A>type elapsed
— START TIME —
Current date is Sat  4-27-1991
Enter new date (mm-dd-yy):
Current time is 12:26:01.97
```

```
Enter new time:
— STOP TIME —
Current date is Sat  4-27-1991
Enter new date (mm-dd-yy):
Current time is 12:30:03.72
Enter new time:
```

With some simple arithmetic, you can compute your elapsed time for the job.

Summary

This chapter began Section II, the Power User's introduction. It explained what a filter is, how to redirect a filters input and output, and how to correct filters within a pipe. Additionally, the chapter provided some practical applications for filters.

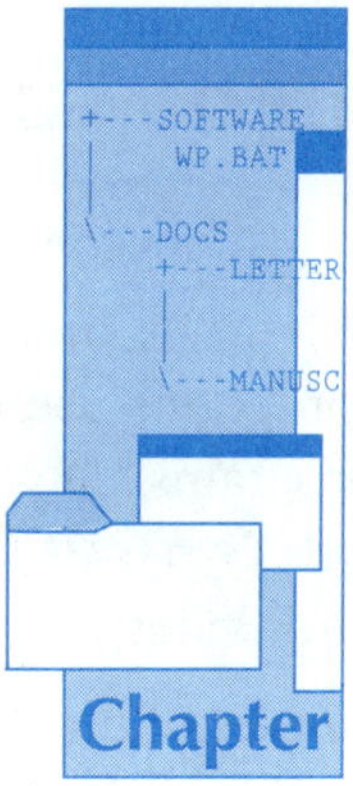

10

Advanced Topics and Commands

This chapter discusses some of the advanced uses of DOS 6.0. These are the toys and tools of the Power User, and learning about them will help you when you might need one or more of them.

You will learn about:

- Environment variables
- Advanced directory displays
- Advanced FORMAT options
- System configuration
- Programs that must run on a different DOS version
- How to move DOS 6.0

Environment Variables (SET)

Many programs use a DOS 6.0 feature called the *environment variable*, which is an ASCII value that DOS 6.0 stores internally and that programs can read. The programs use environment variables to tell how you have installed the programs. DOS 6.0 uses several of its own environment variables. The DOS 6.0 PATH that you learned in about Chapter 6 is actually an environment variable.

As an example of how a program would use the environment variable, consider this. A program cannot dictate the drive or subdirectory into which you will install it. There is no way for it to know that your PC has any particular drive or that another application does not use a subdirectory with the same name. Yet, the programs often need to know where things are. Many programs, therefore, use environment variables to record where their critical files are located. You will need to set these variables before you run the program. (Its user's manual will explain the procedure.)

Programs also use environment variables for complex options that cannot be included on the command line. The installation procedures for programs will specify which ones need environment variables and how to set them. You can experiment with them on your own.

The SET command sets and displays environment variables. To see which ones are set on your PC, enter this command:

```
C>set
```

You will see a display something like this:

```
COMSPEC=C:\COMMAND.COM
PATH=C:\WS;C:\DOS;\
```

The lines of text you see will depend on how your system has been installed. This example shows two environment variables, one called COMSPEC and one called PATH, both are used by DOS 6.0. To set one of your own, enter this command:

```
C>set foobar=123
```

This command establishes an environment variable named FOOBAR that has the value 123. Any program can read this value and modify its own behavior accordingly. If you issued the SET command by itself now, you would see this display:

```
COMSPEC=C:\COMMAND.COM
PATH=C:\WS;C:\DOS;\
FOOBAR=123
```

You can delete an environment variable by setting it to a null value as with this command.

```
C>set foobar=
```

Advanced Uses of the DIR Command

You have used the DIR command extensively in the exercises so far. As you might imagine, the DIR command is the one you use more often than any other. You can add command line options to the DIR command and affect the file selection and format of the directory display.

DIR Display Format

The /p command line option tells the DIR command to pause after every screen of directory listing. This is the same as piping the DIR output through the MORE filter program.

The /w command line option displays the directory in a wide format of five columns of file names. Only file names display. If you use the /w option on the root directory of the TYD Learning Diskette, you will see this display:

```
COMMAND.COM    AUTOEXEC.BAT    [WORDPROC]    [SPRDSHT]
[DOS]
```

Observe that the subdirectory names are bracketed so you can distinguish them from data files.

The /b command line option displays only the file names in a single columns. The root directory of the TYD Learning Diskette is displayed as shown here:

```
COMMAND.COM
AUTOEXEC.BAT
WORDPROC
SPRDSHT
DOS
```

The /l command line option displays the directory in lowercase as shown here:

```
command  com      53022 10-26-92   6:00a
autoexec bat         67 01-09-93   2:54p
wordproc     <DIR>      01-09-93   3:24p
sprdsht      <DIR>      01-09-93   3:26p
dos          <DIR>      01-09-93   3:26p
```

DIR Sort Order

The /o command line option controls the sort order of the directory display. Normally, the display lists the files in the order in which they are in the disk directory. The /o option allows you to list the file in ascending or descending order by file name, extension, date and time, size, or with subdirectories and data files separated. You follow the /o option with parameters taken from Table 10.1. Do not put any spaces between the /o and its parameters.

Table 10.1 DIR /o Parameters

Parameter	Sort Order
N	Name
E	Extension
D	Date and time
S	Size
G	Subdirectories first
Precede with a minus sign (-) to sort descending	

If you use the /o command line option with no parameters, the DIR command displays the subdirectories in name order followed by the data files in name and extension order as shown here:

```
DOS          <DIR>       01-09-93    3:26p
SPRDSHT      <DIR>       01-09-93    3:26p
WORDPROC     <DIR>       01-09-93    3:24p
AUTOEXEC BAT          67 01-09-93    2:54p
COMMAND  COM       53022 10-26-92    6:00a
```

Selecting the Files To Display

You learned earlier how to use wild cards in the DIR command file specification to select groups of file names and extensions for the directory display. Files also have a property called the file attributes. There are five attributes that a file can have. You learned about them in Chapter 8 when you learned how to select from them for the Shell's File List display. To review, the five attributes are:

1. Hidden files
2. System files
3. Directories

4. Archive files
5. Read-only files

The DIR command's /a command line option lets you list only files that match the attribute you select with a parameter that follows the /a. The parameters are: h, s, d, a, and r. If you precede the parameter with a minus sign (-), it means that you want to list files that do not have the attribute. If you use the /a option without any parameters, it lists all files, including hidden files.

The following command lists all files that are not directories:

```
A>dir /a-d
IO       SYS      39590 10-26-92   6:00a
MSDOS    SYS      37416 10-26-92   6:00a
COMMAND  COM      53022 10-26-92   6:00a
AUTOEXEC BAT         67 01-09-93   2:54p
```

Searching Subdirectories

The DIR command's /s command line option lets you search the current directory as well as subdirectories below the current one for the files to list. This is a handy way to locate files on the disk that you have misplaced. Suppose you have forgotten—or never knew—where your word processor put that file named NOVEL.DOC. This command will find it.

```
dir /s novel.doc
Volume in drive A has no label
Volume Serial Number is 3437-15EE

Directory of A:\WORDPROC\DOCS\MANUSCRP
NOVEL    DOC        264 01-16-93  12:11p
1 file(s)        264 bytes
Total files listed:
1 file(s)        264 bytes
1145856 bytes free
```

The DIR command found the file in \WORDPROC\DOCS\MANUSCRP. You can find all occurrences of files with the same name by using the /s command line option. You can also use wild cards to find all files with the same extension or with similar names as shown in this exercise, which finds all the batch files on your TYD Learning Diskette.

```
A>dir /s *.bat

AUTOEXEC BAT          67 01-09-93   2:54p
1 file(s)           67 bytes
Directory of A:\SPRDSHT\SOFTWARE
SS       BAT          70 01-16-93  12:20p
1 file(s)           70 bytes
Directory of A:\WORDPROC\SOFTWARE
WP       BAT          73 01-09-93   4:35p
1 file(s)           73 bytes

Total files listed:
3 file(s)          210 bytes
1144832 bytes free
```

The DIRCMD Environment Variable

You might prefer to use one or more of the DIR command's options all the time. For example, you might want to list files in lowercase and sorted by file name with directories first as the default. You could enter this command every time:

```
A>dir /l /og
```

The display would look like this, which is what you would want.

```
wordproc     <DIR>       01-09-93   3:24p
sprdsht      <DIR>       01-09-93   3:26p
dos          <DIR>       01-09-93   3:26p
command  com       53022 10-26-92   6:00a
autoexec bat          67 01-09-93   2:54p
```

That would work, but most users would rather not have to remember and type all of those keys on the command line for a routine command. You could build a batch file as described in Chapter 13 or a DOSKEY macro as described in Chapter 11.

An alternative is to use the DIRCMD environment variable. You learned about environment variables at the beginning of this chapter. The DIRCMD environment variable tells the DIR command what its default command line options are. Enter this command:

```
A>set dircmd=/l /og
```

Now enter the DIR command alone without any command line options like this:

```
A>dir
```

This display will look just like it did above when you used the /l /og command line options. If that is the way you always want to display directories, put the SET command in the AUTOEXEC.BAT file.

To return the DIR command to its defaults, clear the DIRCMD environment variable with this command:

```
A>set dircmd=
```

FORMAT Revisited

You learned the basics of the FORMAT command in Chapter 5 when you first built the TYD Learning Diskette. You used the /s option to format a diskette and add the DOS 6.0 system files it. You can use a diskette formatted in this manner to boot DOS 6.0 on any PC-compatible computer that has a compatible diskette drive.

The FORMAT command completely erases all data on a diskette. When you use it, make sure that there are no files on the diskette that you want to keep.

You can issue the FORMAT command against your hard disk but you seldom, if ever, want to do so. When you become a full-fledged Power User and system installer you will know when and how to do this.

The FORMAT command has options other than /s. If you issue the command with no options, it will format the diskette in its default configuration without a copy of DOS 6.0 added.

You can tell FORMAT that you are formatting a 5.25-inch, 360K diskette in a 1.2MB drive or a 3.5-inch, 720K diskette in a 1.44 MB drive. You cannot go in the other direction for either disk size, however.

FORMAT will build single-sided 5.25-inch diskettes, but there is little use for this format. Table 10.2 lists the FORMAT command line options.

Table 10.2 *FORMAT command line options*

Command line option	Meaning
/4 or /f:360	Format 360K diskette in 1.2MB drive
/f:720	Format 720K diskette in 1.44MB drive
/v:label	Add "label" as diskette's volume label
/b	Format with room for DOS 6.0
/s	Format and copy DOS 6.0 to diskette
/1	Format 160K diskette (single-sided)
/8	Format 8 sectors per track
/t:n	Format with n tracks
/s:n	Format with n sectors
/q	Deletes system areas of diskette
/u	Destroys all data. Cannot use unformat

The /f: command line option can be followed by 160, 180, 320, 360, 720, 1200, 1440, or 2880. These numbers represent the size of the diskette in K. The drive must be able to format the size you choose. The first six values are for 5.25-inch disk drives. The last two are for 3.5-inch drives.

The /b option is for compatibility with earlier versions of DOS, and is not needed with DOS 6.0.

The /t and /s options must be used together. They may not be used with the /f option, which is the preferred way to specify disk size.

The /8 option formats a diskette that systems with DOS 1.0 can read.

Use the /u option if the diskette has read/write errors.

System Configuration

When you load DOS 6.0, it uses two files to tell it how to set itself up. These two files must be in the root directory of the boot disk. They are text files that you build and their names are CONFIG.SYS and AUTOEXEC.BAT.

CONFIG.SYS

All DOS 6.0 systems should have a CONFIG.SYS file. When DOS 6.0 loads, it uses the entries in this file to modify its configuration, adding device drivers, setting operating parameters, and establishing the sizes of internal tables. The entries in CONFIG.SYS can affect the size of DOS 6.0 and can, therefore, affect the amount of memory available for programs to run.

Minimum Requirements for CONFIG.SYS

You build CONFIG.SYS with a text editor program or by using the COPY CON CONFIG.SYS technique. At a minimum, CONFIG.SYS should have these lines of text.

```
files=20
buffers=20
```

The reason you need these lines is that most applications programs require them. They specify the size of some internal DOS 6.0 tables, which influence DOS 6.0's performance in support of programs. Some programs require larger numbers in the statements. If this is true, the installation procedures for the programs will either say so or will automatically update the file to the values needed.

ANSI.SYS

DOS 6.0 includes a device driver program called ANSI.SYS. You will find it along with the other DOS 6.0 utility programs. The purpose of ANSI.SYS is to enhance screen displays and keyboard input and is of use to you if some of your programs require it. Many systems include ANSI.SYS just in case a program needs it. To include it in your system, add this line to CONFIG.SYS:

```
device=ansi.sys
```

If the file named ANSI.SYS is in a subdirectory other than the root directory of the boot disk, you must include the path in the CONFIG.SYS entry. For example, if your system has all the DOS 6.0 utility programs in the C:\DOS subdirectory, the entry in CONFIG.SYS would look like this:

```
device=c:\dos\ansi.sys
```

When ANSI.SYS is installed, your PC's screen displays react differently to certain sequences of characters written to the screen by programs. You can use this feature to modify the DOS 6.0 prompt by putting these sequences into the PROMPT command. The most frequent use of this feature is to fix the color of the screen colors.

With ANSI.SYS installed, you can use the PROMPT command in this format:

```
A>prompt $e[32;40m$p$g
```

The $e[is a special PROMPT command sequence that inserts the Escape character into the prompt. The 32 and the 40 are graphics codes that set screen colors. The 32 specifics a green characters; 40 specifies a black background. There may be several of these codes separated by semicolons. The last code is not followed by a semicolon but is followed by the letter "m" to terminate the ANSI.SYS command sequence. The

pg sequence tells the PROMPT command to display the current drive and subdirectory with each DOS 6.0 prompt.

Table 10.3 lists the values you can use where the example above uses 32 and 40.

Table 10.3 *ANSI.SYS color values*

Color	Character	Background
Black	30	40
Red	31	41
Green	32	42
Yellow	33	43
Blue	34	44
Magenta	35	45
Cyan	36	46
White	37	47

You can add the values in Table 10.4 to change the video effect.

Table 10.4 *ANSI.SYS video effect values*

Value	Effect
0	Reset to normal white characters on black background
1	High intensity
4	Underscore (Monochrome video only)
5	Blinking characters
7	Reverse video
8	Invisible characters

Other Device Driver Programs

The DOS 6.0 SETUP program may include other device driver programs that you might want to use. Chapter 14 discusses some of them.

Other entries in CONFIG.SYS are dictated by the installation procedures of your applications programs and hardware additions. The most frequent requirement for CONFIG.SYS entries is when you include device driver programs in your DOS 6.0 configuration. If you use a mouse, a digitizing tablet, or other nonstandard hardware devices, they probably require a device driver program to be installed. The CONFIG.SYS entry for installing a device driver is the same as for installing ANSI.SYS.

AUTOEXEC.BAT

After DOS 6.0 loads itself and before it turns the command line over to you, DOS 6.0 executes a file called AUTOEXEC.BAT. DOS 6.0 expects to find this file in the root directory of the boot disk. If no AUTOEXEC.BAT file is there, DOS 6.0 automatically executes the DATE and TIME commands before giving you the command line prompt.

The AUTOEXEC.BAT file is where you execute any commands you want automatically executed when the system starts up. The most common command found in AUTOEXEC.BAT is the PATH command that sets the DOS 6.0 path to point to the subdirectories of all of the software you want to use.

AUTOEXEC.BAT is where you put your PROMPT command, the MODE command, and several custom SET commands. This is also where you load any memory-resident utility programs that are a part of your operating environment. MODE and SET are discussed later in this chapter.

Many users put a command in AUTOEXEC.BAT to start their applications program. If you use your PC exclusively for word processing, you might want to have it always load with the word processor program running. If you are working on a project that you expect will take a long time, you might want to have AUTOEXEC.BAT load the project's document file into the word processor. These comments are relevant to databases, spreadsheets, and other programs.

Some users use the DOS 6.0 Shell program (Chapter 8) rather than the DOS 6.0 command line, preferring to retreat to the command line only when necessary. If you do this, you might want to use AUTOEXEC.BAT to automatically start the Shell when DOS 6.0 is loaded.

You can put any command in AUTOEXEC.BAT that you can execute from the command line. AUTOEXEC.BAT can also use the special batch file commands discussed in Chapter 13.

Selectable Configurations

DOS 6.0 introduces a new feature not found in previous versions of DOS—the ability to control the configuration with a menu that displays when you boot the computer. The menu allows you to select from a number of custom configurations.

Suppose that sometimes you run DOS applications and at other times you run Windows. There are configuration items that you can put in CONFIG.SYS to support these two environments, but the configurations are not the same.

Suppose that you and a co-worker share the computer. You prefer one configuration and your co-worker uses another.

Perhaps sometimes you operate your computer as a workstation in a network and at other times you operate as a standalone desktop computer. The configurations for these two environments are different.

How did users of earlier versions of DOS cope with these differences? They took one of two approaches: either they used one, all-encompassing configuration that included all the device drivers, environment variables, and so on, to support every possible environment; or they managed several sets of CONFIG.SYS and AUTOEXEC.BAT. The first technique overloads the computer with configuration items not needed in each environment. The second technique requires the user to manually replace CONFIG.SYS and AUTOEXEC.BAT with the next appropriate set and reboot.

A Menu in CONFIG.SYS

DOS 6.0 allows you to specify a menu in your CONFIG.SYS file. The menu consists of a number of MENUITEM statements. The CONFIG.SYS file then contains sets of configuration statements, one for each MENUITEM. Following is an example of a simple CONFIG.SYS menu.

```
[Menu]
menuitem=Windows
menuitem=DOS

[DOS]
DEVICE=C:\DOS\HIMEM.SYS
DEVICE=C:\DOS\EMM386.EXE RAM 1024
DEVICEHIGH=C:\DOS\RAMDRIVE.SYS 512 /E

[Windows]
DEVICE=C:\DOS\HIMEM.SYS
DEVICE=C:\DOS\EMM386.EXE NOEMS RAM

[Common]
DOS=HIGH,UMB
SHELL=C:\DOS\COMMAND.COM C:\DOS\ /e:512 /p
BUFFERS=40,0
FILES=60
```

The statements that follow the [Menu] token identify the menu selections. In this example there are two: Windows and DOS. You can name the menu selections anything you want. The statements that follow the [Windows] token identify the CONFIG.SYS statements to be executed for the Windows configuration. The statements that follow the [DOS] token identify the CONFIG.SYS statements to be executed for the DOS configuration. The statements that follow the [Common] token are executed for all configurations.

Choosing a Configuration

When you boot the computer, it displays the menu as shown here:

```
MS-DOS 6 Startup Menu
=====================
1. Windows
2. DOS

Enter a choice: 1


F5=Bypass startup files  F8=Confirm each CONFIG.SYS
line [NO]
```

The first selection on the menu is highlighted with a menu selection cursor. The number next to the choice prompt reflects the current selection. You change the selection by typing its number or by moving the menu selection cursor with the Up and Down Arrow keys. You choose a selection by pressing Enter.

Booting a Bare DOS

If you press F5 instead of choosing a menu selection, none of the CONFIG.SYS and AUTOEXEC.BAT statements are executed, and DOS 6.0 boots in a bare environment.

Choosing Specific Configuration Items

If you press F8 while the CONFIG.SYS menu is displayed, the [NO] token at the bottom right of the screen toggles to [YES]. When you choose a configuration with the [YES] token selected, each CONFIG.SYS statement is preceded by a prompt as shown here.

```
DEVICE=C:\DOS\HIMEM.SYS [Y,N]?
```

Press Y or N to choose whether you want to execute the statement. When all of the CONFIG.SYS statements have been processed this way you will see this prompt:

```
Process AUTOEXEC.BAT [Y,N]?
```

Press **Y** or **N** to choose whether or not to execute the statements in the AUTOEXEC.BAT file.

Note that if CONFIG.SYS does not have MENUITEM statements, you can invoke this feature by pressing F8 once while the Starting MS-DOS... message is displayed.

Selecting Configurations in AUTOEXEC.BAT

Chapter 13 teaches you how to build batch files of DOS 6.0 commands that you can execute. You have already learned that the system uses the AUTOEXEC.BAT file when you reboot the computer. When a CONFIG.SYS file contains MENUITEM statements and you choose one of them, the system sets a special environment variable named CONFIG to the value of the MENUITEM token. If you chose the Windows selection from the menu just shown, DOS 6.0 would set CONFIG to the value Windows just as if you had entered this statement at the command line.

```
set CONFIG=Windows
```

DOS 6.0 does this to allow your AUTOEXEC.BAT file to determine which configuration you have chosen. A batch file uses the IF and GOTO statements to test the value of environment variables. You will learn how to use the IF and GOTO statements and how to read an environment variable's value from within a batch command file in Chapter 13. Here is a simple AUTOEXEC.BAT file that could accompany the CONFIG.SYS file just shown.

```
rem --- commands common to all configs
cls
rem --- Go to the chosen configuration
goto %config%

rem --- Windows is chosen
:Windows
path=c:\dos;c:\windows
share
win

rem --- DOS is chosen
:DOS
path=c:\dos
```

Programs Needing Other DOS Versions (SETVER)

You learned about the DOS version and the VER command earlier in this chapter. Some programs insist on running under a specified range of DOS versions and, although they would run properly under DOS 6.0, they do not know that. A program can test the DOS version, and if one of these programs senses DOS 6.0 when it wants to run under 3.3, for example, the program displays an error message that tells you it cannot run.

Why is this? DOS 2.0 was a major upgrade to DOS and it added features that most programs use. Most programs cannot run with versions less than DOS 2.0. DOS 3.0 added additional features that many other programs use. They cannot run with versions less than 3.0. DOS 4.0 had bugs. Many programs can run with DOS versions 3.0 through 3.3 and cannot run with 4.0. Even though most of the bugs were fixed in DOS 4.1, these programs still have tests to make sure that the version number is 3.0 through 3.3.

The software industry was not prepared for Microsoft to introduce DOS 5.0 much less version 6.0. It was considered acceptable to reject DOS versions less than or greater than 3. Eventually, most of these vendors will release versions of their products that run with DOS 6.0. Until then, and for those users who see no need to buy an upgrade of a program simply to get around a test for a DOS version number, DOS 6.0 has the SETVER command.

The SETVER Device Driver Program

The SETVER command begins as a device driver program. The DOS 6.0 SETUP program adds this line to the CONFIG.SYS file in the root directory of your boot disk.

```
DEVICE=C:\DOS\SETVER.EXE
```

This statement loads the SETVER program into memory each time you boot DOS 6.0. If you never need to use the SETVER facility, you can remove this statement from the CONFIG.SYS file by using a text editor program such as EDIT (Chapter 12). Removing the statement will free the memory normally occupied by the SETVER program.

To learn about SETVER, you must add it to your TYD Learning Diskette. Enter this command and data on the command line:

```
A>copy con \config.sys

device=\dos\setver.exe
files=20
buffers=20
```

Press **F6** and **Enter**. Now reboot DOS 6.0 from the diskette. SETVER is installed.

The SETVER Command

The SETVER command stores a table of program names and the DOS version number to report to those programs when the programs ask for it. As distributed, the SETVER command has a table of program names and version numbers. The developers of DOS 6.0 built this table based on their knowledge of existing programs that needed version numbers other than 6.0. To view the current table, enter the command immediately following and see the list as shown.

```
A>setver
WIN200.BIN      3.40
WIN100.BIN      3.40
WINWORD.EXE     4.10
EXCEL.EXE       4.10
HITACHI.SYS     4.00
MSCDEX.EXE      4.00
REDIR4.EXE      4.00
NET.EXE         4.00
NET.COM         3.30
NETWKSTA.EXE    4.00
DXMA0MOD.SYS    3.30
```

```
BAN.EXE           4.00
BAN.COM           4.00
MSREDIR.EXE       4.00
METRO.EXE         3.31
IBMCACHE.SYS      3.40
REDIR40.EXE       4.00
DD.EXE            4.01
DD.BIN            4.01
LL3.EXE           4.01
REDIR.EXE         4.00
SYQ55.SYS         4.00
SSTDRIVE.SYS      4.00
ZDRV.SYS          4.01
ZFMT.SYS          4.01
TOPSRDR.EXE       4.00
NETX.COM          5.00
EDLIN.EXE         5.00
BACKUP.EXE        5.00
ASSIGN.COM        5.00
EXE2BIN.EXE       5.00
JOIN.EXE          5.00
RECOVER.EXE       5.00
GRAFTABL.COM      5.00
NET5.COM          5.00
NETBEUI.DOS       5.00
LMSETUP.EXE       5.00
STACKER.COM       5.00
NCACHE.EXE        5.00
KERNEL.EXE        5.00
REDIR50.EXE       5.00
```

This table might have more or fewer entries depending on when you obtained your copy of DOS 6.0.

Adding a Program to SETVER

To add a program to SETVER, you must know the name of its executable file. If, for example, you wanted to add the program named

OLDPROG.EXE, and it needed to think it was running with DOS 3.30, you would use this command:

```
A>setver oldprog.exe 3.30
```

You will see a display that tells you that the SETVER strategy may or may not work and that Microsoft assumes no liability if it does not. If you now issue the SETVER command without parameters, you will see the OLDPROG.EXE entry added to the end of the table. You can delete an entry with this command:

```
A>setver oldprog.exe /delete
```

How SETVER Works

SETVER keeps its table in its own executable file, SETVER.EXE, which was installed by the SETUP program. When you add or delete an entry in the table, this file changes in content, but its size and file date/time do not change. There are two items to consider about this technique. The first is that because SETVER is a memory-resident device driver program, the changes you make do not take effect until you reboot DOS 6.0. The second item has to do with viruses. Some virus-checking programs sense when executable files have changed and report a possible virus infection after you modify the SETVER table.

If you are running a network from a diskless workstation where all your DOS 6.0 files are on the file server, SETVER might not work except as a global table for all users, and it might be necessary for the network administrator to make all changes to the table.

Moving DOS 6.0 (SYS)

The SYS command moves the current copy of DOS 6.0 onto the disk specified as a command line parameter as shown here:

```
C>sys c:\ a:
```

The first parameter names the drive and path where the SYS command will find the DOS 6.0 system files to copy. The second parameter specifies the drive where SYS will copy the system. You can omit the first parameter, in which case SYS will expect to find the DOS 6.0 system files in the root directory of the current logged-on disk.

Summary

This chapter introduced you to some advanced DOS 6.0 topics and commands. You learned about environment variables, advanced directory displays, and advanced FORMAT options. Additionally, the chapter taught you about how the system configuration works and how to run programs that need a different version of DOS. Finally, you learned about how to move DOS 6.0 to another disk.

Chapter 11

The DOSKEY Program

The DOSKEY program is a memory-resident utility program that enhances the DOS command line. The program provides command line editing functions beyond those you learned in Chapter 5. DOSKEY also maintains a history buffer of past commands so that you can go back to an earlier command that you typed and re-execute it, perhaps editing it first. The DOSKEY macro facility provides a way to build macros that are similar to the batch files that you will learn about in Chapter 13, but they are memory resident for faster execution.

You will learn about:

- Loading the DOSKEY program
- Editing the DOS command line
- Using the command line with multiple commands
- Using the command history buffer
- Using DOSKEY macros

Loading the DOSKEY Program

You can load the DOSKEY program from the command line. Enter its name like this:

```
A>doskey
```

You can insert the DOSKEY command into your AUTOEXEC.BAT file so that it is loaded every time you boot DOS. The DOSKEY program occupies approximately 4K of memory. There are 512 bytes of that memory that are used as a buffer to store macros and to maintain the command history. You can specify a different buffer size when you load DOSKEY with this command line option:

```
A>doskey /bufsize=1024
```

The 1024 value in this example tells DOSKEY to reserve 1024 bytes of memory for its buffer. The resident size of DOSKEY and, therefore, the memory available for other programs changes when you change this buffer.

Editing the DOS Command Line

When DOSKEY is loaded, the DOS command line edit keys, which you learned about in Chapter 5, behave differently. Enter a DOS command such as this one:

```
A>dir /w *.*
```

After the directory displays, press **F3** to redisplay the DIR command you just executed. F3 works just like it always has.

Now press **Esc**. Instead of displaying a slash and moving to the next line, DOS 5.0 erases the command from the command line and leaves only the A> command line prompt.

Press **F3** again to display the command again. Press the **Left Arrow** key several times. Before you loaded DOSKEY, the Left Arrow key would erase the characters to its left. Now it moves the cursor over the characters in the command without erasing them. Try the **Right Arrow** key, which moves the cursor, too. You are moving the cursor back and forth on top of the command. Press **Ctrl+Right Arrow** and **Ctrl+Left Arrow**. The cursor moves to the previous and next words in the command line. The cursor movement is behaving just like it does in the EDIT program (Chapter 12) and other word processors.

Move the cursor under the slash character of the /w command line option. Press **Del** three times to delete the option. The command now looks like this:

```
A>dir *.*
```

The cursor is still in the middle of the command, but press Enter anyway to execute the command.

Now press **F3** to redisplay the command. Move the cursor under the first asterisk character. Press **Ins**. Observe that the cursor changes to a larger underline character. This format indicates that DOSKEY is in insert mode. Type **/o** followed by **Space**. The characters to the right of the cursor move as you type to make room for the new characters. The command looks like this:

```
A>dir /o *.*
```

Press **Enter** to execute the command.

If you type on top of a command when you are not in insert mode, your keystrokes overwrite the characters that are displayed. You use Home and End to position the cursor at the beginning and end of the command line, respectively. Use Ctrl+End to delete everything from the cursor to the end of the command. Use Ctrl+Home to delete everything from the cursor to the beginning of the line. The Backspace key works just like the Left Arrow key except when you are in insert mode. Then it deletes the character to the left of the cursor as it backspaces. Table 11.1 lists the DOSKEY editing keys.

Table 11.1 The DOSKEY editing keys

Key	Meaning
Home/End	Move to beginning/end of line
left/right arrow	Move the cursor one character
Ctrl+left/right arrow	Move the cursor one word
Backspace	Move left. In insert mode, delete
Del	Delete character to right of the cursor
Ctrl+End	Delete to end of command
Ctrl+Home	Delete to beginning of command
Ins	Toggle insert/overwrite modes
Enter	Execute the command as displayed
Esc	Clear the command

Command Lines with Multiple Commands

DOSKEY allows you to type several commands on one line. The combined length of all the commands may not exceed 128 characters. The commands look just like they would if you executed them one at a time, but you separate them by pressing Ctrl+T, which displays a paragraph mark (¶). Enter the following two commands to change to another subdirectory and list its contents:

```
A>cd \wordproc\docs\letters ¶ dir
```

You will see this display:

```
Volume in drive A has no label
Volume Serial Number is 3437-15EE
Directory of A:\WORDPROC\DOCS\LETTERS

<DIR>      01-09-93   3:28p
<DIR>      01-09-93   3:28p
MILLY01  LTR        123 01-09-93   4:22p
MILLY02  LTR         30 01-09-93   4:23p
4 file(s)         153 bytes
1145344 bytes free
```

The Command History Buffer

As you enter commands, DOSKEY collects them in its command history buffer. When the buffer fills, the oldest command scrolls out of the buffer, and you cannot retrieve it. You can view the contents of the command history, recall and execute one of its commands from the buffer, modify and execute a command in the buffer, save the contents of the buffer into a disk file, and delete all of the entries from the buffer.

Viewing the Command History

To view the contents of the command history buffer, press **F7**. You will see this display:

```
1: doskey
2: dir /w *.*
3: dir *.*
4: dir /o *.*
5: cd \wordproc\docs\letters   dir
```

To view the command history without the line numbers, enter this command:

```
A>doskey /history
```

You will see the command history displayed here. Observe that the command you entered to display the history has become a part of the history.

```
doskey
dir /w *.*
dir *.*
dir /o *.*
cd \wordproc\docs\letters  dir
doskey /history
```

Retrieving Commands from the Command History

Press the **Up Arrow** key. DOSKEY displays the last command in the buffer on the command line just as if you had typed it in yourself. You can press Enter to execute the command or you can use the editing keys to change it before you execute it. If you press the **Up Arrow** key again, DOSKEY retrieves the command immediately preceding the one currently being displayed. The **Down Arrow** key retrieves the command following the current one. PgUp and PgDn display the oldest and newest command in the command history.

You can retrieve a command with its number in the command history buffer as displayed by F7. Press **F9**. DOSKEY will display this message:

```
A>Line number:
```

Type the number that is displayed to the left of the command in the F7 command history list. Press **Enter**, and the command is retrieved and displayed. You can modify the command with the editing keys and execute it by pressing Enter.

You can retrieve commands that begin with a string of characters that you specify. Suppose you know that you executed a DIR command sometime ago, but you are not sure of its exact format. Type DIR in upper or lowercase and press **F8**. DOSKEY displays the most recent command that begins with DIR. Press **F8** again to see the next most recent DIR command. Continue to press **F8** until you see the DIR command you are looking for.

Clearing the Command History Buffer

Press **Alt+F7** to clear the command history buffer.

Saving the Command History in a File

To write the command history to a file, enter this command:

```
A>doskey /history >textfile
```

The text file name can be any DOS file name you want to use. You can build a batch file of the commands in the command history by using the .BAT extension on the file name. You can use the EDIT program (Chapter 12) or another text editor to modify the batch file, perhaps to remove the command that created the text file. The command gets into the command history buffer before DOSKEY writes the file.

This procedure provides a handy way to build a batch file. You can press **Alt+F7** to clear the command history buffer, execute the commands you want in your batch file, and save the command history buffer to the batch file. You will learn more about batch files in Chapter 12.

Command History Buffer Keys

Table 11.2 is a list of the command history buffer keys.

Table 11.2 DOSKEY command history keys

Key	Meaning
Up/Down Arrow	Retrieve previous/next command in buffer
PgUp/PgDn	Retrieve first/last command in buffer
F7	Display contents of command history buffer
Alt+F7	Clear command history buffer
F8	Retrieve command that starts with text
F9	Retrieve command by number within buffer

DOSKEY Macros

A macro is a technique that assigns one or more DOS commands to a single keyboard command. If you have a routine procedure that uses a fixed set of commands, you can build a macro that executes the sequence of commands when you execute the macro's name as a command from the DOS command line.

A macro can consist of any sequence of DOS commands as long as the combined length of the commands does not exceed 127 characters. You can build the macro so that parameters you type on the command line next to the macro's name are inserted into the macro's commands when they are executed.

A macro can assume the name of another DOS command, in which case the macro executes instead of the command. You will learn how to override this feature.

Building Macros

The DOSKEY program builds and stores the macros in its buffer space. When you add macros to DOSKEY, you reduce the amount of buffer space that DOSKEY can use for its command history buffer. To build a macro, you execute the DOSKEY program with the macro definition on the command line. To build a macro named DIR, which uses the options you might prefer for the DIR command, enter this DOSKEY command:

```
A>doskey dir=dir /l /og
```

This macro overrides the DIR command and causes the directory display to be in lowercase and sort the subdirectories apart from the file names. You learned how to do the same thing with the DIRCMD environment variable in Chapter 10.

Executing Macros

When you enter a command on the DOS command line, DOSKEY looks to see if the command is the name of one of the macros. If so, DOSKEY executes the macro. To execute the DIR macro you just built, enter its name on the command line just as you would any other command.

Do not put any spaces on the command line ahead of the macro name. DOSKEY will not find the macro definition if you do. You learned in Chapter 5 that you could use leading spaces on the command line for DOS commands. This is not permitted when you execute DOSKEY macros.

This restriction has an advantage, however. Now that you have redefined the meaning of the DIR command, suppose you want to use the DOS version of that command and bypass the macro version. Put a space in front of the command's name when you execute it. The standard DOS DIR command will execute instead of the DIR macro.

Input/Output Redirection

The DOSKEY macros cannot accept the standard DOS command line redirection symbols because DOSKEY is a filter. You used the greater than symbol to save the command history buffer to a file. If you try to put greater than, less than, or pipe into a macro definition, DOS 5.0 will intercept them and apply them to the redirection of DOSKEY.

To get around this problem, DOSKEY allows you to use the values $l for less than (<), $g for greater than (>), and $b for pipe (|). Thc gg becomes the >> concatenation operator.

To build a macro named FF, which sends a form feed to the printer, enter this command:

```
A>doskey ff=echo ^L $g prn
```

The ^L represents Ctrl+L which is a form feed. You press Ctrl+L and DOS 5.0 displays ^L on the command line. When you execute the macro, it expands to the command as shown here:

```
A>ff
A>echo ^L > prn
```

The $g becomes the greater than sign, and so the echoed form feed is redirected to the printer.

Command Line Parameter Substitution

A macro can have parameters just as a DOS command can. To build a macro that uses DOS commands that need parameters, you enter the tokens $1 through $9 in the macro. When you execute the macro and use command line parameters, DOSKEY will substitute your first parameter wherever the macro contains $1. DOSKEY substitutes the second parameter on the command line for $2, and so on through $9.

Suppose you frequently read long text files on the screen. To prevent the displays from scrolling off the page before you can read them, you pipe the output from the TYPE command though the MORE filter, a program you learned about in Chapter 9. You use TYPE so that the tabs in the file are expanded and you use MORE so that the displays pause between screenfuls. You would type the following command. (Log into the \WORDPROC\DOCS\MANUSCRP subdirectory first.)

```
A>type novel.doc | more
```

You could build a DOSKEY macro named PAGE that does the job for you. Enter this command to build the macro:

```
A>doskey page=type $1 $b more
```

DOSKEY substitutes the file name you put on the command line for the $1 token in the macro. The $b token becomes the pipe redirection symbol when the command executes. Now, instead of using the longer command with the pipe, you can use the shorter PAGE command like this:

```
A>page novel.doc
```

Multiple Commands in a Macro

DOSKEY allows you to have more than one command in a macro. You separate them with the $t token. Remember that the combined length of the commands cannot exceed 127 characters.

To build a macro named PRNT, which prints a text file directly to the printer and follows it with a form feed, enter this command:

```
A>doskey prnt=type $1 $g prn $t echo ^L $g prn
```

The ^L represents Ctrl+L which is a form feed. You press Ctrl+L when you define the macro, and DOS 5.0 displays ^L on the command line.

When you execute the macro, it expands to the two commands as shown here:

```
A>prnt milly01.ltr
A>type milly01.ltr > prn
A>echo ^L > prn
```

The $1 is the command line parameter substitution token. In this example, it is the file named MILLY01.LTR. The $g tokens translate into the greater than symbol (>) to redirect the output of the TYPE and ECHO commands to the printer. The $t token separates the two commands in the macro.

Observe that you did not call the FF macro from the PRNT macro. You cannot call a macro from another macro, so you must repeat its commands in the macro that needs to use it.

Displaying the Macros

The DOSKEY command with the /macros command line option will display all of the macros that DOSKEY currently has in its buffer as shown here:

```
A>doskey /macros
PRNT=type $1 $g prn $t echo ^L $g prn
DIR=dir /l /og
PAGE=type $1 $b more
FF=echo ^L $g prn
```

Writing the Macros to a File

Use the /macros command line option to write the macros to a file by redirecting the DOSKEY output to the file as shown here:

```
A>doskey /macros >macs.bat
```

To permanently install the macros, use your text editor program to add the DOSKEY command to the front of the macros listed in MACS.BAT (or another file name of your choosing) so that the file contains these lines:

```
doskey PRNT=type $1 $g prn $t echo ^L $g prn
doskey DIR=dir /l /og
doskey PAGE=type $1 $b more
doskey FF=echo ^L $g prn
```

You can merge these lines into your AUTOEXEC.BAT file or put a CALL MACS statement into it instead. Then your macros will be installed everytime you boot DOS 5.0.

Be careful of the ^L tokens. Even though they are recorded as the Ctrl+L value in the macros, they are written to the file as the two characters ^ and L. You must use your editor to fix any such characters before you use the batch file to build the macros.

Deleting Macros

To delete a macro from the buffer, enter this command:

```
A>doskey ff=
```

This command deletes the FF macro from the buffer. The memory the macros occupied can now be used by new macros, but DOSKEY does not return macro memory to the command history buffer when you delete a macro.

Some Macro Disadvantages

These are some points about macros:

- Macros are limited to 127 characters in length, including the $t tokens that separate commands.
- You cannot run a macro from within a macro or from within a batch file.
- Macros occupy memory that the command history buffer would otherwise use.
- You cannot use Ctrl+C or Ctrl+Break to terminate a macro. These keys will terminate the current command that the macro runs, but DOSKEY will run the next command in the macro anyway.
- Macros are simple sequential lists of commands. You cannot do any looping or jumping within a macro.
- Macros display all of their commands. You cannot tell one not to.
- You cannot reference the value of an environment variable from within a macro.

If all or any of these disadvantages seem to severely limit the usefulness of DOSKEY macros, or if there is something you want to do that one of these disadvantages prevents, perhaps you should be writing a batch file instead of a macro. Chapter 13 teaches you how to do that.

Summary

This chapter taught you how to load the DOSKEY program. You learned about editing the DOS command line and using the command line with multiple commands. You also learned how to use the command history buffer. Finally, the chapter introduced you to DOSKEY macros, and taught you how to build and use them.

Chapter 12

Text Editing: EDIT

This chapter is about EDIT, the DOS 6.0 full-screen text editor. If you already have a text editor program that you prefer, you may skip this chapter. If you do not, then proceed. You will need some kind of text editor for the exercises in Chapter 13 when you build and test DOS 6.0 batch files. You will learn how to:

- Create a text file
- Make simple corrections

Purpose of EDIT

A program named EDLIN was included with DOS since its first version and through version 5.0. It is what is called a line editor, descending from a tradition of text editors from the early minicomputer consoles, which used paper and keyboards rather than video monitors. Since the console output was on paper, the editors displayed lines of text and the users typed additions and corrections on separate lines.

DOS 5.0 introduced the EDIT program, which is a full-screen editor. In fact, it is the text editor component of the QBASIC program that was also new with DOS 5.0. A full-screen editor uses the entire screen to display a page of the text file. You move the cursor around the screen and change the text where it is displayed.

Most users do not use a line editor when they have a full-screen editor available, and so Microsoft stopped distributing EDLIN beginning with DOS version 6.0. This chapter describes EDIT.

Setting Up the Text Editing Exercises

You will use the TYD Learning Diskette for the exercises in this chapter. Begin by booting DOS 6.0. Insert the diskette in the A: drive and press **Ctrl+Alt+Del**.

The AUTOEXEC.BAT file already has a path to \DOS set up, and now you must copy EDIT to the TYD Learning Diskette. Note that if you are using a 360K diskette for the TYD Learning Diskette, the files for the EDIT program (edit.* and qbasic.*) will not fit, and you cannot run EDIT from the diskette. You will need to skip the part of this chapter that teaches EDIT, run EDIT from your hard disk, or build the TYD Learning Diskette onto a different diskette format.

Copy the EDIT programs to the diskette with these commands:

```
A>copy c:\dos\edit.* \dos
A>copy c:\dos\qbasic.* \dos
```

Now that you have copied the editor into the \DOS subdirectory, the environment is ready. Make a subdirectory for your EDIT practice exercises and change to that subdirectory with these commands:

```
A>md \text
A>cd \text
```

Starting EDIT

To run the EDIT program, you type its name on the command line with or without the name of a text file you want to edit. Enter this command to use EDIT with a file named TEST.TXT.

```
A>edit test.txt
```

The first thing you will see is that it takes a long time to load the program from the floppy diskette. This is because EDIT is really the QBASIC program loaded in a mode that permits text editing only. Most users will not load EDIT routinely from diskettes because they will not have the patience to wait for it to come into memory.

After EDIT is loaded, you will see the screen that is displayed in Figure 12.1.

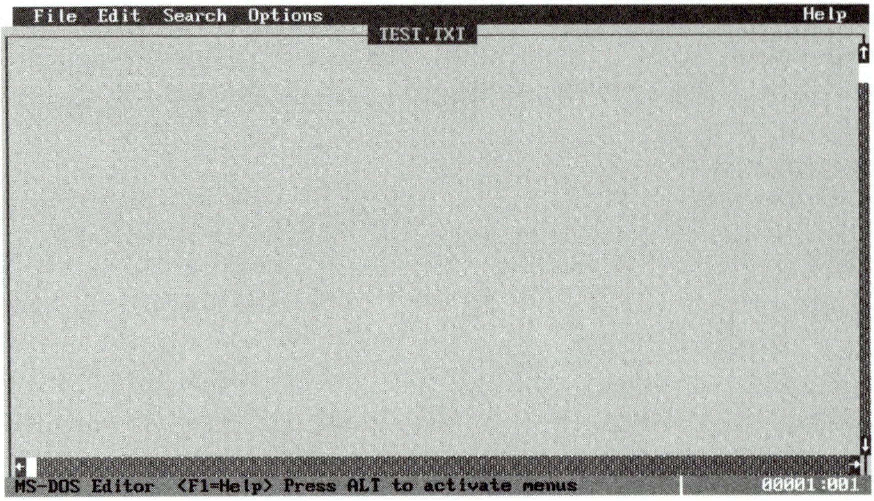

Figure 12.1 *The EDIT screen*

The EDIT Menus

EDIT uses the same Common User Access (CUA) interface as the DOS 6.0 Shell with a menu bar, pop-down menus, scroll bars, and dialog boxes. You use the same techniques for executing EDIT menu commands and filling in dialog boxes that you learned in Chapter 8.

The menu bar contains File, Edit, Search, and Options entries, with the standard Help entry at the right end of the menu bar.

The bottom of the screen is the EDIT status bar, which displays a message pertinent to what you are currently doing. The right end of the status bar displays the current line and column where the EDIT cursor is positioned.

Text Editing

You enter text by typing. EDIT does not have the equivalent of a word processor's word wrap operation, so you must press Enter at the end of each line, just as you would do with an old-fashioned typewriter.

Insert and Overwrite Modes

Your typing is either in insert or overwrite mode. You select the mode by pressing Ins. In insert mode, the characters you type are inserted into the existing text, which is moved one character position to the right for each key you type. In overwrite mode, the keys you type are written over the existing text, which does not shift.

The cursor is a blinking underline character when you are in the insert mode and a blinking box character when you are in the overwrite mode. This convention is the opposite of the one used by the DOSKEY program and the opposite of the convention used by many other text editors, so keep this contradiction in mind when you use these programs.

Moving the Cursor

There are a number of cursor movement operations that you can do. You can use the Up, Down, Left, and Right Arrow keys to move the cursor around the screen and you can use PgUp and PgDn to move to the previous and next screenful of text. Use Home to move to the beginning of the text on the current line, not the beginning of the line. End moves to the end of the text on the current line. Ctrl+Right Arrow and Ctrl+Left Arrow move the cursor to the beginning of the next and previous word, respectively. Ctrl+Home and Ctrl+End position the cursor at the beginning and end of the text file.

EDIT emulates some of the cursor movement control keys of the old WordStar program as well. You may not need these operations, however, Table 12.1 lists all the EDIT cursor movement keys:

Table 12.1 *The EDIT cursor movement keys*

EDIT key	WS key	Movement
Left Arrow	Ctrl+S	Left one character
Right Arrow	Ctrl+D	Right one character
Down Arrow	Ctrl+X	Down one line
Up Arrow	Ctrl+E	Up one line
Ctrl+Left Arrow	Ctrl+A	Left one word
Ctrl+Right Arrow	Ctrl+F	Right one word
Home		Beginning of text, current line
	Ctrl+Q,S	Beginning of current line
End	Ctrl+Q,D	End of text on current line
Ctrl+Enter		Beginning of text, next line
	Ctrl+Q,E	Top of screen window
	Ctrl+Q,X	Bottom of screen window
Ctrl+Up Arrow	Ctrl+W	Scroll up one line
Ctrl+Down Arrow	Ctrl+Z	Scroll down one line
PgUp	Ctrl+C	Scroll to next screenfull
PgDn	Ctrl+R	Scroll to previous screenfull
Ctrl+Home	Ctrl+Q,R	Beginning of file
Ctrl+End	Ctrl+Q,C	End of file
Ctrl+PgUp	Scroll left one screen	
Ctrl+PgDn	Scroll right one screen	

The mouse will position the cursor, too. Move the mouse cursor to a character in the text and click the left button. You can use the scroll bars at the right and bottom edges of the text window to scroll the text. Move the mouse cursor to one of the scroll button arrow characters and hold the left mouse button down to scroll the text.

You can drag a scroll bar's scroll box to a new position on the bar and you can click a position on the bar to pull the box to that position.

Deleting Text

You can delete individual characters of text, all or part of the current word or line, or a marked block of text. This discussion addresses all deletes except block deletes. They will be discussed after the discussion on marking blocks.

Deleting a Character

To delete the character that is under the cursor, press **Del** or **Ctrl+G.** The text to the right of the cursor moves one position to the left to fill the hole left by the deleted character. To delete the character immediately to the right of the cursor, press **Backspace** or **Ctrl+H**.

Deleting a Word

To delete a word, position the cursor on the first character of the word and press **Ctrl+T**. If the cursor is in the middle of the word, only the portion of the word from the cursor to the word's end is deleted.

Deleting a Line

Delete the current line by pressing **Ctrl+Y**. To delete from the cursor to the end of the line, press **Ctrl+Q** followed by **Y**.

Table 12.2 *EDIT text deletion keys*

EDIT key	WS key	Deletes
Del	Ctrl+G	Character under the cursor
Backspace	Ctrl+H	Character to right of the cursor
	Ctrl+Y	Current line
	Ctrl+Q,Y	From cursor to end of line
	Ctrl+T	From cursor to end of word

Selecting Text

There are a number of text manipulation operations that you can do to marked blocks of text. You will learn about them soon, but first you must learn how to mark a block. EDIT allows you to mark blocks in increments of whole text lines.

To mark a block with the keyboard, hold down **Shift** while you move the cursor. The marked block displays in reverse video. When you release the keys, the marked block remains ready to be used in a block operation. If you press any key other than one that executes or leads to a block operation before you use the block, the block is unmarked.

To mark a block with the mouse, click anywhere on the first line of the block and hold the mouse button down. Drag the mouse cursor up or down until you get to the last line of the block. To scroll beyond the limits of the current screen, drag the mouse cursor into the upper or lower border of the text window. Release the mouse button, and the block is marked. If you click the mouse button again before you use the block, the block is unmarked.

Block Operations

After you have marked a block, you can move, copy, or delete it with one of the operations discussed here.

The Clipboard

EDIT includes a feature called the *clipboard*, which is an internal buffer into which you can place text to be retrieved later. Some of the block operations involve the clipboard. When the clipboard has text in it, you can insert that text into the current text file with Shift+Ins or by executing the Paste command on the Edit menu. Pasting text into a file does not delete the text from the clipboard. Neither does closing the file and opening a new one. You can, therefore, use the clipboard to transfer text from one file to another.

Text gets into the clipboard when you mark a block and Cut or Copy it by using the corresponding commands on the Edit menu or with their shortcut keys. Whenever you put text into the clipboard, the new text replaces any text that might already be there. The text that you delete with Ctrl+Y or Ctrl+Q,Y also goes to the clipboard.

Deleting a Block

Press **Del** or execute the Clear command on the Edit menu. If you want to delete the text with the opportunity to retrieve it later, press **Shift+Del** or execute the Cut command on the Edit menu. This deletion also places the deleted text into the clipboard.

Moving a Block

To move a marked block of text, first delete it, placing it into the clipboard by pressing Shift+Del or executing the Cut command on the Edit menu.

If you are moving the text to a different text file, save the current file and open the new one. See the discussion on EDIT Files later in this chapter.

Move the cursor to the line immediately past the place where you want the block to be inserted. Put the cursor anywhere on the line. That line is going to move down, and the text in the clipboard is going to be inserted just ahead of the line where the cursor is. Press **Shift+Ins** or execute the Paste command on the Edit menu.

Copying a Block

Copying is the same as moving except that the original block is not deleted. First you place the marked block of text into the clipboard by pressing Ctrl+Ins or executing the Copy command on the Edit menu.

If you are copying the text to a different text file, save the current file and open the new one. See the discussion on EDIT Files later in this chapter.

Move the cursor to the line immediately past the place where you want the block to be inserted. Put the cursor anywhere on the line. That line is going to move down, and the text in the clipboard is going to be inserted just ahead of the line where the cursor is. Press **Shift+Ins** or execute the Paste command on the Edit menu.

Searching for and Changing Text

You can search for text that matches a text string that you specify. You can, optionally, change one or more occurrences of the text string to a different text string.

Searching for Text

To find a specified text string, execute the Find command on the Search menu. You will see the Find dialog box. Type the string you want to search for into the Find What field. There might already be a string there. EDIT copies the current word under the cursor into the field before it displays the dialog box.

If you want to search for exact matches on upper and lowercase, press **Tab** to move to the Match Upper/Lowercase checkbox and press **Spacebar** to select the checkbox. If you want to search for whole words only (you do not want to find *Maryland* when you search for *Mary*, for example) press **Tab** to move to the Whole Word checkbox and press **Spacebar** to select the checkbox.

Press **Enter** to begin the search. EDIT stops with the cursor on the first match of your search criteria. To search for subsequent matches in the file, press **F3** or execute the Repeat Last Find command on the Search menu.

Changing Text

To change a specified text string to another text string, execute the Change command on the Search menu. You will see the Change dialog box. Type the text string you want to change into the Find What field. Press **Tab** to move to the Change To field and type the replacing text string.

If you want to change text based on exact matches on upper and lowercase, press **Tab** to move to the Match Upper/Lowercase checkbox and press **Spacebar** to select the checkbox. If you want to change based on whole words only (you do not want to change *Maryland* when you search for *Mary*, for example) press **Tab** to move to the Whole Word checkbox and press **Spacebar** to select the checkbox.

Press **Spacebar** to execute the Find and Verify command button to perform the change on the first occurrence of the match. EDIT will ask you to verify the change. If you do, the change takes place, and EDIT searches for the next occurrence of your search string to change. You can execute the Skip command button instead to keep the current occurrence but proceed to the next. This process repeats until you select the Cancel command button or EDIT cannot find further occurrences of the string to change.

To change all occurrences of the search string without being asked to verify the changes, press **Tab** to move to the Change All command button and press **Spacebar**.

Options

The Options menu has two commands: Display and Help Path. The first command allows you to modify the color scheme that EDIT uses. The second allows you to specify a different path for the EDIT help files. You will have few occasions to use the second command.

The Display command shows the Display dialog box. You can tab between the two color list boxes in the dialog box and move their selection cursors up and down to change the foreground and background colors used by EDIT. You can select and deselect the Scroll Bars check box to tell EDIT whether or not to display scroll bars along with its text. You can change the value that edit uses to expand tab characters into spaces when you edit files.

EDIT Files

The File menu contains commands to open an existing text file, open a new file, save the file you are editing, print it, and exit the program.

EDIT can contain only one file in memory, so if you try to exit or open a different file after you have changed and not saved the one that is in memory, EDIT will display a dialog box to ask if you want to save the file first.

Opening a New File

The New command on the File menu clears the editor screen and allows you to begin typing the new text file, which has no title yet.

Opening an Existing File

The Open command on the File menu displays the Open dialog box. You can enter a new file path and name in the File Name field, select from the list of files in the Files field, or use the Dirs/Drives field to navigate the drives and subdirectories of your computer to search for other files. EDIT uses the *.TXT file specification as a default, but you can change this to a different specification. If, for example, you wanted to use EDIT to work with your NOVEL.DOC and other .DOC files in the \WORDPROC\DOCS\MANUSCRP subdirectory, you could enter *.DOC into the File Name field.

Saving the File

The Save command on the File menu saves the file to the disk. If you called the file by entering its name as a command line option to the EDIT program or by using the Open command on the Files menu, the file will be saved into its original subdirectory with its original name. If you initiated the file with the New command, the Save command works just like the Save As command described next.

The Save As command on the File menu saves the text file into the subdirectory and file name that you specify. The command displays the Save As dialog box. You can enter a file name into the File Name field, and EDIT will save the file on the drive and into the subdirectory shown under the File Name field. You can enter a full drive, path, and file name into the File Name field to specify a completely different location for the file. You can use the Dirs/Drives field to select a different drive and directory. As you do so, the changes will be displayed under the File Name field.

Printing the Text

When you select the Print command from the File menu, a dialog box asks if you want to print the entire text file or only the selected text. After you make that selection, EDIT prints the text onto the standard print device. Chapter 7 explained how the standard print device is assigned to your printer output port.

EDIT Help

The Help menu has three commands, Getting Started, Keyboard, and About. The last one displays a message box that tells you that EDIT is a Microsoft program. The other two display help text.

When help displays, it splits the screen into upper and lower halves. The upper half contains the help information and the lower half contains the current text file that you are editing. You can move between the help screen to the edit screen by pressing F6. That lets you edit some text while you look at the help information. You can move the border between the split screens by pressing Alt+Plus and Alt+Minus. (The Plus and Minus keys are on the numeric keypad.)

The top display of the help text contains three command buttons, Getting Started, Keyboard, and Back. The first two buttons execute the same commands as their counterparts on the Help menu. That way, you do not have to return to the menu to get the other help screen. The Back button displays the screen that was displayed before the current one.

Getting Started and Keyboard screens both have command buttons in their text. Selecting one of these calls the help text that describes the topic.

When you press Esc, you erase the help text, and the edit text takes over the entire screen.

Exiting from EDIT

The Exit command on the File menu exits the EDIT program and returns you to the DOS 6.0 command line.

Summary

This introduction to EDIT gives you enough knowledge to create and modify simple text files. If you need to know more, your DOS 6.0 user's guide has all the commands.

Every DOS 6.0 user should have a good text editor readily available for those infrequent, but necessary text entry chores that do not warrant the use of a full-featured word processor. EDIT is a full-featured, full-screen editor and is adequate for most text-editing tasks.

Chapter 13

Batch Files

This chapter teaches you how to design and use DOS 6.0 batch files. Writing batch files is an elementary form of computer programming, and it is remarkably easy and effective.

You will learn:

- What batch files are
- How to use command line parameter substitution
- How to suspend and terminate a batch file
- How to loop, test, jump, and call
- How to build a menu with a batch file

The Basics of Batch Files

Batch files are text files with the file name extension .BAT. They contain DOS 6.0 commands. You have already built several batch files. The WP.BAT and SS.BAT files from Chapters 5 and 6 are simple batch files that you built to simulate some software on the TYD Learning Diskette. AUTOEXEC.BAT is the DOS 6.0 startup batch file.

You build batch files with a text editor program. The EDIT program described in Chapter 12 is such a program. When the batch file is complete, you execute it by typing its name as a command on the DOS 6.0 command line. DOS 6.0 then reads the file and executes each command as if you had typed it on the command line individually.

Batch files have their own set of commands. By using these commands, you can build a batch file that uses command line parameters and executes program-like loops and jumps. Writing a batch file is a form of computer programming.

Setting Up the Batch Exercises

The TYD Learning Diskette has most of what you need to perform these exercises. You added the EDIT program to the diskette in Chapter 12, and you can use it in this chapter to build batch command files. If you prefer to use a text editor program other than EDIT, you should copy it to the diskette or make sure that its executable programs on your hard disk are in the DOS 6.0 path.

You must change the CONFIG.SYS file in the root directory of the TYD Learning Diskette. The file will have these entries:

```
files=20
buffers=20
device=\dos\setver.exe
device=\dos\ansi.sys
```

With the CONFIG.SYS file added, boot the TYD Learning Diskette. Make and change to a new subdirectory that you will name \BATCH with these commands:

```
A>md \batch
A>cd \batch
```

For a test file, copy the NOVEL.DOC file into \BATCH from \WORDPROC\DOCS\MANUSCRP with this command:

```
A>copy \wordproc\docs\manuscrp\novel.doc
```

Command Line Parameter Substitution

You used command line parameter substitution in the WP.BAT and SS.BAT batch files in earlier chapters. The DOS 6.0 batch file processor substitutes the first parameter on the command line for the %1 token that is in those files. Remember that a DOS 6.0 command consists of the command name perhaps followed by one or more parameters. When the command is the name of a batch file (a file with the .BAT extension), DOS 6.0 reads the file, executes the commands in the file, replacing the tokens (such as %1, %2, %3) in the file with the parameters you typed on the command line.

A Single Command Line Parameter

Use your text editor to build this batch file, named DOIT.BAT.

```
type %1
```

The batch file contains a DOS 6.0 command to type something. The %1 is the special batch file token that you use for command line parameter substitution. If you enter the command with a parameter, the batch processor substitutes your parameter for the %1 token in the batch file before it executes the command. So, if you enter DOIT NOVEL.DOC, the batch processor translates and reads the command from the DOIT.BAT file and replaces the %1 token with the NOVEL.DOC parameter. The command with the parameter substitution becomes TYPE NOVEL.DOC, which is a legitimate DOS 6.0 command. The batch processor then executes the translated DOS 6.0 command. Try that now with this command:

```
A>doit novel.doc
```

The translated command executes, typing the NOVEL.DOC file to the screen.

Multiple Command Line Parameters

Now modify DOIT.BAT so that it has these commands:

```
copy %1 %2
type %2
```

DOIT.BAT now has two substitution tokens, %1 and %2. As you might expect, %2 will have the second command line parameter substituted for it. Enter this command:

```
A>doit novel.doc novel.sav
```

The batch processor copies NOVEL.DOC into a file named NOVEL.SAV. Then it TYPEs the NOVEL.SAV file.

The Zero Parameter (%0)

Every batch file knows its own name by the substitution parameter %0. If you use %0 in the batch file named DOIT.BAT, the DOIT portion of the name is substituted. You can use that to display the command's name while the file is being executed. Change DOIT.BAT to these lines:

```
echo %0 is running
copy %1 %2
type %2
echo %0 is done
```

When you run the DOIT program, it displays these lines:

```
doit is running
.
.
doit is done
```

This is a convenience feature. Certainly you could put doit wherever you put %0, and the result would be the same. However, if you ever change the name of the batch file or copied to another file name to modify and use for a different but similar purpose, you will need to change all of those doits. By using %0, the file automatically adjusts to its own name.

Pausing Execution of a Batch File

(This exercise assumes that you have a B drive on your PC. If not, substitute C for B.)

You can tell the batch processor to stop executing commands until you take some action. The PAUSE command is used for this purpose. Suppose you wanted your backup copy to be written to the B drive. Modify DOIT.BAT to have these commands:

```
copy %1 b:
type b:%1
```

This batch file copies the file you specify on the command line to the diskette in the B drive. However, suppose the B drive has no diskette inserted. The copy command would invoke a DOS 6.0 error message. Or suppose you want to always verify that the correct diskette is in the B drive. If you do not do that, you might copy the file to the wrong diskette.

The PAUSE command will stop the execution of the commands and tell you to press any key when you are ready to continue. If you put some text as parameters to the PAUSE command, that text will be displayed with the PAUSE command. Insert the PAUSE command into DOIT.BAT as shown here:

```
pause Put Backup Diskette in B
copy %1 b:
type b:%1
```

Enter this command:

```
A>doit novel.doc
```

You will see this display:

```
C>pause Put Backup Diskette in B
Press any key to continue . . .
```

Make sure that B has the correct diskette in it and press any key when it does. The batch file resumes its execution, and copies and types the data file.

Terminating a Batch Command

The PAUSE command allows you to terminate the batch file execution altogether. Press **Ctrl+Break** when it pauses and you will see this display.

```
Press any key to continue . . . ^C
Terminate batch job (Y/N)?
```

If you press Y, the batch processor terminates the batch job and returns to the DOS command line prompt.

You have just learned the basics of batch files. They are little more than lists of DOS 6.0 commands to be executed in turn. They provide a measure of shorthand to the user who performs routine commands in a fixed sequence. You can put all those routine commands into a batch file and execute them by issuing one command, the name of the batch file.

Next, you will learn about some advanced commands that the batch file processor uses to add the properties of a computer program to a batch file. That's right, you are about to learn computer programming at the elementary level.

Program Logic in a Batch File

The properties of looping, testing, jumping, and calling are the foundation of all logic in all computer programs. Batch files can contain these properties when you use the special batch file commands that implement them. When you do, you are writing the equivalent of a computer program. This next discussion describes what looping, testing, jumping, and calling are. The discussion offers English language expressions of what each of these actions does from inside a batch file. After that, you will learn the batch file command syntax that implements the actions.

Testing

A test is an evaluation of a condition, which tells the batch file processor to execute the next command only if the evaluation is true. You would express a test in English like this: *If such-and-such is so, then do something specific. Otherwise, do not do that thing.*

Normally, a batch file executes each statement in sequence starting with the first one and ending with the last one. Many batch files are written this way. Except for the command line parameter substitutions, the statements in a batch file behave just as if you had entered them one at a time from the command line.

When you put a jump into a batch file, however, you allow it to alter the sequence of commands that it executes. As you will see later, you can make this alteration on the basis of an external condition that might be different for each invocation of the batch file. That external condition is what you test.

Jumping

A jump causes the batch file processor to resume its execution with a statement in the batch file other than the next sequential one. In English: *Do this. Do that. Jump to a statement other than the next one. Do another thing.*

What becomes of the statement just past the jump? Perhaps some other jump elsewhere in the batch file jumps to it. That's what computer programmers call *spaghetti logic*, and they try to avoid it.

A better use of the jump is to use it where the batch file processor evaluates a condition. In English again: *If such-and-such is so then jump to a different statement in the batch file. Otherwise, execute the next one after this test.* Programmers call this practice *structured programming*, and they strive to do it all the time.

Looping

Looping is the behavior of a batch file to repeat the execution of a group of statements. A typical loop repeats until something interrupts it, usually a test and jump or a keypress by the user. A loop is characterized by a jump that occurs at the bottom of the loop and that tells the batch file processor to resume executing statements at the top of the loop. In English: *Do this. Do that. Do the other thing. Jump to the 'do this' statement.*

Calling

A batch file can call another batch file. Well, why not? If a statement in a batch file is a DOS 6.0 command, and a DOS 6.0 command can execute a batch file, why shouldn't a batch file execute another batch file? It can, but if it does so simply by using the other batch file's name, the batch file processor does not return to the calling batch file when the called batch file is complete. DOS 6.0 has a special CALL batch file command that overcomes this problem. In English: *Do this. Do that. Call another batch file. Do the other thing.*

A call to another batch file has the property that when the called batch file is finished, the batch file processor returns to the calling batch file and resumes with the statement that follows the call.

Now you can proceed to learn how to put testing, jumping, looping, and calling into your own batch files.

Testing with the IF Command

You make tests in a batch file with the IF command. The IF command is not a DOS 6.0 command that you would use from the command line. IF is a batch command designed specifically for the batch processor. The IF command has this format:

```
IF <condition> <command>
```

When an IF command is executed, the condition represented by the <condition> parameter is tested. If the condition is true, the command represented by the <command> parameter is executed. If the condition is false, the command represented by the <command> parameter is not executed. In most cases, the statement following the IF statement is executed next, regardless of the condition. The exception is when the <command> parameter is a GOTO command, which is discussed later.

The <command> parameter is any valid DOS 6.0 or batch command, except that pipes and standard input/output redirection may not be used. You will often use the GOTO command as the <command> parameter.

The <condition> parameter can be one of the following three conditions:

- ERRORLEVEL <n>
- <string> == <string>
- EXIST <filename>

The <condition> parameter can also be one of the above three with the word NOT ahead of it as shown here:

- NOT ERRORLEVEL <n>
- NOT <string> == <string>
- NOT EXIST <filename>

The ERRORLEVEL Condition

This condition tests a value returned by many programs. To use it, you must know the possible values returned by the command executed just before the IF statement. Programs return errorlevel values to report their results. By convention, programs return errorlevel 0 to report a successful execution and errorlevel 1 to report an error condition. Some programs, however, return one of several values to report the conditions of their execution.

A batch file tests the errorlevel value by using this format:

```
if errorlevel <n> <command>
```

The <n> parameter is the errorlevel value being tested. If the errorlevel value is equal to or greater than the parameter, the <command> parameter executes. Batch programs typically use a GOTO command in an errorlevel test as in this example.

```
doprog
if errorlevel 2 goto level2
if errorlevel 1 goto level1
rem --- errorlevel is zero
```

The <string> == <string> Condition

This condition tests two string values. It is usually used to test the value of a command line parameter against a constant string. The string can be only one word. Modify DOIT.BAT to contain only these statements. (Make sure that you have a diskette in drive B.)

```
if %1 == novel.doc echo Oh no, not that turkey!
copy %1 b:
```

Enter this command:

```
A>doit novel.doc
```

You will see this display:

```
C>if novel.doc == novel.doc echo Oh no, not that turkey!
Oh no, not that turkey!
C>copy novel.doc b:
1 File(s) copied
```

The two strings must be identical with respect to case. If there is a chance that the user will enter the file name in uppercase, you must test for both values.

The EXIST and NOT EXIST Conditions

A batch file can test to see if a file exists. This feature is useful to prevent the execution of commands that require a particular file. You will find other uses for it as well when you begin to design your own batch files.

Modify DOIT.BAT so that it contains only this line.

```
if exist %1 copy %1 b:
```

Try the DOIT command with NOVEL.DOC and with other file names that do not exist.

Jumping with the GOTO Command

You can insert a statement in a batch file that is called a *label*. A batch file can have several labels, and labels themselves are not executed. The purpose of a label is to give the GOTO statement a place to jump. A label is a single word in a batch file with a colon as the first character. Here are examples of batch file labels:

```
:top
:wp
:exit
```

The GOTO statement has this format:

```
goto <label>
```

The <label> parameter must correspond with a label in the batch file. The label in the GOTO statement does not include the colon prefix.

When the batch processor encounters a GOTO statement, it resumes execution with the statement that follows the label that matches the GOTO parameter. With this feature, you can cause the batch processor to modify its command sequence. When combined with the IF statement, the GOTO statement gives powerful decision-making capabilities to your batch file.

Rebuild DOIT.BAT to contain these statements:

```
if not exist %1 goto exit
copy %1 b:
:exit
```

Run the DOIT command with NOVEL.DOC and with some invalid file names to observe the effect of the IF test.

Complex Tests in a Batch File

You can have multiple IFs, GOTOs, and labels in a batch file. Rebuild DOIT.BAT to contain these statements:

```
echo off
:start
     echo %0 is starting
     if not exist %1 goto nofile
         if %1 == novel.doc goto nocando
              echo copying %1
              copy %1 b:
              goto exit
:nofile
     echo There is no such file as %1
     goto exit
:nocando
     echo I refuse to copy that turkey
:exit
     echo %0 is done
```

There are a couple of style changes to this file. First, the commands are indented. This technique makes it easier to tell where the labels are and which statements are subordinate to IF tests. The START label is included just to preserve the integrity of the indenting style. No GOTO statement references START. Whether to indent is a personal choice, and subject to your preferences and your eye. You will find a style you like.

Second, the file begins with an ECHO OFF statement. This tells the batch processor not to display every statement before it executes it, a technique that cleans up the display considerably.

The following commands and displays show three executions of DOIT.BAT, one with a file name that does not exist, one with the file named NOVEL.DOC, and one with the name of the DOIT.BAT file itself.

Enter the following command to try the DOIT batch file with a file name parameter that does not exist:

```
C>doit nofile.bad
```

You will see this display:

```
C>echo off
doit is starting
There is no such file as nofile.bad
doit is done
```

Enter the following command to try the DOIT batch file with the file name that it rejects:

```
C>doit novel.doc
```

You will see this display:

```
C>echo off
doit is starting
I refuse to copy that turkey
doit is done
```

Enter the following command to try the DOIT batch file with a file name that it will accept:

```
C>doit doit.bat
```

You will see this display:

```
C>echo off
doit is starting
copying doit.bat
1 File(s) copied
doit is done
```

Calling with Nested and Chained Batch Commands

Early versions of DOS did not provide for nested batch commands. A batch file could not call another batch file except as its last operation. Beginning with DOS version 3.30, batch processing includes the CALL command with which one batch file can call another.

If a batch file executes another batch command without using the CALL command to do it, the execution chains to the other batch file, and the first batch file is not resumed when the second one is complete.

You will use the CALL command in the batch file menu shell exercise, which you will find later in this chapter.

Looping with the FOR Command

The FOR command works in batch files or from the command line. Here is an example of a FOR command in a batch file:

```
for %%p in (1 2 3) do echo Please read Chapter %%p
```

The FOR statement is itself a loop. FOR repeats a command some number of times based on what is in the rest of the FOR statement. The

%%p token is what computer programmers call a *variable*, which is a data value that varies with each execution of the loop. The %1 command line substitution parameters—discussed above—are variables that take their values from the parameters on the command line. The %%p variable in the FOR statement takes its value from the set of values that are within the parentheses in the FOR statement. In this example, the set contains three values, 1, 2, and 3.

The %%p variable can be named any anything as long as it is preceded with the %% token.

The FOR statement executes the DOS 6.0 command that follows the word *do* in the statement. FOR executes the command once for each value in the set. The example ECHO command in the batch file example above, therefore, executes three times. Each time it executes, the %%p value will contain the next value from the set. This batch file will display these messages:

```
Please read Chapter 1
Please read Chapter 2
Please read Chapter 3
```

You do not need to use the variable in the executed statements. You can use the set simply as a counter of the number of times the statement will be executed.

The values in the set can contain DOS 6.0 file names with wild cards. In this usage, the number of values in the set is the same as the number of files that match the wild card specification. Build this batch file and name it TYPEALL.BAT:

```
for %%p in (*.ltr) do type %%p
```

Change to the \WORDPROC\DOCS\LETTERS subdirectory and enter the TYPEALL command. You will need a path to the \BATCH subdirectory, or you can issue the command this way:

```
A>\batch\typeall
```

The batch file will type all the letters in the subdirectory.

You can use substitution parameters in the FOR statement's set of values. Build this batch file and call it TYPETHIS.BAT

```
for %%p in (%1) do type %%p
```

Now you can specify on the command line the file or files that you want to type by using this format to call the batch file.

```
A>\batch\typethis *.ltr
```

A set can contain several file specifications. The following batch file would type all files with a .TXT or .DOC extension (which do not exist on the TYD diskette; this is an example) as well as the AUTOEXEC.BAT file in the root directory.

```
for %%p in (*.txt \autoexec.bat *.doc) do type %%p
```

Looping with the SHIFT Command

The SHIFT command in a batch file shifts all of the parameters one position to the left. After the shift command executes, the parameter that was %0 is gone, the value that was in %1 is now in %0, the one that was in %2 is now in %1, and so on. You can use this command to build a loop that performs the same operation on a variable number of parameters. Build the following batch file and name it GREET.BAT.

```
echo off
cls
:top
   if "%1" == "" goto exit
        echo Welcome, %1
        shift
        goto top
:exit
```

Run the GREET.BAT command with several names on the command line as follows:

```
A>greet Tyler Landon Kellie
```

The batch file processor substitutes the %1 token for the first parameter, Tyler. Then it uses the IF command to compare the character string "Tyler" to the null, zero-length character string "". They are not the same, so it does not execute the GOTO statement that addresses the :end label. Instead, it echoes the "Welcome, Tyler" character string. Then it uses the SHIFT command to shift all the parameters one position to the left, putting Landon in the %1 position.

The GOTO statement that addresses the :top label effects the loop by returning to the IF statement. After the SHIFT that follows the "Welcome, Kellie" message, %1 is empty, so the "%1" test compares "" to "", which are equal. The IF condition is true, so it executes the GOTO, which goes to the :exit label at the end of the batch file. The batch command as shown above results in this display:

```
Welcome, Tyler
Welcome, Landon
Welcome, Kellie
```

Remarks

You can insert remarks into a batch file to explain its meaning. The REM command at the beginning of a line turns any line into a remark. Remarks are bypassed by the batch processor. If ECHO is on, the remarks are displayed as they are passed. Here is DOIT.BAT with some remarks and some blank lines inserted to make it more readable.

```
echo off
rem --- Start Processing ---
:start
rem --- display the batch file name ---
     echo %0 is starting
     rem --- test for the file's existence ---
     if not exist %1 goto nofile
         rem --- do not accept NOVEL.DOC ---
         if %1 == novel.doc goto nocando
              rem --- copy the file to the B: drive ---
              echo copying %1
              copy %1 b:
              goto exit
rem -- No such file on the disk --
:nofile
     echo There is no such file as %1
     goto exit
rem -- refuse to copy NOVEL.DOC --
:nocando
     echo I refuse to copy that turkey
rem -- all done --
:exit
     echo %0 is done
```

Environment Variables in Batch Files

You can reference the value of an environment variable in a batch file by referencing its name surrounded by percent signs. For example, build this HUNTPECK.BAT batch file:

```
type %file%
```

Now enter the following commands. The first one sets an environment variable named FILE to the value "a:\autoexec.bat." The second command executes the HUNTPECK batch command.

```
A>set file=a:\autoexec.bat
A>huntpeck
```

The HUNTPECK batch file substitutes the value that is set in the FILE environment variable for the %file% substitution token. You would see this display:

```
A>type a:\autoexec.bat
echo off
cls
echo Teach Yourself DOS 6.0 Learning Diskette
ver
path=a:\wordproc\software;a:\sprdsht\software;a:\dos
```

A handy use for the environment variable substitution feature is for extension of the DOS PATH. Often, you want to add a subdirectory to the path without removing any of the rest of the path. Yet you do not want to type in the entire path every time. Build this XPATH.BAT batch file:

```
path=%path%;%1
```

Use the PATH command to see the current path. You will see this display:

```
PATH=A:\WORDPROC\SOFTWARE;A:\SPRDSHT\SOFTWARE;A:\DOS
```

Enter the following command to add a path to the \BATCH subdirectory you built earlier in the chapter.

```
A>xpath a:\batch
```

You will see this display.

```
A>path=A:\WORDPROC\SOFTWARE;A:\SPRDSHT\SOFTWARE;A:\DOS;
a:\batch
```

The DOS PATH has been extended to include the \BATCH subdirectory.

The CHOICE Command

A batch program can use the CHOICE command to prompt the user to enter one of a specified number of keystrokes. The CHOICE command sets the ERRORLEVEL value to reflect which of the specified keystrokes the user pressed. You would use the CHOICE command to let the user select from some number of keys as shown here:

```
choice /c:abc Enter one of these
```

The batch program will display the text *Enter one of these[A,B,C]?* and would wait for the user to type a key. If the key is not one of the characters specified by the /c: parameter, the program beeps and keeps waiting. If you do not specify a /c: parameter, the program uses Y and N for a yes/no prompt. If you do not specify text, the program prompts with just the question mark.

If you use the /s parameter, the user input is case-sensitive. Otherwise it is not. The /t parameter allows you to specify a timeout period and a default value to use if the user does not enter a key as shown here

```
choice /c:abc /t:b,3 Enter one of these
```

In the example just given, the program defaults to the b selection after 3 seconds.

A Batch File Menu Shell

This exercise shows you how some imagination and an understanding of batch files can be put to work to do creative things. You will build a menu system that will demonstrate more of the power of batch files.

The menu you build will be in the \BATCH subdirectory of the TYD Learning Diskette. This menu will execute the simulated word processor and spreadsheet upon your selections. Begin by building MENU.BAT, which looks like this:

```
echo off
:menu
cls
echo Snappy Computer Menu System
echo ---------------------------
echo 1 = Word Processing
echo 2 = Spreadsheet
echo 3 = DOS Prompt
choice /c:123 Selection

if errorlevel 3 goto dos
if errorlevel 2 goto ss

rem ----- word processing
:wp
cls
cd \wordproc\docs\manuscrp
call wp novel.doc
pause
goto menu

rem ----- spreadsheet
:ss
cls
cd \sprdsht\sheets
call ss taxes92.sps
pause
goto menu

rem ----- DOS
:dos
```

You can test the MENU.BAT file now. Execute the MENU command, and you will see this display:

```
Snappy Computer Menu System
---------------------------
1 = Word Processing
2 = Spreadsheet
3 = DOS Prompt
Selection[1,2,3]?
```

When you run MENU.BAT, the menu is displayed, and you must enter 1, 2, or 3 to make a selection.

The batch commands following the :wp label are executed when you select 1 from the menu. The commands in the file change to the \WORDPROC\DOCS subdirectory and use the batch CALL command to call the WP.BAT command with the NOVEL.DOC filename as a parameter. In an actual environment, the WP command might not be a batch file, in which case, you would execute the word processor program using whatever command it requires.

The batch commands following the :ss label are executed when you select 2 from the menu. The commands in the file change to the \SPRDSHEET\SHEETS subdirectory and use the batch CALL command to call the SS.BAT command with the TAXWS92.SPS filename as a parameter. As with word processing, in an actual environment, the SS command might not be a batch file, in which case you would execute the spreadsheet program using whatever command it requires.

When you select 3 from the menu, the batch file jumps to the :dos label which exits from the batch file and returns to the DOS 6.0 command line prompt.

Summary

This chapter taught you about batch files and how to use them. You learned about using the command line parameter substitution, and suspending and terminating a batch file. Additionally, the chapter explained looping, testing, jumping, and calling in batch files. Finally, you learned how to build a menu with a batch file. You have now completed your Teach Yourself DOS 6.0 tutorial lessons. You are prepared to go out and practice your skills with confidence and ability.

Chapter 14

Memory Management and Optimizing

This chapter describes procedures to modify and optimize the way DOS 6.0 operates with the memory installed in your computer. These procedures require a better understanding of PC/AT architecture than you have needed so far. You need to know about conventional, extended, and expanded memory. You also need to understand the fundamental differences between the 8088, the 80286, and the 80386 microprocessors from the advanced user's viewpoint. This chapter introduces these subjects and describes how DOS 6.0 provides ways to for you to optimize its use of memory. By using these techniques, you can tune DOS 6.0's performance to match your hardware and your operating requirements. You will learn about:

- PC/AT memory architecture
- Conventional, extended, and expanded memory
- Upper- and high-memory areas
- How to load device drivers and memory-resident programs in high memory
- Using MEMMAKER to optimize 386 memory
- How to install a RAM disk
- How to build a disk cache

PC/AT Memory

First, you must understand the PC/AT memory architecture. There are three kinds of physical random access memory in a PC/AT. The first two are conventional memory and extended memory. The third kind of memory involves one or both of the first two and often some extra hardware. This memory is called expanded memory.

Conventional Memory

All PC/AT computers have conventional memory with a maximum of 640K. They can address up to 1MB, but the space above 640K is used by devices such as video cards, network cards, and the BIOS read-only memory.

Conventional memory contains some hardware-specific, BIOS-specific, and DOS-specific data areas at the lowest memory locations. DOS 6.0 loads just above these data areas. Above that are the device driver programs that DOS 6.0 loads from entries in your CONFIG.SYS files. DOS 6.0's COMMAND.COM command line processor program comes next. Above that are the memory-resident programs that you load from the AUTOEXEC.BAT file or from the DOS 6.0 command line. These programs include network shells, DOS-resident commands such as DOSKEY, MODE, and DOSSHELL, other operating environment shells such as Windows 3.1, and third party utility programs such as Borland's Sidekick. The address space from just above the memory-resident utility programs to the top of the 640K address line is where DOS 6.0 loads your applications programs.

Upper Memory Area

The 384K that occupies the space from 640K to the top of conventional memory space is called the upper memory area. All but the last 64K of the upper memory area is used by hardware adapters such as video, network, scanner, and FAX cards. The address space used by these cards varies depending on what cards you have. Often a PC/AT has holes—unused blocks of memory addresses—in this space. Those holes are called *upper memory blocks* (UMBs). The PC/AT's ROM BIOS firmware occupies the top 64K of the upper memory area.

If you have an 80386 or 80486 computer with extended memory, you can load device drivers and memory-resident programs into the UMBs. The EMM386.EXE program—addressed later in the expanded memory discussion—manages this for you.

Typical Memory Organization

Figure 14.1 shows the organization of a typical PC/AT that uses DOS 6.0 with no consideration given to memory management. The figure is, in effect, an example of how earlier versions of DOS necessarily organized memory. A PC/AT with a network shell and a significant number of memory-intensive resident programs often had too little conventional memory remaining to support the requirements of large programs that manipulate large blocks of data.

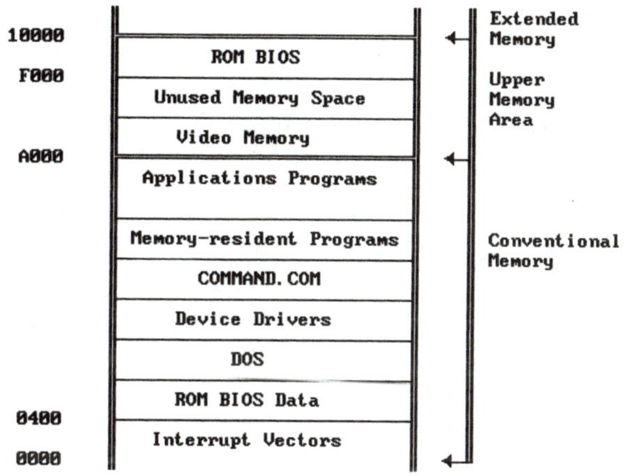

Figure 14.1 *DOS 6.0 memory organization*

DOS 6.0 provides a number of memory management tools to allow you to relocate some programs from conventional memory into other memory locations so that your applications have more space. Some of these tools are put into place by the SETUP program when you install DOS 6.0. These tools and others are available for you to modify. You will learn how to do that later in this chapter.

Extended Memory

Computers that use 80286, 80386, and 80486 microprocessors can have extended memory. These processors have an operating mode called the *protected mode* where they can address memory above the 1MB range. DOS 6.0 does not run in protected mode, but in *real mode,* which can address only the first 1MB of memory. DOS 6.0 runs this way because the 8086 and 8088 microprocessors do not have the equivalent of protected mode, and DOS 6.0 must work with all PC and AT machines regardless of the microprocessor.

Inasmuch as DOS 6.0 is a real mode operating system, programs that run under it are in real mode as well. As such they cannot directly access extended memory without slipping into protected mode. If every program did that for itself and read and wrote extended memory, its use of extended memory would interfere with DOS 6.0's use of extended memory and the use of it by other programs that could be resident at the same time. To define how programs may use extended memory, Lotus, Intel, Microsoft, and AST Research developed a standard specification, which is called the *extended memory specification* (XMS). DOS 6.0 implements that specification with a device driver program called HIMEM.SYS, about which you will learn later in this chapter. The 8086 and 8088 microprocessors run only in real mode and, therefore, cannot access and do not have extended memory. Since computers that use these microprocessors do not have extended memory, they cannot use the HIMEM.SYS program.

A typical use of extended memory is for a so-called RAM disk—a device that resembles a disk drive to the DOS command line, the DOS 6.0 Shell, and programs, but that uses extended memory rather than an actual disk device. The DOS 6.0 RAMDRIVE.SYS device program implements such a RAM disk.

The High Memory Area

A characteristic of the 80286, 80386, and 80486 is that they can address the first 64K of extended memory without switching into protected mode. This extra memory is called the *high memory area* (HMA). Most of DOS 6.0 can be loaded into the high memory area to make more conventional memory available to applications. The HIMEM.SYS program manages the use of the HMA, just as it manages the use of all other extended memory.

This characteristic that allows real-mode access to what is usually protected-mode address space was originally a bug in the first 80286 integrated circuits. Someone discovered it, and the industry began to use it in beneficial ways. Rather than fixing the bug in later microprocessors, Intel perpetuated it so that its benefits could continue. The nature of the way in which a program can use the memory precludes more than one program from using it. Therefore, HIMEM.SYS allows only one use of the HMA. Usually, DOS 6.0 itself loads into the HMA.

Expanded Memory

Expanded memory is a technique whereby a PC/AT computer has extra memory that it cannot normally address. Programs can use the memory, however, by having small segments of it temporarily mapped into one of the UMBs. A program that uses expanded memory requests it by "pages." The expanded memory manager maps the requested page of expanded memory into one of the UMBs. The program can then read and write the memory by using the address of the UMB, which it can legitimately access in real mode because the UMB is below the 1MB memory address range.

The management of expanded memory pages is the responsibility of a memory-resident program called the *expanded memory manager*. There is a standard method for implementing expanded memory. This standard is the Lotus/Intel/Microsoft Expanded Memory Specification Version 4.0, commonly abbreviated as LIM EMS 4.0, and often called, simply, EMS. The expanded memory manager program that you use depends upon your hardware.

The expanded memory manager appropriates one of the UMBs when you install the manager and uses the UMB for all requests for expanded memory pages. By definition, only one expanded memory page is active and accessible at any time.

Any PC/AT can have expanded memory. Computers that use the 80386 and 80486 microprocessors can implement EMS by using extended memory. These microprocessors can map any range of memory addresses into any physical memory hardware, so requests for EMS pages by programs cause areas of extended memory to be mapped into the designated UMB. The 386 expanded memory manager for DOS 6.0 is a program called EMM386.EXE, which is a device driver program that you install from your CONFIG.SYS file. Since EMM386.EXE uses extended memory, that use must be arbitrated by the HIMEM.SYS XMS manager. Therefore, use of EMM386.EXE assumes that you have loaded HIMEM.SYS in advance.

Computers that use 8088, 8086, and 80286 microprocessors do not implement EMS by using extended memory. The first two do not have any extended memory, and the 80286 cannot map its extended memory into the UMBs above 640K. Therefore, these processors must use other methods to implement EMS. These methods use an EMS board with memory that is, at first, nowhere within the address range of the microprocessor. The board can, however, be told to map pages of its memory into one of the UMBs. An expanded memory manager program accompanies the board, and it works only with the kind of board for which it was designed. DOS 6.0 does not include expanded memory manager programs for any of these boards, but those portions of DOS 6.0 that use EMS use this kind of expanded memory if its implementation complies with LIM EMS 4.0.

Memory Management Analysis

The first step in managing your memory is to figure out what kind of memory you have and whether you can run DOS 6.0 or any device drivers or memory-resident programs in upper memory. After you know that, you can begin to modify your system to make the best use of its resources.

If the DOS 6.0 Setup program senses that you have extended memory, it adds lines to your CONFIG.SYS file to load HIMEM.SYS into conventional memory and to load DOS 6.0 in the HMA. The Setup program does not do this if it finds another XMS driver program running when Setup runs. Setup also adds a line to install the SETVER device driver program. There are many different configurations that a DOS 6.0 installation can install as a default.

Beginning with this chapter, the exercises in the book abandon the TYD Learning Diskette. The number and size of the system files prohibit its use any further. The exercises assume that you have installed DOS 6.0 in its default configuration and that no memory or disk optimization programs are installed. This might not be the case. An upgrade from DOS 5.0 to DOS 6.0 uses the optimizations that were in the original. Device drivers, such as those for the mouse, scanners, CD-ROM drives, and other devices from the original installation are installed into DOS 6.0 as well. The numbers that you see with these exercises might be quite different from those you see on your own computer. Nonetheless, the principals are the same.

Determining Conventional and Extended Memory

Run the MEM command to find out about your computer's memory configuration. Enter this command:

```
C>mem
```

You will see a display similar to this one:

```
Memory Type        Total  =  Used  + Free
----------------   ------    ------  ------
Conventional         640K      21K    619K
Upper                  0K       0K      0K
Adapter RAM/ROM      384K     384K      0K
Extended (XMS)      7168K      64K   7104K
----------------   ------    ------  ------
Total memory        8192K     469K   7723K

Total under 1 MB     640K      21K    619K

Largest executable program size       619K (633680 bytes)
Largest free upper memory block         0K (0 bytes)
MS-DOS is resident in the high memory area.
```

This display tells you that there are 619K free and available for your programs. This is a bare-bones load of DOS 6.0.

The Extended (XMS) entry is important. It tells you that you have some extended memory, in the case of this example, 7MB. If you do not have extended memory, you cannot load DOS 6.0 into the high-memory area or load device drivers and memory-resident programs into the upper memory area. In that case, proceed to the discussion about analyzing expanded memory.

If your computer is not an 80386 or 80486, skip this section, too.

Loading the Expanded Memory Manager

Add this entry to the CONFIG.SYS file.

```
device=\dos\emm386.exe noems
```

This entry loads the EMM386.EXE Expanded Memory Manager but tells it not to emulate EMS. Reboot the computer. If you now execute the MEM command, you will see this difference in the display:

```
Memory Type        Total =  Used  +  Free
----------------   ------   ------   ------
Conventional         640K     24K     616K
Upper                151K      0K     151K
Adapter RAM/ROM      384K    384K       0K
Extended (XMS)      7017K    221K    6796K
----------------   ------   ------   ------
Total memory        8192K    629K    7563K
Total under 1 MB     791K     24K     767K
Largest executable program size       616K (630544 bytes)
Largest free upper memory block       147K (150592 bytes)
MS-DOS is resident in the high memory area.
```

The EMM386 program is resident in memory, reducing the total memory available to the other programs from 619K to 616K.

Loading DOS 6.0 into the High Memory Area

Observe in the displays just shown the message that says:

```
MS-DOS is resident in the high memory area.
```

You might see this message instead:

```
The high memory area is available.
```

If so, DOS 6.0 is not loaded into the high memory area, and you can add 64K to the memory available to your applications programs by adding this line to the CONFIG.SYS file.

```
dos=high,umb
```

Reboot the computer and execute the MEM command to see that DOS 6.0 is in the high memory area and that the available memory is increased by 64K.

Loading Programs into the Upper Memory Area

You can load many of your device driver and memory-resident programs into the upper memory area. You cannot load HIMEM.SYS or EMM386.EXE into the upper memory area, because they are the programs that manage access to it, and they must run in conventional memory. You might have problems loading some third-party, memory-resident programs into the upper memory area as well because they might not be designed to operate correctly in that configuration.

Device driver programs normally load from the CONFIG.SYS file, and memory-resident programs normally load from the AUTOEXEC.BAT file. You can tell all of these programs to load into the upper memory area, but they might not all get there. DOS 6.0 loads programs in this order: first, it loads the ones in the CONFIG.SYS file; next, it loads the ones in the AUTOEXEC.BAT file. Within those files, the programs load in the order in which you see them. DOS 6.0 loads a program into the biggest UMB it can find. That UMB is no longer available, and the excess memory from the UMB that the program does not need becomes a new, smaller UMB.

Which Programs To Load into Upper Memory

To decide which programs to load, first load them into conventional memory to see how much memory they require. Insert these lines into the CONFIG.SYS file at the end of the file.

```
device=\dos\ansi.sys device=\dos\ramdrive.sys 2048 /e
```

Insert these lines at the end of the AUTOEXEC.BAT file:

```
doskey fastopen c:=40
```

There might already be device drivers and memory-resident programs installed due to your previous configuration with an earlier version of DOS. These benefit from the procedures that follow as well.

At this point in earlier version of DOS you had to do some detailed analysis and experimentation to figure out which programs load into upper memory and which ones do not. DOS 6.0 introduces MEMMAKER to take the worry out of that. You will learn about MEMMAKER later in this chapter.

Setting Up Expanded Memory

If you are using an expanded memory adapter board on your 8088, 8086, or 80286 computer, you can leave it configured the way it was installed and continue to the next discussion. It might, however, have some impact on how much upper memory area your system has, and you might want to modify it. The discussion on EMM386.EXE gives you some insight on how EMS affects the upper memory area.

If you have an 80386 or 80486 computer and want to use the EMM386.EXE program to emulate expanded memory with extended memory, you must do some planning. First, you must consider how your programs use expanded memory, if at all. Many programs run more efficiently if they find expanded memory installed in the system. If you run such programs, you should read their documentation to determine how much EMS they need. If you set up enough EMS to support the biggest requirement, that should be sufficient.

When you use EMM386.EXE to emulate EMS, it reserves enough extended memory from the HIMEM.SYS XMS manager to support the amount of EMS you specify. You could tell it to take all of the extended memory. If you do, not enough extended memory remains for other uses, such as the RAM disk, which is described later in this chapter.

To tell the EMM386.EXE program to support emulated EMS, change the command in the CONFIG.SYS file to this value:

```
device=\dos\emm386.exe ram
```

The RAM parameter tells the program to support the upper memory area as well as EMS. If you omit the RAM parameter, the program supports EMS alone, and none of your programs load into the UMBs. Reboot the diskette with the modified CONFIG.SYS and use the MEM command to see the effects.

Using MEMMAKER To Optimize Memory

In DOS 5.0, you had to experiment with the placement of device driver and memory-resident program loads, using the DEVICEHIGH and LOADHIGH command in order to get the best combination that left the most memory available for your applications. DOS 6.0 adds the MEMMAKER utility to analyze your memory and memory requirements and to build the best possible configuration for loading device driver and memory-resident programs. MEMMAKER makes several passes through your configuration, modifying the load sequence and rebooting the computer each time until it finds the best combination. Then it changes your CONFIG.SYS and AUTOEXEC.BAT files to reflect that combination. To run MEMMAKER, type its name on the command line like this:

```
C>memmaker
```

You will see a series of screens with which you run MEMMAKER. Press **Enter** to get past the first one. The second screen allows you to select from the Custom and Express Setup options. For now, use the Express Setup option. It does a reasonable job of configuring your computer. Later, when you understand the process better, you can experiment with a Custom Setup.

Read each screen and answer its questions as well as you can. Do not worry if you get an answer wrong. You can always run MEMMAKER at a later time to try other options.

MEMMAKER analyzes your running system and then displays the screen shown in Figure 14.2. Follow its instructions to reboot the computer.

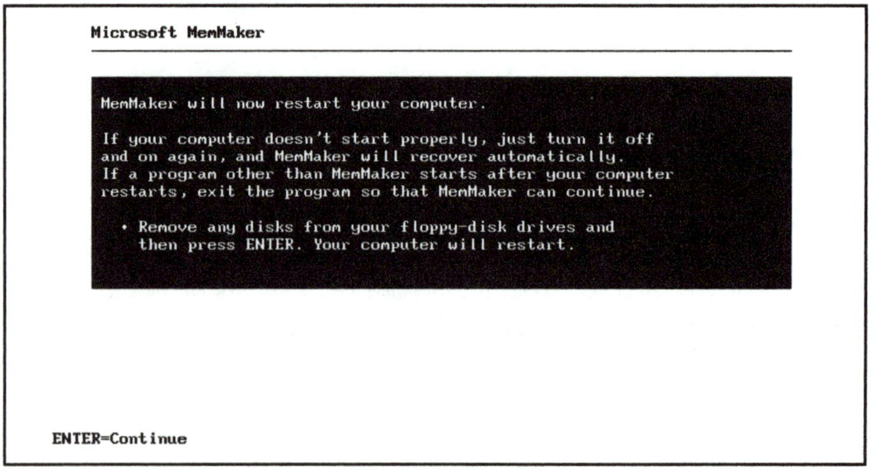

Figure 14.2 *Memmaker*

MEMMAKER goes through a second reboot. It shows you again the screen in Figure 14.2. When it is done, MEMMAKER asks you if your computer is running properly. It's hard to know, because all it does is display the screen that asks the question. Press Enter. If anything happens, your computer is probably working OK. MEMMAKER displays the before and after values of memory. If you press Enter, you have selected the changes, and your CONFIG.SYS and AUTOEXEC.BAT are updated. If you press Esc, the MEMMAKER changes are discarded.

Loading Other Memory-Resident Programs into Upper Memory

The procedure just described loads DOS 6.0 device drivers and memory-resident programs into the upper memory area. However, most users have other memory-resident programs from other vendors. Many of these programs originated long before the concept of loading high was developed, and they do not operate properly in the high memory area. In some cases, they hang up the computer as soon as you boot it. You must test each one to see if it works.

If you build a configuration that does not boot because a device driver or memory-resident program hangs up during system initialization, press F8 after the initialization program displays the Starting MS-DOS... message. You can then choose to not load the offending device driver or not execute the commands in the AUTOEXEC.BAT file. This procedure gets you past the initialization process so that you can repair the CONFIG.SYS and AUTOEXEC.BAT files with your editor.

Building a RAM Disk

In the exercises above, you installed the RAMDRIVE.SYS device driver into the high memory area. The RAMDRIVE.SYS device driver program builds a RAM drive into your system. A RAM drive uses conventional or extended memory to emulate a disk drive and store data. The drive's advantage is speed. Reading and writing RAM is much faster than reading and writing disks.

The contents of a RAM drive are not permanent. When you reboot the computer the contents are no longer there. Therefore, you cannot use a RAM drive for permanent files. RAM drives are typically used by programs that use temporary files for work space. When the programs terminate, they delete the temporary files. By using a RAM drive, the program runs faster and it does not risk exhausting the space on your disk drive with its temporary files.

Many programs that use temporary files follow a convention that uses the TEMP environment variable to tell them where the temporary files should go. The DOS 6.0 Shell's Task Swapper feature uses temporary files to swap images of program memory in and out, and it uses the TEMP environment variable convention. You can significantly improve the performance of the Shell by building a RAM drive into your system and setting the TEMP environment variable to point to the RAM drive.

You build a RAM drive by installing the RAMDRIVE.SYS device driver in your CONFIG.SYS file with a statement such as this one:

```
device=c:\dos\ramdrive.sys 2048 /e
```

The 2048 is the RAM drive size. This example specifies that the RAM drive is 2048K—or 2MB. You can follow this number with a value that specifies the sector size as 128, 256, or 512. The default is 512, and there is little reason to make it anything else. If you do specify a sector size, you can follow that number with one that specifies the number of entries that the RAM disk can have in its root directory. The valid numbers are 2 through 1024. The default is 64. If you do not specify this number, and you expect to have more than 64 files on the RAM drive, you must create one or more subdirectories on the RAM drive in which programs store their temporary files.

The /e parameter tells the RAMDRIVE program to use extended memory for its data storage. If you prefer to use expanded memory, you can use the /a parameter. If you use neither, RAMDRIVE positions its data storage at the top of conventional memory. In this case, you must specify a RAM drive size that fits into conventional memory. RAM drives of 64K, 128K, and 512K are typical values for conventional memory RAM drives.

If you have extended memory and use the /e option, the DEVICE= HIMEM.SYS statement must precede the DEVICE=RAMDRIVE.SYS statement in the CONFIG.SYS file. If you use the /a option, the DEVICE=EMM386.EXE statement—or the statement that loads your third-party expanded memory manager program—must precede the DEVICE=RAMDRIVE.SYS statement.

You should use conventional memory for a RAM drive only if you do not have extended or expanded memory. The amount of conventional memory available to applications programs is reduced by the size of the RAM drive.

If you have extended and expanded memory, put the RAM drive into extended memory so that it works more efficiently. You can have as many RAM drives as you want by putting successive DEVICE=RAMDRIVE.SYS statements into CONFIG.SYS as long as the total number of disk drives and RAM drives do not exceed 26. Each successive RAM drive is assigned the next available drive letter. For example, you have a C: hard drive, the first RAM drive becomes D:.

To use the RAM drive for the temporary files of programs that use the TEMP environment variable, put the following statements into your AUTOEXEC.BAT file. This example assumes that your RAM drive is D:.

```
md d:\temp set temp=d:\temp
```

Optimizing Performance with SMARTDRV

The SMARTDRV.SYS device driver implements what is called a *disk cache*, which improves the performance of a PC by storing disk data in extended or expanded memory. When a program reads a disk record, the SMARTDRV driver copies that record into its cache. If the same or another program reads the record again, SMARTDRV transfers the cache copy of the record to the program rather than rereading it from the disk.

When a program writes a disk record, SMARTDRV writes the new data into the cache and writes it to the disk as well. If a program reads a disk record, and the cache is full, SMARTDRV copies the new record to the space in the cache that the oldest record occupies.

SMARTDRV works only on systems that have extended or expanded memory. You cannot build a SMARTDRV cache in conventional memory.

The effectiveness of the cache depends on how much memory you dedicate to it. The more memory it has, the more cached disk records it can contain, and the fewer disk accesses are involved supporting disk reads from programs. The optimum size for the cache is 2MB. A larger cache than that does not significantly improve performance.

To install SMARTDRV, put the following statement into your CONFIG.SYS file after the statement that loads HIMEM.SYS:

```
device=\dos\smartdrv.sys 2048
```

The 2048 in this example tells the SMARTDRV program to build a 2048K (2MB) cache in extended memory.

By default, the SMARTDRV program uses extended memory for its cache storage. If you prefer to use expanded memory, you can put the /a parameter after the cache size parameter. You should do this only if your system has no extended memory. SMARTDRV is more efficient when the cache is in extended memory. If you use expanded memory for the cache, you must put the statement that installs the SMARTDRV.SYS program after the one that installs the expanded memory manager.

Optimizing Performance with FASTOPEN

The FASTOPEN program keeps a list of the files that your programs access on a specified disk drive. Along with the entry for each file, FASTOPEN keeps information about the location of each file on the disk. This list allows subsequent accesses to the same files to bypass the normal search of the disk's directory for the file, thereby improving the performance of accesses to that disk.

FASTOPEN is a memory-resident program. You loaded it in the exercise above that taught you about loading programs in the high memory area. FASTOPEN cannot work with network drives, floppy drives, or RAM drives.

To install FASTOPEN, put the following statement into your AUTOEXEC.BAT file:

```
fastopen c:=40 /x
```

The c: parameter tells FASTOPEN to work with the C: drive. The 40 tells it to support a list of 40 files. This value works best on a 40MB disk. Make the value the same as the MB size of the disk. You can specify several disk drive parameters to have FASTOPEN work with several disk drives. The /x parameter tells FASTOPEN to use expanded memory for the name list. If you do not specify the /x parameter, FASTOPEN builds the list in conventional memory. If you load it with the LOADHIGH command as you did in the earlier examples, FASTOPEN builds the name list in the UMB in which it loads.

Loading Memory-Resident Programs from the CONFIG.SYS File

You can use the INSTALL command in the CONFIG.SYS file to load memory-resident programs into conventional memory rather than executing them in the AUTOEXEC.BAT file. Do this when you want a memory-resident program loaded ahead of a device driver program or when the program does not use environment variables. The INSTALL command loads the programs without copies of the environment variables, so the programs occupy less conventional memory than they do when you load them from the AUTOEXEC.BAT file.

There is no way to use the INSTALL command to load memory-resident programs in the upper memory area. Therefore, you would use the command only for programs that are going to be in conventional memory anyway and that do not use environment variables, hot keys, or use the critical error processing features supported by the COMMAND.COM program. Many of the DOS 6.0 memory-resident programs—FASTOPEN and SHARE, for example—fall into this category.

To use the INSTALL command to load the FASTOPEN program into conventional memory with the same parameters as above, put the following statement in your CONFIG.SYS file:

```
install=fastopen.exe c:=40 /x
```

Summary

This chapter taught you how to use the features of DOS 6.0 to optimize the performance of your system and to manage its use of memory. You learned about PC/AT memory architecture and conventional, extended, and expanded memory. The chapter also taught you about upper and high memory areas and how to load device drivers and memory-resident programs in high memory. Finally, you learned about installing a RAM disk and disk caching.

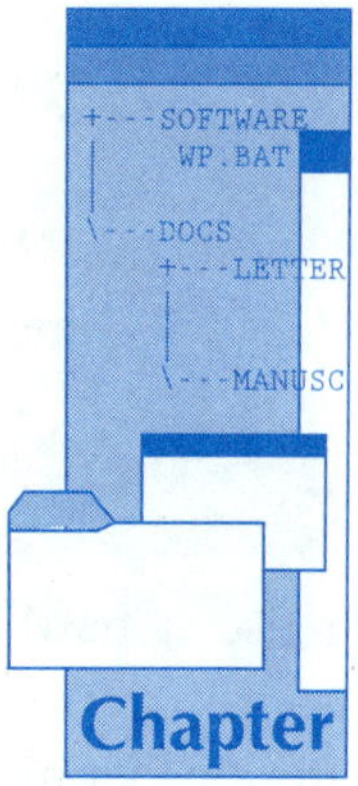

Chapter 15

Disk and File Management

This chapter teaches you about the advanced DOS 6.0 commands that you use to manage and maintain your disks and files.

You will learn about:

- Setting up your hard disk
- Operating procedures for disk and file management
- Copying, saving, and restoring your work
- Defragmenting a hard disk
- Virus protection

Setting Up Your Hard Disk

This section is about the DOS 6.0 commands that help you to set up your disk and file environment to support the way you want to work.

Preparing a Hard Disk

Before you can use a hard disk in a DOS 6.0 environment, you must prepare it. This preparation requires, at a minimum, three steps: the deep format, partition definition, and the FORMAT command.

The Deep Format

If necessary, you complete the first stage of preparation at the hardware level. This step is called the low-level or deep format. This procedure writes the track and sector information that the PC uses to physically transfer data to and from the disk medium. This procedure is outside the realm of DOS 6.0, and there are disk utility programs from third-party vendors that perform it. Often, the source for a hard disk sells it already formatted at the deep level. Maintenance organizations can perform deep formats to repair old disks that have developed surface defects.

FDISK

The FDISK command allows you to manage the partitions on a hard disk. A PC/AT can have one or two physical hard disk drives. These drives can consist of one or more partitions. Each drive can contain a primary DOS 6.0 partition, an extended DOS 6.0 partition, and nonDOS partitions. The extended DOS 6.0 partition can consist of from 1 to 23 logical DOS 6.0 drives.

A disk drive may contain nonDOS partitions, which could be used by other operating systems such as XENIX and OS/2, but FDISK cannot create them.

If you are going to use the FDISK command to change the partition or logical drive assignments of a hard disk that already has data on it, you must back up the data if you want to keep it. FDISK destroys all of the data on any partition that you change or delete.

Most users install DOS 6.0 as an upgrade from earlier versions of DOS that did not support partitions greater than 32 MB. DOS 6.0 supports much bigger partitions, and you might want to take advantage of that feature by using FDISK to increase the size of the primary partition, eliminating the other ones. However, you must make copies of all of your files first, or you will lose them.

The FDISK program uses a simple menu-driven display that leads you through its processes. You can create DOS 6.0 primary and extended partitions. A primary partition is one from which you can boot DOS 6.0. An extended partition is one that consists of one or more logical drives and that appears to DOS 6.0 to be a unique drive letter. You use FDISK to delete partitions and logical drives as well. When you delete a partition, you lose its data.

To change the size of an existing partition, you must delete it and create a new one. To make it bigger, you must delete more than one partition to make room for the new one.

You can change the active partition on the C: drive. The active partition is the one from which the PC boots. If you change the active partition to a nonDOS partition, the operating system in that partition must have an equivalent program to change the active partition back to your primary DOS 6.0 partition.

You can use the FDISK program to view the current partition and logical drive configuration.

FORMAT

You have already learned about using the FORMAT command for diskettes. You can FORMAT a hard drive as well. Since this measure has potentially drastic consequences, the FORMAT command displays a warning that all of the data on the hard disk will be lost if you proceed and asks you to verify your action. The command to format a hard disk is as follows.

```
C>format c:
```

You can use the /v:label command line switch to specify a volume label and the /s command line switch to transfer a copy of DOS 6.0 to the drive.

The /u command line switch performs an unconditional format. This switch destroys all of the data on the disk. You cannot recover any of the data from an unconditionally formatted disk.

If you do not use the /u command line switch, FORMAT performs a safe format, which rewrites the file allocation table (FAT) and root directory and scans the disk for bad sectors, marking them so that DOS 6.0 does not try to use them.

The /q command line switch performs a quick format of a previously formatted disk. This command writes the file allocation table and root directory and does not scan the disk for bad sectors.

LABEL

The LABEL command lets you give a hard disk or diskette a label. The disk label is displayed whenever you use the DIR command on the disk. Some software programs use the label on their diskettes to ensure that you have the correct diskette mounted when you are installing the software. Not much use has been made of disk labels on hard disks. You can create a label by entering this command:

```
C>label c:judy's disk
```

The c: specifies the drive that you want to label, and the text that follows is the label, which can be from 1 to 11 characters.

If you enter the LABEL command without a disk drive and label, the program displays the label for the currently logged-on disk and prompts you to enter a new one. You can enter up to 11 characters for a label. To enter no label, press **Enter** once.

Fooling the File System

You have learned how you address files by preceding their file names with a path. The path can specify the drive and subdirectory where the file exists. DOS 6.0 has commands that allow you to fool the file system into thinking that a file exists somewhere other than its actual location. These measures support programs that are inflexible about file locations.

Virtual Disk Drives: the LASTDRIVE Command

Some of these commands allow you to substitute drive letters for other drives or paths. You might not want to use an existing drive letter because they are in use during the effective time of the substitution. In that case, you can use a virtual drive letter.

A *virtual drive letter* is one that does not otherwise exist. For example, if you have floppy disks A: and B:, hard disks C: and D:, and RAM drive E:, then F: through Z: are virtual disks. To use a virtual disk, you must tell DOS 6.0 that the drive letter exists. DOS 6.0 maintains a table of valid drive letters that it builds when it boots, getting the information from the physical drives and the RAM drives you build. The highest drive it finds is the highest valid drive letter you can use in a file specification. To set up virtual drives, put this statement into the CONFIG.SYS file to increase the highest valid drive letter to F:, for example.

```
lastdrive=f
```

SUBST

The SUBST command substitutes a drive and subdirectory specification for a drive letter alone. Some older software programs work only on files that are on A: and B:. Others work with drive designations, but do not allow you to specify subdirectories on the command line. To use these programs with files that are in your file system, you can use the SUBST command to tell DOS 6.0 to substitute the specified path for the drive. Suppose that you use an old word processor that works with drives and not with paths. You can build the following batch file, called WP.BAT.

```
subst a: c:\wordproc\docs ws a:%1 subst a: /d
```

The first SUBST command tells DOS 6.0 to substitute the C:\WORDPROC\DOCS path for any references to drive A:. The second statement runs the word processor program with the A: and the file name taken from the command line when you ran the WP batch file command. The third statement is a SUBST command that deletes the substitution for A: so that you can use the drive in its usual configuration.

You can use the SUBST command with no parameters to view a list of the current substitutions.

APPEND

The APPEND command appends directories to the current directory. You can use the APPEND command to put one or more directories within reach from anywhere in the file system. APPEND is the data file's equivalent of the PATH command for executable files.

Recall the subdirectory structure on the TYD Learning Diskette. The word processing documents are in A:\WORDPROC\DOCS\LETTERS and A:\WORDPROC\DOCS\MANUSCRP. If you want to get to those documents from anywhere in the system, regardless of where you are logged on and what you are doing, you can use the APPEND command. To append the paths to those documents to the current path, enter this command:

```
C>append a:\wordproc\docs\letters;a:\wordproc\docs\letters
```

Assuming you have the PATH set to your word processor, you can now call the word processor from anywhere in the file system and specify the name of a document in either of those subdirectories, and DOS 6.0 finds the file.

You can use the APPEND command by itself to view the current list of appended subdirectories. To remove all of the appended subdirectories, enter this command:

```
C>append ;
```

You cannot add a new appended subdirectory to the existing list. You can only replace the existing list with a new one. This restriction means that the combined length of the APPEND command and its subdirectory parameters may not exceed the 127-character limit of the DOS 6.0 command line.

The APPEND command has three command line switches. If you specify /X:ON, DOS 6.0 searches the appended subdirectories during directory searches for programs to execute. Without /X:ON, or with the default /X:OFF, DOS 6.0 searches the appended subdirectory only for files to open. Observe, however, that the DOS 6.0 DIR command is unaffected by the APPEND command. The /PATH:OFF command line switch tells DOS 6.0 not to use the appended subdirectories when a file specification includes a path. The /PATH:ON switch, which is the default, uses appended subdirectories even when the file specification has a path.

The /e command line switch tells APPEND to copy the current append list to an environment variable named APPEND. You can use this switch only the first time you execute the APPEND command and only when the APPEND command has no other command line parameters.

APPEND loads a 9K memory-resident program that remains resident until you reboot the computer. You might want to execute it by using the LOADHIGH command, which loads it into the Upper memory area. Do not use the CONFIG.SYS INSTALL= command to load APPEND because APPEND accesses the environment variable table, which DOS 6.0 has not built when CONFIG.SYS entries are being processed.

Disk and File Management Operating Procedures

The commands in this section are for the routine operations of your disk and file system.

CHKDSK

The CHKDSK command tells you some interesting things about a disk and about DOS 6.0's memory usage. To use this command, you execute it with some optional command line parameters. Enter the following command to see the basic CHKDSK report:

```
C>chkdsk
```

You see a display like this:

```
Volume Serial Number is 1A54-5C7A
 340746240 bytes total disk space
   6373376 bytes in 3 hidden files
    303104 bytes in 37 directories
  55328768 bytes in 1216 user files
 278740992 bytes available on disk
      8192 bytes in each allocation unit
     41595 total allocation units on disk
     34026 available allocation units on disk
    655360 total bytes memory
    529696 bytes free
```

The numbers vary depending on your memory size and the size of your hard disk.

If the display reports fragmented clusters, you can rerun the CHKDSK command with the /f option. The fragmented clusters are written into dummy files in the root directory. The dummy files are given names with the extension .CHK. You can then delete them to reclaim the disk space they occupy.

A fragmented file results when you reboot or power down while a program has an output file open. DOS 6.0 has not had the opportunity to associate the disk space it has allocated with the updated file. As a result, the disk contains allocated space that is not assigned to any file. The CHKDSK program cleans up these files and gives them names.

ATTRIB

The ATTRIB command allows you to change the attributes of a file or group of files. You learned about file attributes in Chapters 8 and 10.

You execute the ATTRIB command with command line switches that set or clear specified attributes for specified files. The switches consist of plus (+) to set and (-) to clear followed by one of the letters, R, A, S, and H to set or clear the read-only, archive, system, and hidden attributes. For example, to set the read-only and hidden attributes for all of your document files, enter this command:

```
C>attrib +r +h *.doc
```

To display the attributes of a file or files, enter this command:

```
C>attrib novel.doc
```

Put the /s command after the file specification parameter to process files in the current directory and its subdirectories.

VOL

The VOL command displays a disk's label. Type VOL at the DOS 6.0 command line and see the volume label that you created when you formatted the disk or with the LABEL command, described earlier.

FC

The FC command is a file comparison program. To perform a byte-by-byte comparison of two binary files, execute this command:

```
C>fc /b c:\command.com a:\command.com
```

The /b command line switch says that the comparison is on binary files. The two file names are the files to be compared. In this example, you are comparing the COMMAND.COM program on your C: drive to the one on your A: drive. The FC command displays a list of file offsets in hexadecimal notation along with the values of the differences in the two files.

An ASCII comparison omits the /b command line switch, but may have several others. First, consider the comparison of two small ASCII files with this command.

```
A>fc autoexec.bat autoexec.old
Comparing files AUTOEXEC.BAT and AUTOEXEC.OLD
***** AUTOEXEC.BAT
@echo off
cls
echo Teach Yourself DOS Learning Diskette
ver
path=a:\wordproc\software;a:\sprdsht\software;a:\dos
***** AUTOEXEC.OLD
@echo off
rem cls
rem echo Teach Yourself DOS Learning Diskette
rem ver
path=a:\wordproc\software;a:\sprdsht\software;a:\dos
*****
```

This comparison shows the locations where the two files differ. The first and last line of both blocks are the lines where the files are back into synchronization with respect to comparisons.

You can put one or more command line switches before the file names. The /a command line switch abbreviates the display so that you only see the first and last line of each block. The /c switch performs a case-insensitive comparison. The /LBn switch specifies the length of the line buffer at n lines. The default is 100. The /n switch displays the line numbers. The /t switch suppresses the default conversions of tabs to spaces. The /w switch compresses all contiguous white space–tabs and spaces–into a single space before comparison. This switch also removes leading and trailing white space on a line.

The /nnnn switch specifies nnnn as the number of lines that are equal before FC puts the file back into synchronization.

DISKCOMP

The DISKCOMP command compares the contents of two floppy disks that have the same format. The command format is as follows:

```
C>diskcomp a: b:
```

If the two diskettes are the same, DISKCOMP displays the *Compare OK* message. Otherwise, it displays the diskette side and track where the differences occur. The comparison does not include the diskettes' unique volume numbers.

You can specify the same drive for both parameters to compare two diskettes. DISKCOMP lets you know when to insert the two diskettes. This feature supports computers that have only one diskette drive or two drives with different formats.

Copying, Saving, and Restoring Your Work

The most important task you do with DOS 6.0 is your work. Whether you are an accountant, a farmer, a writer, an administrator, a bookie, or a musicologist, your vested interest in the PC is in the data files you have created, nurtured, and grown.

If your most important task is your work, then your most important obligation is the protection of that work. Aside from the usual protection from vandals, plagiarists, and competitors, there is the requirement that you protect your work on the PC from the PC itself.

A PC is an electromechanical device subject to failure. The degree of failure and the degree to which you can recover vary. When a PC quits, it can take your work with it. Your only protection is a measure of prevention. If you make periodic copies of your work onto media that are separate from the PC, you have a form of recovery. Even if the house burns down, if you have copies of your work on diskettes–kept in another house–you can take those diskettes to another PC and resume work. The amount of real loss is a matter of how much work you have done since your last backup.

DOS 6.0 provides a number of commands that help you to make backups onto diskettes. These are discussed here. These discussions assume that you normally store your data files on the C: hard drive and that you make backup copies onto diskettes in the A: drive.

COPY

You already learned and used the COPY command in the exercises in earlier chapters. The most common use of COPY is to backup small numbers of critical data files. Suppose your word processing documents for a project are together in a subdirectory. You can use COPY to make periodic backups of those files. If you have grouped them into files with a common file name extension, .DOC, for example, you can use this command to make backup copies.

```
C>copy *.doc a:
```

If your work involves different kinds of files, documents, figures, and tables, for example, you could make a batch file named COPIES.BAT that had these commands in it.

```
copy   *.doc a:
copy   *.fig a:
copy   *.tbl a:
```

You can do most, if not all, of your backup operations with COPY. You need the other methods described next when your backup requirements become more complex.

XCOPY

XCOPY is an advanced form of the COPY command that works better when your data files are organized in a subdirectory structure. On the TYD Learning Diskette, you organized the \WORDPROC\DOCS subdirectory into the lower LETTERS and MANUSCRP subdirectories. XCOPY provides a way to use a single command to make copies of these sets of data files. XCOPY copies groups of files including files in lower subdirectories, if you so specify.

Assume the same subdirectory structure on your hard disk. To make backups of all of the word processing documents, you could use this command:

```
C>xcopy \wordproc\docs a:\ /s
```

This command creates two subdirectories, LETTERS and MANUSCRP, on the A: drive and copies to them the files from the corresponding subdirectories under C:\WORDPROC\DOCS. If you want the target diskette to have the higher subdirectories, you must specify them on the command line. If you specify a different subdirectory in the target specification of the XCOPY command, that subdirectory is created, and the files and subdirectories from the source are copied into the new target subdirectory.

XCOPY has several other command line options as shown in the following list.

```
Option        Meaning
/A            Only copy files with archive bit on, do not
              turn off
/D:mm-dd-yy   Only copy files on or later than mm-dd-yy
/E            Copy empty subdirectories to the target
/M            Only copy files with archive bit on, then turn
off /P        XCOPY prompts with (Y/N?) before each file copy
/V            Verify sector copies
/W            XCOPY waits for a source diskette to be inserted
```

REPLACE

The REPLACE command is handy when you are dealing with a large number of files only a few of which change at a single work session. This command is also convenient when several people work on the same project at different PCs and need to keep their collective copies of the work current. Finally, REPLACE is helpful when you are working on the same data files in two different locations, perhaps at home and at work, and you transport the changed files back and forth.

The REPLACE command matches the files in the source specification with files of the same name on the target specification and transfers the files according to the options you choose. REPLACE has several command line options, but the one you are most likely to use is the /u option, which replaces files on the target only if they are older than the matching files on the source. The effect of that option is that if you use the same diskette for backups, only files that have been changed since the last backup are copied. Consider the situation where you work at two different locations. While at work, you modify some of your document files for a project. Before leaving for home, you make a backup with this command:

```
C>replace *.doc a: /u
```

The diskette now has all of the latest files. You go home and transfer the files to the hard disk on your home computer with this command.

```
C>replace a:*.doc c: /u
```

This writes the changed files to your home computer. You can work at home and repeat the procedure to take the files to work the next day. Be aware that the two computers must agree on the date and time for this procedure to work reliably.

You can get the same result with COPY *.* but every file would always be copied, wasting time. The other command line options for REPLACE are shown here.

Option	Meaning
/A	Copy only files that do not exist on the target
/P	Prompt for each file before copying
/R	Replace read-only files on the target
/S	Search subdirectories on the target for matching file names
/W	Wait for a source diskette to be inserted

MSBACKUP

If you have a large number of files on a hard disk to copy to a diskette, the files might not fit. The COPY, XCOPY, and REPLACE commands go as far as they can and then let you know that there is no more room. If you are using wild cards, you must then manually figure out how to get the remaining files onto the next diskette. The same COPY, XCOPY, or REPLACE command would not work; it would start over at the beginning of the list of files.

The MSBACKUP command allows you to make backups of large volumes of files onto diskettes. To backup or restore files on your hard disk enter this command:

```
C>msbackup
```

MSBACKUP is a full-screen, menu-driven program that uses a menu bar, popdown menus, and dialog boxes similar to those of DOSSHELL and EDIT. The first time you run MSBACKUP, it runs an automatic compatibility check on your hardware to make sure that backups may be reliably performed. You need two diskettes for the compatibility test. Once the test is completed, MSBACKUP does not need to make it again.

MSBACKUP uses a setup file to describe the files you want to backup or restore. You can have different setup files for different routine backup operations. You specify the setup file name as a command line parameter when you run MSBACKUP. If you do not specify a setup file, MSBACKUP uses the file named DEFAULT.SET, which it creates the first time you use it. After starting MSBACKUP, you choose whether you are making backups to or restoring from the diskettes. You may also choose to compare the diskettes with the hard disk files.

DISKCOPY

The DISKCOPY command is used to make copies of diskettes. For example, you would use this command to make working copies of the distribution diskettes of a new software package. You can also use DISKCOPY to make backup copies of any critical files that are kept on diskettes.

You do not need to format the target diskettes before you run DISKCOPY and you do not even need two diskette drives to use the command.

To make a copy of a diskette enter this command:

```
C>diskcopy a: b:
```

Follow the instructions on the screen.

VERIFY

The VERIFY command tells DOS 6.0 to verify every disk write. You turn the option on and off with these commands:

```
C>verify on
C>verify off
```

You can see the current setting of the VERIFY command by entering it without a parameter. When VERIFY is on, every disk write is followed by a disk read so that DOS 6.0 can compare the disk contents with the contents of the memory buffer from where the record was written.

Disk and File Recovery

DOS 6.0 contains several tools that help you recover from a damaged disk or a disk that you have inadvertently formatted. This section explains these tools.

UNFORMAT

If you inadvertently format a disk, you can try to use the UNFORMAT command to recover the data that it contained. You stand a better chance of recovering your data if you formatted the disk without the /u switch and you run the UNFORMAT command immediately after the FORMAT command.

The UNFORMAT command has this syntax:

```
A>unformat c:
```

The UNFORMAT command has several command line option switches, as follows.

The /test switch displays what UNFORMAT would do if you ran it without the switch. The /l switch lists all of the files and subdirectories found by UNFORMAT. The /p switch prints UNFORMAT's output to the LPT1 device.

UNDELETE

The UNDELETE command recovers files that you inadvertently deleted with the DEL command. Use this command:

```
C>undelete novel.doc
```

If you specify no file name, UNDELETE attempts to undelete all of the files in the current directory. You can use wild cards to specify the files.

The /list command line switch lists the files that could be recovered. The /all switch recovers files without prompting for each one. Deleted file names have lost the first character. The /all switch substitutes a number sign (#) for the first character unless that would create a name collision, in which case it selects a character from this list: %, &, -, the digits 0 through 9, the letters A to Z.

Defragmenting the Hard Disk (DEFRAG)

DEFRAG is a utility program that defragments your hard disk. You should run it every now and then. Defragmentation improves your computer's performance.

DOS 6.0 allocates physical disk space in fixed-length clusters of disk tracks. When a new file is created, DOS 6.0 finds the first available cluster to write the new file. If the file length is greater than the cluster length, DOS 6.0 finds the next available cluster and links it to the current one, continuing to do so until enough clusters have been allocated and the complete file has been written. When you delete a file, DOS 6.0 returns the clusters the file occupies to the pool of available ones. This scheme will, over a period of time, result in a fragmented pattern of cluster-to-file allocations where the clusters for a given file are not contiguous. In fact, they will be in a random sequence–scattered about the disk. Reading these files involves a lot of disk head activity as the system jumps back and forth collecting the file's clusters of disk tracks.

DEFRAG scans the whole disk and reorganizes it so that all of the files are in contiguous, sequential clusters. You should not interrupt DEFRAG while it is in progress. You should run DEFRAG only when you are sure that there will be no interruption in power, if one can ever be sure of that. If you do not have an uninterruptable power supply (UPS), run DEFRAG only when there are no atmospheric disturbances that could turn off the lights.

Virus Protection (MSAV and VSAFE)

DOS 6.0 offers two virus detection and removal programs. One is a program that you run periodically to scan for virus programs. The other is a memory-resident program that maintains a constant watch for virus infection.

A virus is a computer program written and distributed by mischievous vandals. The virus program attaches itself to system and applications disk files and perpetuates itself when these files are copied among machines. Distribution on a network can infect many computers. A common source of viruses is found in unauthorized copies of commercial software. The DOS 6.0 virus detection and removal programs watch for the symptoms of virus infection and deal with them accordingly.

MSAV

MSAV is the Microsoft Anti-Virus program. You run it from the command line to make periodic tests for the presence of viruses. The program displays a menu with selections to detect and clean viruses. You can switch drives to scan and set options. The detection program scans computer memory and the currently selected disk drive.

Use MSAV in a closed environment where few outside files are used and where other people seldom use your machine. Such an environment does not need constant vigil, and an occasional check for viruses suffices.

VSAFE

VSAFE is a memory-resident program that maintains a constant watch for virus infection. When you load it, you can pop up a menu of options by pressing **Alt+V**. The menu includes a command to unload VSAFE from memory. If VSAFE detects a virus infection, it alerts you immediately with a popup window that explains the error and allows you to stop the system or proceed.

You would use VSAFE in a highly volatile environment where you process many diskettes from uncontrolled sources, where you frequently download files from bulletin boards and on-line services, or where other people have frequent, uncontrolled access to your computer.

Summary

This chapter has taught you how to use the facilities of DOS 6.0 to manage and maintain your disk and file systems, and it brings to an end the tutorial sessions of Teach Yourself DOS 6.0.

Appendix A

DOS 6.0 Command Summary

This is an alphabetical list of the DOS 6.0 commands that you can enter on the command line. Each command has a brief description of its purpose and the chapter references where the command is discussed.

APPEND..........makes references to specified directories appear as if they were in the current directory. Chapter 15.

ATTRIB...........sets, clears, and views file attribute flags. Chapter 15.

CD...................changes the currently logged-on subdirectory. Chapter 5.

CHCP.............displays or changes active code page.

CHKDSK.........displays capacity and file space of a disk. Chapter 15.

CLS.................clears the screen. Chapter 5.

COMMAND....runs another copy of the command line interpreter.

COPY.............copies files. Chapter 5, Chapter 15.

COUNTRY......uses international dates, times, currency, and so forth.

CTTY..............changes the console device to a communications port.

DATE..............displays and changes the current date. Chapter 5.

DEBUG............is a programmer's tool to debug programs.

DEFRAG.........defragments disk volumes. Chapter 15.

DEL.................deletes files. Chapter 5.

DELTREE........deletes subdirectories and files. Chapter 5.

DIR.................displays the files in a directory. Chapter 5, Chapter 9, Chapter 10.

DISKCOMP....compares two floppy disks. Chapter 15.

DISKCOPY.....copies a diskette to another diskette. Chapter 15.

DOSKEY.........is a enhanced command line processor. Chapter 11.

DOSSHELL.....is a full-screen DOS 6.0 operating environment. Chapter 8.

EDIT................is a full-screen text editor. Chapter 12.

EMM386.........displays the current EMS status. Chapter 14.

ERASE.............is the same as DEL.

EXIT................returns from secondary execution of COMMAND.COM.

EXPAND.........decompresses DOS 6.0 installation files. Chapter 4.

FASTHELP......displays all of the DOS commands.

FASTOPEN.....is a memory-resident utility to speed up file opens. Chapter 14.

FC....................is a file compare utility program. Chapter 15.

FDISK.............is a disk partition maintenance program. Chapter 15.

FIND...............is a text search filter. Chapter 9.

FOR.................runs a command for each file in a set. Chapter 13.

FORMAT.........prepares a disk for use. Chapter 5, Chapter 10, Chapter 15.

GRAPHICS......enables screen print of graphics images. Chapter 7.

HELP..............displays help for DOS 6.0 commands. Chapter 5.

INTERLNK......connects the computer to a computer running INTERSVR.

INTERSRV......establishes the computer as a server to be accessed by a computer running INTERLNK.

KEYB.............sets up the keyboard for a different language convention.

LABEL............writes a disk's volume label. Chapter 15.

LOADFIX........loads and runs a program above the first 64K boundary.

LOADHIGH....loads a memory-resident program into the upper memory area. Chapter 14.

MD..................makes a subdirectory. Chapter 5.

MEM...............displays the DOS 6.0 memory layout. Chapter 14.

MEMMAKER..modifies CONFIG.SYS and AUTOEXEC.BAT to optimize memory. Chapter 14.

MODE ....controls serial port, printer, screen display, and keyboard behavior. Chapter 5, Chapter 7.

MORE ....writes screen output a screenful at a time, pausing between pages. Chapter 9.

MOVE.............moves disk files and renames subdirectories. Chapter 5.

MSAV..............scans for viruses. Chapter 15.

MSBACKUP....backs up and restores disk files. Chapter 15.

MSD ....displays hardware and software configuration data.

NLSFUNC......provides National Language Support for specific countries.

PATH..............sets the path to executable programs. Chapter 6.

POWER..........operates laptop power management functions.

PRINT ....prints text files while running other programs. Chapter 7.

PROMPT.........changes the DOS command line prompt. Chapters 5, 10.

QBASIC..........is the BASIC programming language interpreter.

RD ....removes a subdirectory. Chapter 5.

REN.................renames a file. Chapter 5.

REPLACE........replaces files from one disk to another disk. Chapter 15.

RESTORE........restores files backed up by previous versions of DOS.

SET..................sets an environment variable. Chapter 10.

SETVER..........fools specified programs into thinking other versions of DOS are running. Chapter 10.

SHARE ....installs file sharing and locking.

SORT..............sorts a text file. Chapter 9.

SYS..................transfers DOS 6.0 from one disk to another. Chapter 15.

TIME ....displays and set the time. Chapter 5.

TREE ....displays a file and subdirectory tree. Chapter 5.

TYPE ....displays the contents of a text file on the screen. Chapter 5, Chapter 9.

UNDELETE.....recovers a deleted file. Chapter 15.

UNFORMAT....recovers a formatted disk. Chapter 15.

VER ....displays the DOS version. Chapter 5.

VERIFY ....turns file write verification on and off. Chapter 15.

VOL ....displays a disk's volume label. Chapter 15.

VSAFE ....watches for viruses. Chapter 15.

XCOPY...........copies files and subdirectories. Chapter 15.

Appendix B

Glossary

This is a glossary of words and phrases heard among DOS users. You will read about some of these terms in this book. Others are common parts of the DOS user's vocabulary. This glossary briefly explains the terms so you will know what they mean when you hear them.

ANSI.SYS

This is a special device driver program that comes with DOS 6.0 in the file named ANSI.SYS. To use it, insert this statement into the CONFIG.SYS file of the root directory on the same boot disk:

```
device=c:\dos\ansi.sys
```

When ANSI.SYS is installed, certain character sequences, when sent as displays to the screen, control video characteristics such as colors and cursor position.

applications programs

An applications program (commonly called a *program*) is one that you run to operate your computing application—the reason you have the computer. The applications program is different from the *utility* program. Typical applications programs are word processors, spreadsheets, and database management systems.

ASCII

This is an acronym that means *American Standard Code for Information Interchange*. The code was established by the American National Standards Institute (ANSI) in their ANSI Standard X3.4-1977 (Revised 1983) publication. ASCII specifies the character codes used by many computer and communications systems, including the PC. The ASCII character set uses numbers from 0 to 127 to represent characters in the computer's memory, on disk, and across modem communications. The set includes values for the letters, numbers, and punctuation characters common to most text-based computers. ASCII also includes nondisplayable characters to represent the carriage return, horizontal tab, line feed, form feed, backspace, and a set of communications characters.

Text files consist of ASCII characters. You can build and maintain text files with a text editor program.

The PC extends the ASCII character set to include values 128 to 255. These extensions are graphics characters to build international characters, scientific characters, window borders, playing card symbols, happy faces, and other special characters.

attribute

One of five file characteristics: read-only, hidden, system, archive, and directory.

AUTOEXEC.BAT

AUTOEXEC.BAT is a text file in the root directory of the boot disk. The file contains DOS commands that DOS 6.0 executes when it is first loaded. This file is optional, but most DOS installations include one.

backup

This is a term that means to save your files on separate media—usually diskettes—for safe storage and possible recovery after a loss. DOS 6.0 includes the MSBACKUP program to assist in this process. The term, however, refers to any technique used to make copies of your files. The copies are called *backups*.

batch files

Batch files contain ASCII DOS commands. You build batch files with a text editor program. A batch file has the file name extension .BAT. To execute the commands in a batch file, you enter the file's name (without the .BAT extension) on the DOS command line and press **Enter**.

BIOS

BIOS means *basic input output system*. BIOS is a set of programs in the PC's read-only memory (ROM). The BIOS programs manage the PC's hardware and are executed from within other programs. Users do not usually need to concern themselves with BIOS.

bit

A bit is the smallest unit of information that a computer stores. A bit can contain the values 0 and 1. Bits are combined to form characters. One character consists of eight bits. The 256 possible combinations of ones and zeros constitute the 128 codes of the ASCII character set and the 128 codes of the extended graphics character set.

boot

When you load DOS 6.0, you boot it. DOS 6.0 is booted when you turn power on or when you press **Ctrl+Alt+Del**. Users often call this latter method *rebooting*.

boot disk

This is the disk DOS 6.0 is loaded from when you boot. If the A: floppy disk drive has a diskette inserted during a boot, the PC loads DOS 6.0 from the diskette. Otherwise, the PC loads DOS 6.0 from the C: hard disk drive.

byte

A byte is an 8-bit unit of storage. Memory sizes, file sizes, and device capacities are expressed in bytes (B), kilobytes (KB), and megabytes (MB). See also *character*.

cache

Temporary RAM storage for frequently read disk records.

character

A character is the value contained in one byte, which equals 8 bits. You think of these contents as characters when you consider their value. You think of them as bytes when you think of the unit of storage. A byte holds 1 character.

chip

A chip is an integrated circuit, a miniature electronic device that serves a specified purpose. A chip is made of a silicon wafer that has thousands of semiconductor logic circuits. The wafer is housed in a plastic case with conductor pins that allow the chip to be inserted into sockets or soldered onto an integrated circuit board. The microprocessor is a chip. The math coprocessor is a chip. Internal memory is a series of RAM and ROM chips.

clock speed

See *megahertz*.

clone

A clone is any personal computer that is not made by IBM but that can run all of the software that runs on an IBM PC. Some American manufacturers have become so prominent with their PC-compatible lines of computers that their brand names have their own identities. COMPAQ is an example. The term clone has come to imply PC-compatible computers made from parts manufactured in Asia.

command line

The DOS command line is on the screen at the DOS prompt where you type in DOS commands. The command line usually looks like this:

```
C>
```

command line switch

A command line parameter is preceded by minus (-), plus (+), or slash (/). The parameter is usually one alphanumeric character.

COMMAND.COM

To load and run DOS 6.0, you need several files in the root directory of the boot disk. COMMAND.COM is the program that DOS 6.0 uses to operate the command line and process your typed commands and batch files.

communications port

A hardware device to which you can connect a modem, a terminal, a plotter, or a serial printer.

CONFIG.SYS

To load and run DOS 6.0, you need several files in the root directory of the DOS 6.0 boot disk. CONFIG.SYS is a text file found in the root directory of the boot disk. The file contains parameters that tell DOS 6.0 how to configure itself when DOS 6.0 is first loaded. This file is optional but most DOS installations include one.

conventional memory

The 640K RAM memory from hex address 0000 to 9FFF.

coprocessor

See *math coprocessor.*

copy protection

Some applications are *copy-protected,* a phrase that means many things. The purpose for copy protection is to prevent or discourage the use of the program by software pirates, people who copy programs and use them without paying for them.

There are numerous copy protection schemes, and utility programs to defeat copy protection schemes have proliferated. Copy protection is viewed as an unacceptable inconvenience for the users who own legitimate copies of the programs because of the problems involved in making backup copies of the software disks.

Most major software publishers have dropped copy protection because of criticism the practice receives in the press and because of user complaints. Many users steadfastly refuse to use programs that are copy-protected.

Ctrl+Alt+Del

To reboot DOS 6.0, press these three keys simultaneously. This key combination is also called the *three-finger salute.*

cursor

The blinking line that points to the place where keystrokes will display. It also refers to the box or arrow that indicates where mouse actions take place.

daisywheel printer

A daisywheel printer prints by striking the paper through an inked ribbon with a fully formed character embossed on a removable wheel. The wheel resembles a daisy. Daisywheel printers are capable of letter-quality printing, which means that you cannot tell the result from that produced by a typewriter. Daisywheel printers are not capable of graphics printing.

database

One of your application programs might be a database management system. Your database is the set of files that contain records of in formation relative to how you use the computer.

desktop publishing

Desktop publishing programs combine the text from word processors, the pictures from graphics processors, and the document specifications of the desktop publishing program to produce a publication-quality document, usually on a laser printer.

device driver program

Some software and hardware additions to the PC include a device driver program. These programs are in files with the file name extension .SYS, and are installed by this kind of statement in the CONFIG.SYS file:

```
device=mouse.sys
```

DOS 6.0 includes several such programs that you can optionally install. These are ANSI.SYS, DISPLAY.SYS, DRIVER.SYS, EGA.SYS, EMM386.SYS, HIMEM.SYS, and RAMDRIVE.SYS. Most of these device drivers are discussed in this book.

device names

DOS 6.0 uses device names as substitutes for file names in many commands. These names are CON, PRN, LPT1, LPT2, LPT3, COM1, COM2, COM3, COM4, AUX, and NUL.

dialog box

A displayed box with various kinds of fields for the user to enter data.

directory

Files on a DOS disk are organized in a hierarchical structure of directories and subdirectories. A subdirectory is also a file that contains a list of the subordinate file names and their locations. The directory at the top of the hierarchy is called the *root* directory. All directories below the root are called *subdirectories.*

With typical computer ambiguity, the term directory also describes the file list displayed by the DOS DIR command.

disk drive

A disk drive is a device that houses a magnetic disk platter. The platter records information. You can remove the platter from a floppy disk drive: The medium is removable. The platter in a fixed disk drive is not removable. Many fixed disk drives contain several stacked platters to increase capacity.

disk operating system

DOS is the disk operating system, so called because it is disk based. The primary storage medium is a disk. DOS 6.0 itself is stored on and loaded from a disk device. DOS 6.0 is also called PC-DOS if it came from IBM and MS-DOS if it came from Microsoft or a clone manufacturer.

diskette

A diskette is a removable disk cartridge, which is made of a flexible, magnetic oxide-coated disk inside a paper or plastic envelope. The disk rotates on a spindle and its recording surface is exposed through an aperture in the envelope. See also *disk drive* and *floppy disk*.

DOS

See *disk operating system*.

dot matrix printer

A dot matrix printer prints by forming its characters in a matrix of dots. Each dot is printed by a tiny pin that strikes the paper through the inked ribbon. Dot matrix printers are usually capable of near-letter-quality printing, which means that you can readily discern the result from that produced by a typewriter. Dot matrix printers are often capable of printing graphics pictures.

editor

See *text editor*.

environment variables

The DOS 6.0 environmental variables are text values that you assign with the DOS SET command and that are read by applications programs. An environment variable has a name and a value. Applications programs react to the value assigned to the variable with the chosen name in a manner defined for the program by its documentation. The installation procedures for applications programs will specify the requirements for environmental variables.

DOS 6.0 uses several environment variables. One is the PATH variable, which tells DOS 6.0 what drives and subdirectories to search for programs to run. Another is the COMSPEC variable, which tells DOS 6.0 where to find the COMMAND.COM program (or a substitute) during a reboot. The DIRCMD environment variable tells the DIR command the default format chosen by the user. The APPEND variable shows the current effect of the APPEND command. The PROMPT variable controls how the DOS prompt displays. The TEMP and TMP variables tell DOS 6.0 where to write temporary files.

EMS

See *expanded memory*.

expanded memory

Memory that is external to the 1MB address range of the PC but that can be mapped one page at a time into a 64K page segment in the upper memory area. It is abbreviated EMS for expanded memory system. EMS requires an expanded memory manager program for other programs to access.

extended memory

Memory on 80286/386/486 computers beginning at the 1MB address. It is not accessible to DOS 6.0 except through an XMS driver program. Abbreviated XMS for *extended memory specification*.

extension

The one to three-character extension to a file name. The file name and its extension are separated by a period. See also *file name.*

file

A collection of information stored into one logical file on a disk.

file name

The 1- to 8-character name of a file. See also *extension.*

filter

A filter is a program that reads its input from the standard input device and writes its output to the standard output device. You can redirect the input and output of filter programs to devices, files, and other programs.

fixed disk

See *hard disk.*

floppy disk

A floppy disk is a diskette in an envelope that you insert into a disk drive to be read and written. The diskette is a removable medium and is the primary medium for software distribution and backups.

format

Before they can be used, diskettes must be prepared, or formatted. FORMAT is a DOS command that formats a diskette.

graphics

PCs can display information in one of two ways: as text or as graphics. Text displays consist of letters, numbers, punctuation, and the special character set that includes borders, happy faces, and the like. Graphics displays can be pictures, maps, charts, and other nontextual displays. Graphics displays often contain text as part of the pictures.

hard disk

A hard disk is an internal, nonremovable disk device, usually with much more storage capacity than a floppy disk.

hidden files

DOS 6.0 can record files that are hidden on a disk—they do not show up when you issue the DIR command unless you use the /ah command line switch.

You cannot delete a hidden file from the DOS 6.0 command line. Applications programs hide files for reasons of their own, usually as a part of some copy-protection scheme. DOS includes two hidden files in the root directory of the boot disk. These are named MSDOS.SYS and IO.SYS.

high memory area (HMA)

The HMA is the first 64K of XMS, addressable by DOS 6.0 through a quirk in the microprocessor's addressing circuitry. The HMA is controlled by the XMS manager program.

hot key

You activate most memory-resident utility programs by pressing a key sequence that is set aside for the program. This sequence is called a *hot key* and usually consists of the combination of Ctrl, Alt, and/or Shift along with another key. A more recent name for the hot key is the *shortcut key*.

laser printer

A laser printer prints by using the technology of copier machines. Laser printers are capable of letter-quality printing, which means that you cannot discern the result from that produced by a typewriter. Laser printers are the mainstay of desktop publishing, capable of printing with many different character fonts and with complex graphics renditions.

math coprocessor

The math coprocessor is a device that can speed up mathematical operations in a PC. To be effective, the coprocessor must be known to the applications programs. A program that uses a coprocessor can perform mathematical operations much faster than a program that does not use a coprocessor.

Math coprocessor chips are expensive and do not provide any advantage to programs that do not need or use them.

megahertz

The speed at which a PC can operate is measured in megahertz (millions of clock cycles per second). Megahertz is the equivalent of an automobile's horsepower or a stereo's power output rating. The first PC ran at 4.77 megahertz. Subsequent releases of ATs and 386 machines have progressed through 6, 8, 10, 12, 16, 20, 25, 33, 50, and now 66 megahertz.

The faster a machine runs, the faster it processes your data. If you calculate a lot of big spreadsheets, a fast PC make a difference. See also *wait states* and *nanosecond.*

memory-resident utility program

A memory-resident utility program is resident in the PC's RAM, but does not run until you request it, usually by pressing a key sequence, called a *hot key,* that is reserved for the utility. The advantage of the memory-resident program is that it is available at all times, even when another program is running. The disadvantage is that it occupies memory, even when you do not need it.

modem

A modem is a device that allows you to connect your computer to another computer through the telephone lines. You will need a communications program to use the modem.

There are many on-line services available by modem. Some of them, such as CompuServe, are available by subscription—you pay a one-time connect fee and then only for the time you use the service. Others are operated by hobbyists and are available for the cost of the phone call.

mouse

A mouse is a device that you roll around on the desk or mousepad to move the computer's cursor around. Many graphics, computer-aided design, and desktop publishing systems use a mouse.

MS-DOS

See *disk operating system*.

nanosecond

A nanosecond is one billionth of a second. It is a measure that rates the speed of memory chips. Typical ratings are 200 nanoseconds and 150 nanoseconds. The higher the PC's speed in megahertz, the lower the nanosecond rating of the memory chips must be.

network

A configuration of computers connected by cables and organized into a file server and workstations. The workstations support users. The file server is unattended. The users share files in and printers connected to the file server. In a peer-to-peer network, there is no file server, and the users at work stations share the disks and printers of each other.

page frame

The memory segment address in the high memory area that EMS uses to map extended memory in and out.

parameter

A value that controls or affects the operation of an application and is displayed on the applications command line following the application's executable file name.

path

The DOS path is the route through the subdirectory structure that DOS searches when you command it to execute a program. You specify that path with the DOS PATH command.

PC-DOS

See *disk operating system*.

pipe

The DOS 6.0 pipe is the mechanism through which filter programs are connected. The first program writes its output to the pipe, and the second program reads its output of one program automatically becomes the input to another.

pop-up program

See *memory-resident utilities*.

prompt

The DOS prompt is the sequence of characters that DOS 6.0 displays to tell you that it is ready for a command. Unless told otherwise, DOS 6.0 displays the prompt as the drive letter of the currently logged on disk drive and a greater than sign (for example, C>). You can modify the DOS prompt with the PROMPT command.

protected mode

An operating mode available to 80286 and higher microprocessors that allows them to access memory addresses greater than 1MB. DOS 6.0 does not run in protected mode.

PS/2

The PS/2 is a generation of IBM PC. To the DOS user, the PS/2 is the functional equivalent of other PCs. There are architectural differences in the hardware, but these are mainly of concern to those who set up the machine and add internal expansion boards.

RAM

Random access memory (RAM) is the name of the memory chips used in the PC for volatile program and data storage. When you turn off the power, the contents of RAM are lost, so it is used for temporary matters, such as programs that are reloaded whenever they are needed.

RAM disk

A virtual disk device implemented in conventional, expanded, or extended memory through the inclusion of the RAMDRIVE.SYS device driver.

read-only file

DOS 6.0 can mark a disk file as read-only. You can neither delete nor change such a file. The program that creates the file might mark it as such, or you can mark any file as read-only or read-write by using the DOS ATTRIB command.

real mode

The operating mode of the 8088 and 8086 microprocessors. Allows addresses up to 1MB. The operating mode for DOS 6.0.

redirection

Programs that are written to be filters read their input from the standard input device and write their output to the standard output device. You can redirect these devices from the command line when you run the programs. You can redirect the devices to files or other devices or to other programs by way of the DOS 6.0 pipe.

ROM

Read-only memory (ROM) is the name given to the nonvolatile memory where the PC records the BIOS. When you turn off the power, the contents of ROM are preserved. A program cannot change the contents of ROM.

root directory

DOS 6.0 manages disk files in a hierarchical tree structure of directories and subdirectories. The topmost directory in the tree is called the *root directory*.

setup

The DOS 6.0 installation program.

shareware

Most software is expensive. You buy it and try it. With shareware, you get it for nothing or for a small copy charge. If you decide to keep it and use it, you register it with its vendor by paying a nominal registration fee. The software and documentation are usually contained on a diskette. You can print the documentation and use the software. Sometimes you get a printed manual when you register the software.

The advantage of shareware is that you can try something before you buy it, and the cost is low, reflecting the low overhead involved in its distribution.

The disadvantage is that the quality of the programs vary widely, and you may have to try out many programs before you find one that meets your needs.

shell

The DOS 6.0 Shell program is an operating environment that displays a directory tree, file list, program list, and active task list in screen windows. Supports task swapping.

shortcut key

See *hot key.*

standard input device

Filter programs read their input from the standard input device. Unless you specify otherwise, the standard input device is the keyboard. You can use input redirection to redirect the standard input device to a file, a device, or a pipe from the standard output device of another filter program.

standard output device

Filter programs write their output to the standard output device. Unless you specify otherwise, the standard output device is the screen. You can use output redirection to redirect the standard output device to a file, a device, or a pipe to the standard input device of another filter program.

subdirectory

A subdirectory is a DOS 6.0 file directory that is subordinate to another DOS 6.0 file directory. See also *directory, root directory,* and *tree.*

surge protector

Occasionally, the voltage from commercial power companies surge. A surge protector is a device that you plug into the wall and plug your computer into. It protects your equipment from the damage that such surges can cause. A surge protector is a wise investment.

task swapping

A feature of the DOS 6.0 Shell program that permits more than one program to be active on the active task list. A user can switch from program to program without terminating and restarting them.

text editor

A program that permits the modification of text files. EDIT is a text editor programs.

tree

The DOS 6.0 tree is the hierarchical file directory structure. To view the tree, you use the DOS TREE command.

TSR program

See *memory-resident utility program*.

uninterruptable power supply (UPS)

A UPS is a device that plugs into the electrical outlet and into which you plug your computer. If the electricity goes out, the UPS continues to provide current to the computer for enough time to allow you to save your files and shut down.

upper memory area

The memory in the address range from segment A000 to EFFF. Occupied by video memory, network cards, some disk controllers. The upper memory area has blocks of unused memory, called *upper memory blocks* when DOS 6.0 uses them to load device drivers and memory-resident programs into them.

upper memory block

An unused portion of the upper memory area where DOS 6.0 can load device driver and memory-resident programs. Only available on 386 or 486 computers.

utility program

A utility program is one that you use to perform a utility job, usually related to the operation of the computer. Other utility programs are used for small secondary tasks that support your applications software, such as pop-up calculators and calendars.

version of DOS

DOS has been released in several versions ranging from 1.0 to 6.0 (as of this writing). To see the version of DOS you are running, use the VER command.

virtual disk

See *RAM disk*.

volume label

A hard disk or diskette can have a magnetic label. You can read and set the label of a disk medium with the VOL or LABEL command.

wait states

You will often hear the expression *zero wait states* in the explanation of a PC's processor performance. This means that the RAM chips can respond to the PC's memory accesses at the speed of the PC. When this is not the case, the memory circuits halt the processor with one or more *wait states* so the processor waits for the memory to respond. You do not often hear this measure expressed because it is considered a disadvantage, and the writers of advertising copy do not like to accentuate the negative.

wildcard

When you call out a file name on the command line, you can sometimes include asterisks and question marks as wildcards to form an ambiguous file name. The usual intent is to specify a group of similarly named files as opposed to only one.

Windows

The Windows extension to DOS 6.0 adds a common graphical user interface and multitasking to DOS and all applications programs.

word processor

A word processor is a program that lets you develop textual document files. This type of program usually has far more features than a text editor program, with complex formatting and printing modes, spelling checkers, and other functions of use to those who write documents and manuscripts.

XMS

See *extended memory*.

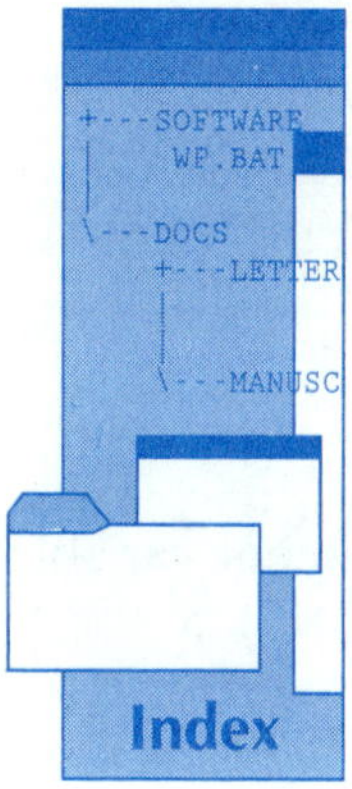

Symbols

A

B

C

D

E

F

G

H

I

J

K

L

M

N

O

P

Q

R

S

T

U